"Jenny Evans is a master communicator. Her book is insightful, thoughtful and exceptionally practical. An important read for anyone who wants to perform at higher levels, deal with stress in a positive way, and experience better health in the process."

Dan Buettner
New York Times Bestselling
author of *Blue Zones*

"This is the most effective book I have seen that combines hard scientific evidence with simple, pragmatic strategies to live a more resilient life. It's a new pathway to optimum performance. Executives and professionals looking for improved resiliency, performance and health can find it here."

Ken Fenoglio
Vice President
AT&T University

"The Resiliency rEvolution has done a spectacular job of shining light on a new approach to dealing with stress. It is filled with scientific insights, enlightening stories, real life examples and practical tools to improve our lives and work."

Martin Scott
Executive Director
High Potential Talent Development
Comcast University

"Today's 24/7 accessibility of people and information causes stress in all of our lives. Anyone seeking to increase resilience and optimize their potential will greatly benefit from The Resiliency rEvolution. It captures the essence of how the body responds to stress, how it affects our physical and mental performance, and how to use it to our advantage."

Niki Leondakis
CEO
Commune Hotels + Resorts

"Over the course of six months, Jenny stood in front of more than 3,500 executives at AT&T for four hours at a time. Her obvious passion around the material and her genuine concern for the participants in the room created a tidal wave of action. This response was consistent from coast to coast in the United States and didn't skip a beat when we took the program to London and Hong Kong. We could not be more proud to call Jenny Evans our friend and our trusted partner. She has changed our culture for the better and we are forever grateful."

Alyson Woodard
Director of Executive Development
AT&T University

"I want to thank you again for giving us such an amazing presentation. People are still raving about what a life changer it has been for them, how it came at just the right moment, and how they have taken the lessons learned home with them to share with loved ones and colleagues. I have run conferences for 20+ years and your session was the best I've ever seen. The survey results are rating this year's conference a 96% score—the best we've ever had—and it's mainly because of you and your message."

Catherine Viglas
President, Canadian Institute
of Traffic and Transportation (CITT)

"Jenny delivers a keynote that is intelligent, inspiring, and vital, while wrapped in humor and high energy. When she spoke to our international group of educators, she captivated the entire audience with her unique perspective. In today's fast-paced, stress-filled, and economically challenging times, Jenny's message is crucial to helping individuals discover how truly simple balance can be to obtain."

Erik Arveseth
Senior Manager, Education
Aveda Corporation

"Yesterday was outstanding, to the point of flawless. Your humor, authenticity, deep knowledge of the material, and warmth combined to make it an incredible day for our folks, who absolutely loved you. Thanks for giving us your best, and for successfully bringing extraordinary energy and performance to our team."

Jon Anastasio
V.P. Learning & Development
Nordstrom, Inc.

The

Resiliency
rEvolution

YOUR STRESS SOLUTION FOR LIFE
60 SECONDS AT A TIME

Jenny C. Evans, BS, CPT, CFT

ISBN 13: 978-1-940014-26-5
eISBN 13: 978-1-940014-44-9
Library of Congress Number: 2014953080

Printed in the United States of America

11   12   13   14   15   5   4   3   2   1

Cover Design by Nupoor Gordon.
Interior Design by Lift Creative.

Published by Wise Ink Creative Publishing
Minneapolis, Minnesota
www.wiseinkpub.com
To order call (800) 901-3480. Reseller discounts available.

The author of this book does not dispense medical advice or prescribe the use of any technique as a form of treatment for physical, emotional, or medical problems without the advice of a physician, either directly or indirectly. If you suspect that you have a medical problem, we urge you to seek competent medical help. The information given here is designed to help you make informed decisions about your health. Always consult your physician before beginning any exercise program. The author and the publisher disclaim any liabilities of loss in connection with the exercises and advice herein.

TO MY WIFE, TIFFANY

Your unwavering support and confidence have helped keep me always pushing forward.

Every Dolly needs a Carl.

AND TO ISABELLA

You'll always be the best thing I've ever done.

Contents

Introduction

Your career is on an upward trajectory, but so is your stress. With each hard-won achievement comes a greater amount of obligation and sense of responsibility. Your job is never going to ask less of you, nor are your loved ones. The years pass, and your life becomes increasingly more complex, not less. At a certain point, you're no longer responsible for just yourself. Perhaps you start a family. You take on a mortgage. You've got debt. You're managing a team. A loved one's health begins to fail. You're trying to balance a successful career and a fulfilling personal life. Your parents are getting older and need to be taken care of. The future is uncertain.

Your stress continues to increase, and there's not much you can do about it.

You've spent a lot of time and resources training to develop your talent and skill so you can perform well in the workplace. But you've most likely spent little to no time training to *sustain* high performance, to be able to handle the ups and downs of your work over the thirty- to forty-year span of your career. Because of this, you're less resilient, and your high performance at work may be coming at a cost to your health, personal relationships, and happiness.

STRESS DOES NOT DISCRIMINATE

I've spoken to people in almost every industry—consumer goods, pharmaceuticals, government, telecommunications, insurance, finance, technology, energy, personal-care products, and hospitality. These are people living and working in North and South America and Europe, in Japan, India, and the United Arab Emirates. I've worked with a diverse mix of people, for sure. It doesn't matter where in the world I go or to whom I speak—I see the same things over and over again.

I've learned two very important tenets that transcend culture, race, and industry: we all want the same things out of life and struggle with the same major challenges, and what's most private is most universal.

We want fulfilling careers that afford us comfortable lifestyles. We want to raise happy, healthy families. We want to realize our full potential. But we struggle with balancing work and home. The pressure to perform at work continues to build. It's hard to find time to take care of our health. More often than we care to admit (or sometimes more often than we are even consciously aware) we're plagued by self-doubt, anxiety, and fear. There are pits in our stomachs while we lay awake in our beds at night, bathing in silent panic as the list of to-dos and worries continue to play out like a broken record.

We don't realize how universal this is. Stress does not discriminate. I recently did a speaking engagement for a smaller group, and we got into an interesting conversation. One by one, the participants remarked about how other people "seem to have it all together and are successful," while they were struggling so much. When I shared the survey information the participants had completed about the stressors they were facing and how they were coping, they were shocked by how much they all had in common. They were all on the same playing field, and they all felt as if they were losing. We often don't get the opportunity to see behind other people's curtains. The outside world doesn't see the stress, the struggle, and the negative side effects we each face. Often times, people themselves don't see them until it's too late.

In my work with corporate executives from all over the world, I typically see two scenarios in response to sustained levels of high stress. The first scenario is when people's seemingly very successful careers—they've got the titles, the salaries, the power, and the respect of their peers—come at a very expensive cost to:

Their health. They're on multiple medications for high blood pressure, high cholesterol, type 2 diabetes, and anxiety. Their body fat is in the "excess" to "risky" range. They're battling insomnia and getting by on four hours of sleep per night. They drink to relax and caffeinate to get going, and their nutritional habits are literally killing them.

Their personal relationships. Their marriages are on the rocks, or they're divorced. Their kids don't really know them. Or perhaps they're single and don't want to be, but don't have the time or energy to meet others. Friends have long since dropped off the radar, and they only see family on rare special occasions.

Their happiness. They keep thinking another promotion will bring the happiness they've been searching for. They mistakenly think more money, more toys, and bigger houses will make them feel fulfilled.

The second scenario I see happens to the people I *don't* see—they've dropped out of the workforce. They were being pulled in dozens of directions, trying to do it all. They realized they were doing too many things, but none of them very well. The long-term exposure to stress and the pressure to perform well both at work and at home became too much. They got burned out and they quit.

The dEvolution Dilemma

I'm not listing these facts to make you feel bad or depressed or to point out the obvious. It's time to make a change because what we're currently doing isn't working. In the twenty-plus years I've been in this industry, I've watched the decline in our overall health and the steady increase in our daily stress, our waistlines, and the number of medications we're taking. Things are getting worse, *much* worse, not better.

We may think evolution is over, but it's not. We're continually dE-volving to our high stress, mainly sedentary lifestyles, and it's not good.

One hundred thousand generations of hunter-gatherers have been on the planet, along with five hundred generations of agricultural ancestors. During this time, the environment didn't change much, and if it did, it happened quite slowly, giving us plenty of time as a species to adapt.

Contrast this with the drastic and rapid changes we've experienced in our modern history. There's been much less time for our bodies to evolve and adapt: there have only been ten generations of humans living since the industrial age reduced the amount of physical work we do each day, and only two generations since the modern food industry began producing processed, fast, and junk foods.

Our overall genetic makeup has changed very little in the past ten thousand years, but our environments have changed dramatically in the last hundred years.[1] We are hunter-gatherers living in a twenty-first-century environment, and this mismatch is a huge source of ongoing physiological and psychological stress.

You would think living in the modern world would afford us a sense of security, predictability, and safety our ancestors could only dream of. Most of us don't have to worry about our basic survival: we have shelter and food, and our lives are rarely in danger.

Then why are our stress levels so high? Why are life satisfaction and happiness so elusive? According the World Health Organization's World Mental Health Survey Initiative, anxiety disorders are the most common disorders in all countries of the world but one, and mood disorders are the second.[2] The leading cause of disability worldwide is depression.[3] According to the American Psychological Association's *Stressed in Amer-*

ica report, most Americans are suffering from moderate to high levels of stress, and 44 percent are reporting their stress levels are continuing to increase.[4]

Continuing to talk about "reducing stress," "getting healthier," and "losing weight" is a waste of time and resources. It's a strategy we've been trying for decades without any success. That's a great example of insanity: doing the same thing over and over and expecting different results. More education about nutrition isn't the answer. More exercise videos aren't the answer. More pills aren't the answer.

Instead of dEvolution, It's Time for a rEvolution

If the stress in your life will continue to increase, your only option is to train to recover from it more quickly and efficiently and to raise your threshold for it. *You've got to build your resiliency.* In order to be the leader you want to be, the significant other you want to be, the parent you want to be, and the best version of yourself—in the face of your mounting stress—you've got to be diligent about how your habits and routines affect your performance.

RESILIENCY IS THE KEY TO SUSTAINABLE PERFORMANCE.

Over the past twenty years, I've trained thousands of business professionals to improve their resiliency to the relentless stresses they face. This allows them to achieve high levels of performance both professionally as well as personally—and to do it in a way that's *sustainable.* Professional success does not have to come at a cost to your health, your personal relationships, or your peace of mind.

The Resiliency rEvolution is going to be much different than anything you've ever seen. First of all, it's not going to *add* stress. Before learning about exercise physiology and psychology, I spent a lot of time doing stressful things to myself because they seemed to make sense and I thought they were the "answer." For instance, I exercised on an empty stomach, thinking it burned more fat. Or I continually "turned over a new leaf" with a complete lifestyle overhaul each Monday morning. I didn't understand these behaviors were in opposition to how the body and mind work. It was incredibly frustrating and added a lot of unnecessary stress.

This book contains feasible training tools dealing with exercise and nutrition, but I want to make one thing very clear: *this book is NOT about counting calories on a diet or how much you weigh.* It's bigger. It's about training to build the resiliency essential for performing to your absolute best—professionally and personally—in the face of stress.

Stress is often seen as a mental or emotional state. We think stress is when we snap at a coworker or loved one, lie awake at night mulling over an upcoming presentation, or have trouble staying focused. The truth is, stress starts as a physical event, secreting hormones that cause a tsunami of physiological responses:

- Increased breathing, heart rate, and blood pressure

- A rapid mobilization of energy from storage sites around the body

- Blood diverting away from nonessential functions

- Changes in immunity, as well as brain function, memory, and learning

It drastically changes the entire chemical makeup of our body, and these changes can have many negative physiological effects.

You may have tried "stress management" techniques, like breathing or meditation, to deal with the negative effects of stress. As an exercise physiologist, I see "stress management" in a completely different way. I'm going to teach you how to change the chemistry and physiology of your body to stop the negative consequences of stress from happening in the first place. Deep breathing is great . . . *after* the hormonal tsunami. But I'll help you work with stress the moment the floodgates open. Stress management is sending out the cleanup crew after the tsunami; resiliency training is having a preparedness plan in place to prevent a natural disaster.

As part of the rEvolution, you're going to learn there are positive aspects to the stress response and how to use them to your advantage. You'll put into practice specific training techniques that will build your resiliency to stress. Your body will recover from stress more quickly and efficiently, and you'll raise your threshold for it. You'll understand how the brain responds to stress and change, and how to implement a successful training plan that will work for the long term. You will be able to perform better in the face of all the stress you're up against on a daily basis. If these benefits aren't enough, your health will improve, you can lose weight, you'll sleep better, and you'll have more energy.

The book you hold in your hand is organized into three major sections. Section one includes the first two chapters, which will help you understand more about stress. You'll be introduced to a caveman named "Sneaky Pete," and you'll learn about the traits you share with him, how they may be hindering your performance, and how you can better utilize your biological functioning to improve your resiliency, performance, and health. You'll also learn how stress negatively affects cognitive function, memory, and learning—things critical to performing well in the workplace.

The second section of the book provides you with specific tools and training strategies to use on a daily basis. It's the how-to section. In chapter three, you'll learn how to strategically use short bursts of movement to Play It Out. In re-creating critical components of Sneaky Pete's day, you'll hit the "reset button" on stress. You'll train to become more resilient, and in the process, you'll build a body that's stronger and healthier instead of weaker and sicker. Chapter four will cover common eating patterns and behaviors that inadvertently add more stress to the body and will offer ways to eat that will mitigate stress and support sustainable performance and health.

The third section consists of the last two chapters of the book, which teach you to successfully implement what you learn here—and to do it in a way that uses the best of your conscious and unconscious minds. Only enrolling your conscious mind in the rEvolution is like bringing only half your brain on the journey, and you'll need to utilize all your assets. In my experience, getting the knowledge and tools is the easiest part of the equation when it comes to change. The most challenging part of the process is putting the knowledge and tools into practice on a regular basis.

In chapter five, you'll learn how to create a microclimate conducive to change. Your environment consciously as well as unconsciously affects your behavior in significant ways, and you'll understand how to create an environment that *literally* makes change a no-brainer. Chapter six teaches you how to effectively introduce change to Sneaky Pete. Otherwise, changing too much, too soon, stimulates the stress response, and you'll end up seeking comfort and security through old habits and routines—pushing you back to the starting line, or even further behind.

Between the chapters you'll be reading success stories about people just like you. These are individuals who struggled for years with stress and making the appropriate changes to their lifestyles, until they started incorporating the things you'll be learning about. They became a part of the rEvolution, and it benefitted them in a myriad of ways. I hope to be able to share your success story after you join rEvolution as well.

I'm excited to share this information with you because it has the potential to change your life in some amazing ways. I know it has in mine.

Welcome to the rEvolution.

Between the chapters, you will find success stories featuring some of my clients. Success comes in many forms. One person's first step toward their goal might be step four to another. One person's primary goal might be something another person inadvertently achieves as a secondary side effect. The people I've coached work in very different fields and have every kind of goal you could imagine for their personal lives and careers. But all of them share one desire: to become more resilient to stress.

The real people I interviewed for these success stories made two simple commitments over the course of sixty days. First, they worked out five times each week, using Hit the Deck at least four times per week. They averaged fifteen to thirty-five minutes of training per day. Second, they stepped back, evaluated their eating patterns, then made one or two small changes in line with the nutritional advice in this book. For instance, they decided to eat breakfast every day or schedule a lunchtime "meeting"—complete with alarms and reminders—so they couldn't forget to eat lunch or schedule over it. (And don't worry: you'll learn plenty about Hit the Deck and the nutrition advice soon. In the meantime, the key thing to understand is that these are simple but powerful ways to get more movement and eat better.)

For those who want hard numbers, each client has shared his or her training and accountability logs from the sixty days. I calculated changes in perceived stress from their daily self-evaluations of how often they felt nervous or stressed, how often they felt upset by an unexpected event, and how often they felt overwhelmed, angry, or unable to cope with the things they needed to do. I calculated sleep quality from self-evaluations of how long it took to fall asleep, number of sleep interruptions per night, and, when available, information from tracking devices. I calculated energy levels from self-evaluations of how often each person felt "on top of things," or confident about facing challenges, as well as from overall feelings of well-being. And I calculated changes in body fat and muscle from their baseline and sixty-day measurements.

These are real people who joined the rEvolution and have shared their struggles and triumphs with me. They show just a few of the many ways we can build resilience and reclaim time and energy from stress. I hope you find their stories an inspiration to reach your own goals!

Success Story

SCOTT

Scott's Story

"My biggest source of stress?" Scott laughs. "Selling on 100 percent commission. The challenge can be energizing, but the pressure is immense." At thirty-seven years old, Scott is married and has two daughters, ages one and three. As an outside sales representative selling hotel supplies, he travels every week and feels a lot of pressure to find new business accounts while providing high-quality service to his current customer base.

"My wife and I both work full-time, but we agreed early on that we would make the kids a priority," he says. However, he admits their work-life balance comes at the expense of time for him and his wife to focus on their relationship. "We have a lot of fun together, and I wish we could make date nights happen more often—who doesn't want that?"

Around the house, days often start with frustration and low-grade anxiety. Scott realizes there's more yelling and hustle than he would like as he and his wife get the girls ready to go.

Like many high-powered business travelers, Scott finds it hard to stick to a rigid plan for food and exercise. "I'll be the first to admit that my eating habits are not the greatest," he says. "I got a gym membership, which was great, but I would spend two hours there one day and then not have a chance to get back for a week. It was too expensive to maintain when I'm in another state twenty days a month."

Life on the road also means eating out the vast majority of the time: entertaining clients, hitting the drive-through between meetings, or grabbing fast food at an airport.

He has a hard time falling asleep and typically feels listless and tired in the morning. "I started getting these headaches from the stress," he says, "almost every day, like clockwork. That's the point where I thought, this isn't working, I need to fix this."

Scott's rEvolution

After sixty days of resiliency training with Hit the Deck and changing his eating patterns, Scott finds himself falling asleep more easily and sleeping more soundly. The headaches have disappeared, and he feels more focused at work and at home—able to deal with stress more productively than ever.

While still traveling more days than not each month, Scott uses Hit the Deck to stay active on his own schedule, without the expensive gym membership or relying on hotel gyms that lack the right equipment. He has lost more than ten pounds of fat.

Most importantly, he faces each day with renewed energy. "The energy is the best part," he says. "I don't find myself wishing that the girls would fall asleep so that our quality time could be a nap."

SCOTT AFTER SIXTY DAYS OF RESILIENCY TRAINING

- 40 percent decrease in perceived stress

- 32 percent increase in energy

- 20 percent improvement in quality of sleep

- 40 percent improvement in ability to fall asleep

- Lost 11.1 pounds (4.6 percent) of body fat

- Lost 5.75 inches

Chapter 1

....

CAVEMEN HAD NO LOVE HANDLES

I'd like to introduce you to someone very special. This is Pete. Actually, he needs no introduction because you already know him. In fact, you've spent your entire life with him.

© Craig Sjodin/American
Broadcasting Companies, Inc.

Pete
a.k.a. Sneaky Pete

When you got stressed-out in that meeting last week, he's the one who made you blurt something you later regretted. He's responsible for keeping you awake at night, unable to stop thinking about whether you'll hit your numbers this month or how you can continue to do the work of two people at your job. Pete's the one who planted the big idea to pig out on that cheeseburger and fries you grabbed in the drive-through on your way to see your next client. And that spare tire around your waist you can't seem to get rid of, no matter what you do? That's entirely his fault. He's also the one who gave the finger to the driver who cut you off while you were late for yoga. (Okay, that last one only happened to me, and the irony of the situation was laughable . . . *after* I got my Zen on.)

If that's not enough, Pete is completely taking over when it comes to making important business decisions. He's clouding your focus and concentration, he's inhibiting your memory, and he's distracting you from your goals and objectives. He's also dating your significant other and raising your children, if you have them.

Pete sounds like a total bastard, and you're probably wondering why anyone would ever want to hang out with someone like him, right? Believe it or not, he has your best interests in mind and does all these things for a very important reason: your survival.

Pete represents your primitive, biological, evolutionarily-driven stress response—also known as the fight-or-flight response. (Throughout the book, I will use the terms "stress response" and "fight-or-flight response" interchangeably.) We're all hardwired to respond in a very particular way to the many stresses, demands, and strains we face on a daily basis. How our distant ancestors responded to stress successfully restored balance to the body. It was like hitting the "reset button" after the release of stress hormones. It was a healthy response.

Today, most of us no longer hit the reset button in that same way, mainly because of the environments we're living in. This is what Pete is trying to get you to do. From this point forward, we're going to refer to him as "Sneaky Pete," because however misguided he sounds, he's doing everything in his power to help you with stress.

Sneaky Pete possesses the key to improved resiliency to the stress in our lives. Throughout this book he will be our reference point, guide, and coach in building resiliency to stress. You'll also understand what he's doing and why, so you can learn how to work *with* him instead of *against* him.

Why Cavemen?

Several years ago, I was driving down the freeway and saw a billboard from the health insurance company Blue Cross Blue Shield. It was part of their "Do" campaign to get people to move more often. It said: "Cavemen. They had no cars. They had no escalators. They had no love handles."

I thought to myself, how clever—funny, but gets a point across.

You know how when you're driving, you go into this stream-of-consciousness sort of thinking—it's just one thought to another? I started thinking more about the billboard. And the more I thought about it, the more I realized how brilliant it really was.

Cavemen's waistlines were different than ours not just because they were more active than we are. They were under a lot of daily stress, and as part of the stress response, they released a large amount of cortisol. As you will learn in more detail later in the book, cortisol is a stress hormone that, among other things, is responsible for depositing fat around the midsection. I got to thinking that cavemen did a lot of fighting and fleeing in response to their stress—such as attacks from predators—that used up cortisol. Because of this, if they *did* have some extra fat stored on their body, it probably wasn't all settled around their waist. No love handles.

I have no idea if this message is what the makers of the billboard actually intended, but it's been the jumping-off point for much of the work and research I've done since. It's the cornerstone of the Resiliency rEvolution, and at the center of it all is the fight-or-flight response.

Fight-or-Flight in Sixty Seconds

There are many longwinded, scientific definitions of *stress* I could cite here, but I like to keep things simple. A **stressor**, or **stress**, is anything that pushes the body out of homeostatic balance. The **stress response** is what your body does to restore balance. The stress response is a *very good thing*.

Stress can be good, bad, physical, psychological, or even just imagined. There are the obvious stressors, such as being under a deadline, missing a sales goal, or having to give an important presentation. But even positive life events can push us out of balance: moving into a new home, having a child, getting married, or getting a promotion. There's the stress of being sleep deprived or going too long without eating, along with the stress from what we process in our heads, either responding to our current environments, what may happen in the future, or what happened in the past.

Every time we're exposed to stress of any kind, the stress response is stimulated. I often refer to it as the "stress tsunami" because it's a tidal wave of hormones released into the body. It's very powerful, and once it starts, it can't be stopped.

You'll learn more details about the fight-or-flight response in chapter two, but here is the CliffsNotes version: the core of the stress response is built around the fact that your muscles need immediate energy to fight or flee in response to stress. (Again, think about Sneaky Pete and the predator.) The brain tells the pituitary gland to secrete stress hormones, which signal the release of energy from storage sites around the body. This stored energy flows into the bloodstream so your muscles can immediately use it for fuel. The subsequent intense physical activity of the fighting or fleeing uses up those stress hormones and causes a new set of hormones—like endorphins—to be released. These new hormones slow things back down and make you feel calm. The end result is that balance is restored. You've just hit the reset button.

STRESS
↓
STRESS HORMONES
↓
ENERGY
↓
FIGHT OR FLEE
(PLAY IT OUT)
↓
BLISS MOLECULES
↓
BALANCE RESTORED

The stress response

The stress response is a beautifully designed system—when it plays itself all the way out. The critical component to the system, however, is the fighting or fleeing, the short burst of intense physical activity. I call that key step "Play It Out," as it allows the stress response to play itself out as it was designed to restore balance. (You'll be learning how to do this in chapter three.) We are all genetically hardwired this way:

STRESS + APPROPRIATE PHYSICAL
RESPONSE = BALANCE RESTORED

Sneaky Pete's Stress vs. Our Stress

For the vast majority of living creatures, stress is a short-term crisis, after which either *it's* over with or *we're* over with. Many of the survival issues humans faced in our first few million years did not take days, weeks, or years to play out. For this reason, our physiological stress response system adapted to deal with short-term emergencies. For example, let's take a look at Sneaky Pete's main sources of stress:

- Predators

- Physical injury

- Food

- Climate

The predator stressor is short-term, with a very definitive end: Sneaky Pete was either killed or he ran away. The whole thing lasted about thirty to sixty seconds and played itself out as he fought or fled. The stress of physical injury also played itself out fairly quickly. Losing the ability to hunt, gather, travel, or fight would soon bring his life to a close. Becoming ill from eating bad food or starving from lack of food took just a bit longer to resolve. Climate was the one stress that was truly long-term.

Let's fast-forward from Sneaky Pete to us:

- You have two or even three overlapping workdays. You have your regular, scheduled workday consisting of meetings, servicing clients and customers, managing communications, and connecting with colleagues scattered around the globe. You squeeze in another "workday" before, after, and in between your scheduled workday. You get up early to get a jump on emails, you stay late to work on tasks you didn't have time to do earlier, and you multitask during the day in an attempt to be as productive as possible. Your third "workday" begins when you leave the office. You have to pick up food, get the kids to practice, run a load of laundry, and make sure the house hasn't fallen apart. After everyone goes to bed, you see the opportunity to get on your computer to get more work done.

- Your job is continually asking you to do more with less. Resources are tight, businesses are downsizing, and you may be doing the jobs of two or three people who were let go and never replaced. US worker productivity has increased rapidly since 1995, while median family income has stayed stagnant.[1]

- The job market is very competitive. If you have a complaint about your job, you're told to just be happy you *have* a job, even if it sucks, so be quiet—and get back to work. According to Gallup's *State of the Global Workplace* report, 62 percent of employees are not engaged in their jobs, are emotionally detached, and are doing little more than necessary on the job.[2]

- Smartphones, laptops, iPads, and video conferencing allow you to always work or be available. It's also a global marketplace that never sleeps: you have conference calls in the middle of the night with Asia or midnight launches that require troubleshooting into the wee hours.

- You might travel frequently, making it even more difficult to be healthy. Crossing time zones messes up your sleep pattern, you don't know what kind of food will be available, and you don't have room in your suitcase to pack your workout gear.

- You've got more debt than you're comfortable with. Perhaps the combination of taking on too much debt and not saving enough for retirement means you have to work longer than you thought.

- You turn on the news, and story after story is about the negative, horrible things happening in the world: reports on missing children and natural disasters. The stock market is unpredictable. You're at the airport, and the threat level is orange.

What do all your sources of stress have in common? And how are they different from Sneaky Pete's stressors? Most of your stressors are long-term and ongoing, with no definitive end or closure. They often result in a constant stream of stress hormones. You have the feeling of never "resolving" anything—there are *always* more emails, voicemails, meetings, reports, and bills. We have chronic worries like money, promotions, deadlines, competing priorities, office politics, relationships—and chronic health issues. We're facing a completely new set of stress factors Sneaky Pete couldn't have even fathomed. It all adds up to never-ending stress, and we're not doing a very good job of handling it.

OUR STRESS RESPONSES WERE DESIGNED TO SOLVE PROBLEMS FOR SECONDS, NOT FOR YEARS.

When our jobs become extremely demanding, and we're under the gun to meet critical deadlines, we typically respond to stress in ways that go against how we're physiologically designed to function. We're gradually dEvolving. We *add* to our stress, not diminish it.

We wake up early and stay up late to get things done, getting by on far less sleep than needed. Our workouts are the first things cut from a busy schedule. We end up skipping meals or grabbing whatever food is fast and convenient. In an attempt to get relief from stress, we self-medi-cate with sugar, fat, alcohol, nicotine, or caffeine, all of which actually *add more stress* to the body, not less.

The Consequences of Not Playing It Out

We're exposed to frequent bouts of stress all day long, yet fight-or-flight is still alive and well in all of us, just as it is in Sneaky Pete. But when we get stressed, can we fight? No. It's considered inappropriate to punch our bosses. Can we flee? Sorry. We can't take off running from the con-ference room to escape the situation, either. How many opportunities do we have to Play It Out? Typically none, and our systems were not designed for this.

Then how do we use up the stress hormones? Unfortunately, most of us don't. The problem is, when we don't Play It Out, we short-circuit the design of the stress response system. The stress hormones don't get flushed out, and they continue to circulate in the body and brain. And that can lead to what one stress expert calls the "Toxic Broth of Dread," a state of stewing in our own stress hormones.[3]

Prolonged exposure to high levels of stress hormones has many negative short- and long-term consequences. You'll learn more about these consequences later in the book, but here are the quick facts: Stress hormones affect your mental and emotional capital. They literally shrink the area in the brain associated with memory, learning, working toward a defined goal, predicting outcomes, and forming strategies and planning. In addition, they increase the portions of the brain responsible for fear, anxiety, and aggression.[4]

Long-term exposure to stress hormones is also tied to insomnia, and it makes us crave sugary, fatty foods. It deposits more fat around the abdominal region and blood vessel walls, increasing our risk of cardio-vascular disease, diabetes, and many other serious health issues. A large body of evidence suggests that stress-related diseases result from turning on the stress response and leaving it on for long periods of time, as compared to turning it on, playing it out quickly, and recovering from it. In addition, we have much longer life spans, which only increases the amount of time our body is exposed to stress.

The reason for these consequences can be found if we examine and compare Sneaky Pete's lifestyle to our own.

Sneaky Pete's Workout and Diet

From an evolutionary perspective, the human brain and body developed while our early ancestors "worked out"—and these exercise sessions weren't optional. Sneaky Pete walked up to twelve miles per day just in search of food and resources.[5] He got cardiovascular interval training by stalking and sprinting after prey—or away from predators. His resistance training consisted of carrying heavy loads of food and water. Foraging for food demanded bending, climbing, digging, and lifting. He constructed his own shelter and built the tools needed to do so. That was quite a daily workout, burning roughly three to five times the number of calories than we do today.[6] He also had to quit working when it got dark, allowing him ample time to rest up and recover for another day of high-energy expenditure.

Sneaky Pete had to work *hard* to cover the basics of survival. The level of physical activity required to provide food, water, and shelter resulted in what is referred to as "effort-based reward." The work Sneaky Pete did was difficult, but it was rewarding not only from a resources perspective, but also from a mental, emotional, and chemical one. He saw the results and benefits of what his work produced each day, and it made him feel good to know that how he was spending his time and energy mattered. It was an evolutionary adaptation to keep him working even when it was expensive from an energy standpoint.

In addition to working hard to get food, what Sneaky Pete ate was whole, natural, organic, and high in nutrients and fiber. The wild plants our ancestors gathered and ate were markedly higher in vitamins, minerals, essential fatty acids, and phytonutrients—elements necessary for good health.[7] They were also lower in sugar content. For instance, the wild ancestral versions of bananas, corn, and carrots were nowhere near as sweet as the ones we consume today.

I'm not suggesting we go back to our caveman ways—it was a short and difficult life. However, taking into account how our body was designed to function, we've slowly created an environment that's making us weaker as a species.

The Caveman Body in a Modern World

Today's modern world doesn't match the design of our caveman body and brain. Just looking at the twentieth century alone, there was a huge shift from labor-intense production industries to professional, service-related, and technological ones, requiring little physical exertion or movement. At the beginning of the century, farmers made up 38 percent of the workforce, but only 3 percent at its end. Even at the end of the century, service-related jobs grew from 31 percent of all workers in 1990 to 78 percent in 1999.[8]

In addition to our workplaces changing rapidly, technology also entered our homes and decreased our amount of physical activity. We have clothes washers and dryers, dishwashers, vacuum cleaners, leaf blowers, and snow blowers. We have televisions and computers in many rooms of our homes, providing hours of entertainment to be consumed while sitting. We expend 8,800 fewer calories per month because of these modern conveniences (which equates to about thirty pounds of fat over a year, if we don't modify our food intake).[9]

Today, many of us measure distance not in miles but in feet—from the closest parking spot to our desk or from the couch to the refrigerator and back. The muscles that get the most exercise are those in our index fingers, swiping and clicking a tablet or smartphone. Because of this, our average energy expenditure is 38 percent less than our Stone Age ancestors'.[10]

We're mainly sedentary, stuck behind desks for ten to twelve hours a day. We don't get to fight or flee to Play It Out after stress. Instead of being burned off, the stress hormones continue to circulate throughout the body, wreaking havoc on our performance and health. The sedentary nature of many of our societies also means we're not activating areas of the brain critical for reward and pleasure, motivation, problem solving, and effective coping strategies. We're missing out on the effort-based reward Sneaky Pete's hard work earned.

Our genes expect us to be physically active if they are to function normally. Even if we did thirty minutes of physical activity every day, we'd still be at less than half the energy expenditure for which our genes are encoded.[11] We were not designed to sit behind desks for ten hours a day. If Sneaky Pete sat around on the savannah for ten hours—or even ten minutes—he would be someone's dinner.

OUR BODY WAS DESIGNED TO MOVE!

If you wanted to create an environment directly opposed to what the brain and body were designed to do, you'd create something like a cubicle or classroom. Our body was designed to move, and integrating movement into our workday or school day should be *normal*!

We've also dEvolved into a chronically sleep-deprived society. Electricity allows us to stay up well beyond sunset, and we've got more options for entertainment than ever before. We may stay up late to watch a favorite show, binge-watch episodes online (just one more!), or watch TV or go online as a way to try disconnecting from a busy day. We might view evenings as a window of time to get caught up on work, when people aren't constantly popping into our offices or we don't have to be in endless strings of meetings. When we do get to bed, we're physically tired but find our mind racing, continuing to process, making to-do lists, and worrying. We can't get to sleep, or if we manage to do so, it's only to find ourselves awake again at 2:36 a.m., struggling to get back to sleep. We then wake up exhausted.

We now live in an obesogenic society, where food is abundant and available in large portions. Getting food is as quick as picking up the phone and having it delivered right to our front door, or as easy as driving up to the fast food drive-through. Much of our food has been altered with artificial flavorings, colorants, preservatives, salt, sugar, and fake fats. Many foods are high in calories, but low in nutrients and fiber. We also have perpetual access to drugs that alter our mood states, energy levels, and balance, riding the roller coasters of caffeine, alcohol, and tobacco throughout the day.

Inactivity is abnormal considering our evolution and results in abnormal expression of our genes, such as disease. This mismatch between our current environments and how we were designed to function has created preventable "diseases of civilization" responsible for an estimated 75 percent of all deaths in Western nations.[12] That's dEvolution at its best. The rates of most chronic diseases are far lower in countries where physical work is a large part of daily life.

So What Can We Do about It?

We have to Play It Out, and physical activity is key. The good news here is that it's not going to require an hour at the gym or even thirty minutes on a machine. Sneaky Pete didn't have time for that, and neither do you! When we tap into our body's innate and ancient intelligence, it's possible to balance our primitive operating system with today's advanced world—and to do it in a way that's sustainable.

We need to look back a bit to successfully move forward. Sneaky Pete is your BFF, not your mortal enemy. Taking the best of what he does and combining it with the assets you've developed will make you more resilient.

In the next chapter, you'll learn more about what's going on in your body and brain during stress, why most of it is good, but also where things go bad.

 For more information about the mismatch between you and Sneaky Pete, visit www.ph-performance.com/caveman

Success Story

LORI

Lori's Story

When Lori decided to start resiliency training, she was forty-five years old and the mother of three kids (ages ten, sixteen, and seventeen). She owned a small business requiring a few hours of face-to-face client time each week.

Her husband had recently been laid off, and both of them were hunting for full-time work while managing the kids' busy schedules. During that time, her father's health began declining, and he had moved into a nursing home. Lori took responsibility for his care and visited as often as she could. He died a few months after her husband lost his job.

"Wow," she says, "now that I look back, it was a time with a lot of changes in my life, but it didn't seem that stressful as I was going through it."

Lori recalls having trouble sleeping and never feeling rested during that time. Tempers frayed as both she and her husband followed lead after lead, but never got employers to bite.

Leaning increasingly on her business for income while taking care of the kids—who often needed to be in three different places at the same time—she frequently delayed or skipped meals to make more time. "I was going way too long without eating," she says, "but I didn't realize it."

She also felt physically weak and she tired easily, something she thought she just had to accept as part of getting older.

Lori's rEvolution

After sixty days of resiliency training, Lori says, "I feel like I'm twenty-five again. I've got more energy to do more, and I *want* to do more, too." She falls more easily into a deep, sound sleep and wakes up feeling refreshed and ready to tackle the day.

"Simply shifting when and how I ate made such a big difference. It was thinking about food in a whole new way, as fuel for my body." She has lost body fat, gained muscle, and best of all, she says, "I feel strong again!"

Although it took a year, Lori's husband has finally landed a new job, and everyday stress has declined to more manageable levels. But that doesn't mean Lori will cut back on her resiliency-building habits. "I've made a life change," she says, "and resiliency training is a necessary part of my day now. It's something I'll do forever."

LORI AFTER SIXTY DAYS OF RESILIENCY TRAINING

- 50 percent decrease in perceived stress

- 31 percent increase in energy

- 60 percent improvement in quality of sleep

- 60 percent improvement in ability to fall asleep

- Lost 14 pounds (5.8 percent) of body fat

- Gained 6 pounds of muscle

- Lost 5.25 inches

Chapter 2

THE CHEMISTRY OF STRESS

Jeff heads the human resources department of a large investment banking company. His job involves handling complex and emotionally intense employee problems, including firing executives in the C-suite. How people react to the news of losing their high-paying jobs runs the gamut from breaking into tears to threatening physical violence. The nature of his work takes him around the globe, which has him on the road about 40 percent of the time. His wife also works full-time.

For the past several years, Jeff has had a lot of sleep and energy problems in addition to quite a bit of weight gain. He has a history of diabetes and does not exercise very often. He feels he doesn't have any time or energy for it, and it seems impossible when he's traveling. To make matters worse, his job involves a lot of sitting behind a desk or in long meetings.

In addition to regularly traveling to different time zones, he's a night owl who likes to stay up late to get work done. When he goes to bed, it takes him a long time to fall asleep, then he wakes up several times during the night. In the morning, he feels completely exhausted. He drinks a lot of caffeine during the day as well as eats a lot of sweets and candy in an attempt to keep his energy going.

Jeff regularly eats at restaurants with colleagues or has room service when he's traveling. He and his wife are very social and love to entertain, and their evening hours are spent either having big dinners with friends or making elaborate meals at home. Both scenarios involve a good amount of alcohol, in addition to his nightly bedtime ritual of a drink or two to relax.

Colleagues have great things to say about Jeff's work ethic and commitment to his job, and he's rapidly advancing in the company. His wife knows he's trying his best at home to be a great husband. But Jeff feels he's not putting in his best work at home or at the office. He's tired of being tired and stressed all the time.

Jeff doesn't realize it, but Sneaky Pete has wrestled control over much of his life, and Jeff is functioning in survival mode much of the time. He doesn't comprehend how much his stress is affecting his physiology, nor how his attempts at coping are actually making the stress worse, not better.

What Is Stress?

Most of us would answer this question by describing feelings, such as anxiety, frustration, irritability, fear, or worry. We'd say stress can make us feel short-tempered. We may snap at a coworker, get impatient with a loved one, or lie awake at night playing through all sorts of scenarios that may or may not happen. All of these things are mental and emotional states that come from our brain, and because of this, we often think of stress as a cognitive event that happens in our head.

But as we briefly discussed in chapter one, the reality is that stress is a significant **physical** event that begins with the brain. Once our brain registers that a stressful event is happening or has the potential to happen, it sends chemical and electrical messages through nerves to the rest of our body. This results in a release of many different categories of hormones that produce very quick and dramatic changes to our entire chemical makeup and affect all types of systems in the body. These changes influence brain function, energy, metabolism, appetite, sleep, immunity, and more.

STRESS IS A CHEMISTRY PROBLEM.

It's vitally important to understand how the stress response works so we can recognize what it's trying to do and learn to use it to our advantage. Let's dig into the chemistry of stress, beginning at, of course, its source.

Where It Starts

Your brain is the starting point. A network of nerves from the brain connects to both the somatic and autonomic nervous systems of the body. The somatic, or voluntary, nervous system is used when you make conscious decisions to control movement of the large muscle groups of the body. The autonomic nervous system is related to unconscious and involuntary movement. As environmental factors change, the autonomic nervous system reacts in an attempt to maintain homeostatic balance. It adjusts the internal environment of the body by regulating smaller muscles related to heart rate, breathing, digestion, and perspiration. (I'm big on word association. For me, it helps to remember that the autonomic nervous system *automatically* adjusts.)

The autonomic nervous system is further divided into two parts that synchronize to maintain balance: the sympathetic and parasympathetic nervous systems. The sympathetic nervous system is activated during the stress response. We should think of it as the gas pedal that speeds things up. The instant your brain senses or anticipates stress, the sympathetic nervous system takes over, and the gas pedal is punched to the floor. It's the fight-or-flight response in action. (More word association for you: the sympathetic nervous system is *sympathetic* to our stress.)

The parasympathetic nervous system is the counterbalance, or the brake. It slows things down, stimulates relaxation, and recharges the batteries for the next stressful event—which is often referred to as "rest and digest."

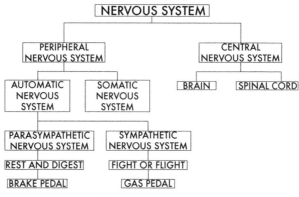

The nervous system

The gas and brake pedals of these two systems work together with give-and-take to balance each other out. The sympathetic nervous system speeds up heart rate when needed, then the parasympathetic slows it down. The sympathetic diverts blood flow to the muscles and tenses them during stress, then the parasympathetic sends blood flow away from the muscles and relaxes them afterward. It's a highly regulated ebb and flow dependent on whether we perceive external stimuli as either stressful, potentially stressful, or safe.

Earlier on I referred to the stress response as a stress tsunami: a release of hormones that sets off a powerful wave of chemical events that change our physiology. In reality, this tsunami is actually made of two waves that happen almost simultaneously. The first wave targets immediate, short-term issues, whereas the second wave deals with longer-term concerns.

A portion of the brain called the hypothalamus is responsible for maintaining constant body states, such as food and water intake, temperature regulation, hormones, and mediation of emotional responses.

The hypothalamus signals a part of the adrenal glands called the adrenal medulla. The adrenal medulla pumps out the hormones adrenaline and noradrenaline as the first wave of defense in a stressful situation. This first wave happens in a matter of seconds.[1]

> Adrenaline and noradrenaline are also known as epinephrine and norepinephrine. The difference in the terminology is mainly geographical: Americans use the terms adrenaline and noradrenaline, while many other countries use the terms epinephrine and norepinephrine.

The second wave of the stress response begins over the course of minutes.[2] It's referred to as the hypothalamic-pituitary-adrenal, or HPA, axis. It's a feedback loop between the hypothalamus, the pituitary gland, and the adrenal glands. The hypothalamus stimulates the release of corticotropin-releasing hormone, which in turn induces the pituitary gland to release adrenocorticotropic hormone. This hormone then stimulates the adrenal cortex (another part of the adrenal glands) to pump out cortisol. Cortisol is a glucocorticoid, a longer-acting hormone in the body.

HPA Axis

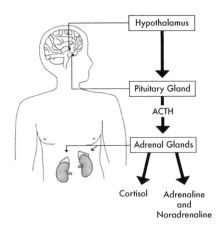

The hypothalamic-pituitary-adrenal (HPA) axis

The stress hormones adrenaline, noradrenaline, and cortisol signal rapid changes to the entire body. They are all *good* changes, perfectly designed to help us meet the challenges of stress—so long as we follow through with the next step of the cycle. We do that when we fight or flee, or more realistically in today's world, when we Play It Out.

That's the *good* news. As you will see later in the chapter, there's a lot of *bad* news about these stress hormones when we don't hold up our end of the deal.

But before we get into the detailed actions of these stress hormones, we need to cover the basics about two very important substances the hormones affect: glucose and insulin. (We'll be talking more about this in chapter four, too.)

Glucose and Insulin

Glucose, or blood sugar, is the primary circulating free sugar in the bloodstream. It's the source of energy for many cells in the body. Glucose is obtained from the foods we eat and is a major factor in metabolism. Not only is it important for supplying energy to muscle cells, but it's also critical for brain function. In fact, glucose is the *only* thing we eat that our brain can utilize as energy to function. The brain requires about 25 percent of the body's glucose supply.[3]

The body is very specific about where it wants blood glucose levels to be, and it will go to great lengths to keep them balanced. Two hormones that help regulate this balance are insulin and glucagon. The pancreas secretes both of these, and they work in opposition to each other to either increase or decrease blood glucose levels, depending on needs.

When blood glucose levels rise, so does the output of insulin. Its job is to take the glucose out of the bloodstream and put it into the cells. As blood glucose levels drop, so does the amount of insulin produced by the pancreas. When glucose levels get too low (from things such as going too long without eating or during exercise), the pancreas produces glucagon. That in turn stimulates the release of glucose from the liver into the bloodstream, where it's also delivered to the cells. The liver synthesizes this glucose from other nutrients in the body, primarily protein.

HIGH BLOOD GLUCOSE = INSULIN RELEASE
LOW BLOOD GLUCOSE = GLUCAGON RELEASE

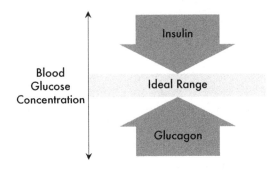

How insulin and glucagon affect blood glucose

Insulin is highly influenced by the stress hormones adrenaline, noradrenaline, and cortisol. It plays a very important role in metabolism and the regulation of the carbohydrates, proteins, and fats we eat. Our body breaks these nutrients down into usable forms of energy, such as glucose, amino acids, and lipid molecules, respectively. When needed, the body can store these types of energy as well as transform them into more complex forms.

Insulin's number one job is to lower blood glucose levels by removing it from the bloodstream. It does this through several different means:

- **It feeds glucose to the cells of our muscles and brain.** When glucose enters the bloodstream, it doesn't just flow right into our cells. It needs something to help it be absorbed. Think of insulin as the gatekeeper with a key. Without insulin to unlock the door to the cells, glucose would continue to circulate in the bloodstream and build to dangerously high levels. Too much blood glucose can ultimately lead to seizures, coma, and death. Also, without insulin to let energy into the cells, you could eat a lot of food and still be in a state of starvation, as the cells wouldn't actually be getting fed.

- **It stores glucose in the liver and muscle cells.** Insulin can signal the liver to convert glucose into glycogen (a polysaccharide that is the principle storage form of glucose). This form of energy is stored in the liver as well as the muscle cells for future use.

- **It converts glucose to fat.** When the liver has reached its glycogen-storing limit, insulin is involved in synthesizing the excess glucose into fatty acids, which are then converted into lipoproteins. High-density lipoproteins (HDL) and low-density lipoproteins (LDL) enable fats and cholesterol to be carried in the bloodstream. These lipoproteins can be broken into free fatty acids that are used as energy by other tissues.

- **It stores fat in our fat cells.** Insulin controls fat storage and metabolism. Lipoproteins are also converted to triglycerides, and insulin can stimulate the storage of this form of fat in the fat cells. When muscle and brain cells reach their capacity to utilize blood glucose, the fat cells become the primary storage site for this excess energy in the bloodstream. Insulin can also put the body in fat-storage mode. It sends a signal to stop any breakdown and usage of fat stored in adipose tissue. This ensures that fat doesn't get released into the bloodstream to add to usable energy levels.

Instant Response

Let's go back to Jeff to see this process in action. It's early afternoon, and he's sitting in an empty conference room, waiting for a meeting to begin. In this meeting, he'll be terminating a high-level executive who's been with the company for over ten years.

He knows from past firing experiences that this person could get very combative, very quickly. As Jeff is waiting, he plays through several possible scenarios in his head. He starts feeling a bit sick to his stomach and notices his palms are getting clammy. No matter how many times he does this, it never gets easier.

The executive walks into the room, sees Jeff sitting there, and immediately understands what this meeting is about. As Jeff begins the process of firing him, the now-former executive's face gets red and he starts to tremble. He begins to yell, pound his fist on the desk, and rise out of his chair.

Jeff realizes this meeting has real potential of getting out of control. By this time, Jeff's brain and autonomic nervous system have already shot off electrical signals that told the adrenal glands and the HPA axis to do their jobs. The gas pedal has been punched.

The entire stress response is built around the fact that muscles will have to work at a very intense level to successfully fight or flee. Those muscles need large amounts of energy, right away, and in the most readily available form, which is glucose. The body very quickly switches from energy-saving mode to energy-spending mode. The stress hormones signal the release of energy from storage sites on Jeff's body. Glucose, proteins (in the form of amino acids), and fats (triglycerides) come pouring out of his liver and out of his muscle and fat cells and rush into the bloodstream.

Blood circulation is critical in delivering these forms of energy to his muscles, so heart rate and blood pressure increase to pump this energized blood to the muscle cells more quickly. Blood is now roaring through Jeff's body. His muscles will also need enormous amounts of oxygen for the physical exertion of fighting or fleeing, so his breathing becomes very rapid.

Because his muscles need so much energy-rich blood to fight and/or flee, it's being diverted away from nonessential body functions that don't support his immediate survival. Less blood is going to his stomach to digest his lunch; growth and tissue repair take a backseat; and less blood is traveling to his genitals, decreasing sex drive (not that it would be appropriate at this particular moment, anyway).

Jeff's body is also preparing for the possibility of injury that may happen during the fight-or-flight process. Two significant shifts happen to his immune system: his short-term immunity increases, while his long-term immunity decreases. There's no point in putting energy into the long-term immune system that may no longer be needed if things don't go well in the next minute or two. His body makes white blood cells available and ready to travel to any location that may become injured so they can start to immediately permeate the site of the potential injury. Fibrinogen is also released, which speeds up clotting in case of a loss of blood due to injury.

His perceptions of pain become blunted. His body doesn't want him to stop fighting or fleeing just because he took a punch to the face or twisted his ankle while running out of the conference room. In fact, this response can be so strong that soldiers on the battlefield can sustain a life-threatening injury and not notice it until the heat of the battle is over.

There are also large shifts in Jeff's cognitive and sensory functions. More blood flows to his brain, and certain aspects of his memory improve. His senses heighten, and his pupils dilate to let in more light as he tries to focus on his environment to perceive and receive cues about what is happening and what the appropriate response should be.

Because Sneaky Pete has taken over, raw emotion and immediate action are the primary drivers of whatever happens next. Forget being politically correct, choosing his words carefully, or taking into consideration how these next few minutes may affect the future of his job. Jeff is in survival mode, and Sneaky Pete just wants to get him out of the meeting without being harmed.

Both Jeff and the former executive are in fight-or-flight mode. Having two Sneaky Petes going head to head is a precarious scenario. Even though Jeff and the other man are trying to maintain professional demeanor, the caveman portion of their brains is overriding their advanced part.

Adrenaline and Noradrenaline—The Bad News

It required two pages to explain what happened inside Jeff's body, but it took only seconds for all of it to happen. How did Jeff's body do all those things almost immediately? The answer is the stress hormones adrenaline and noradrenaline. The stress hormones were responsible for everything that happened to Jeff's body before and during the meeting, and all of it was *really good* for the short term. The changes and responses were all very well suited for preparing his body for a proper reaction to a stressful event—one that plays itself out.

However, because Jeff didn't actually fight or flee or Play It Out, the result was *really bad* for the long term. All the wonderful preparatory and reactionary things Sneaky Pete did to help him with stress begin to have negative side effects. To make matters worse, the side effects compound every time Jeff has a stressful event—day after day.

Instead of Jeff's muscles quickly gobbling up the massive increase in blood glucose, they didn't use much at all with him sitting in the chair. The muscle cells can't store much of the glucose, so the excess needs to go somewhere. The body is very averse to high levels of glucose circulating in the blood stream for long periods. It can lead to nerve and blood vessel damage, heart disease, kidney disease, and vision problems.[4]

Fat cells have almost unlimited potential to store energy, so they gladly volunteer to take all the excess glucose, transform it to fat, and stash it away for possible use in the future. This is one of the reasons why Jeff has gained so much weight over the last few years.

The significant influx of glucose into the bloodstream also means Jeff's pancreas had to produce a large amount of insulin in order to deal with it. When the pancreas regularly produces high amounts of insulin, the body becomes less sensitive to its effects. In a word, the body becomes resistant to the actions of insulin. It's similar to becoming less affected by the intoxicating effects of alcohol or the buzz from caffeine after regular consumption. The body builds up a tolerance, and to achieve an altered state, we must consume more.

This continued strain of the pancreas working harder and harder over time adds stress to the organ. Eventually the beta cells that produce insulin in Jeff's pancreas wear out from all the stress. Long term, being resistant to insulin leads to diabetes and heart disease.

Jeff's high level of body fat also affects insulin's ability to do its job. This cycle is unfortunate: too much glucose without physical activity means increased fat storage and decreased insulin sensitivity. And decreased insulin sensitivity leads to even more increased fat storage. In particular, central, or visceral, body fat located around the internal organs is especially detrimental. It specifically diminishes insulin sensitivity.

Another piece of bad news is that Jeff lost muscle mass. Trying to get as many sources of energy into the bloodstream as possible, adrenaline and noradrenaline broke down and converted some of Jeff's muscle tissue into glucose. It did this by transforming stored protein in the muscle into amino acids that could be taken up by the liver for glucogenesis, the process of making glucose.[5] Any change in muscle mass has a critical effect on the body's ability to regulate energy stores. Losing it is detrimental for many reasons.

First, muscle tissue increases sensitivity to insulin, better allowing it to do its job of getting glucose into the cells. In fact, skeletal muscle accounts for 70 to 95 percent of insulin-mediated glucose removal.[6] Unfortunately, then, less muscle mass means the body is less sensitive to insulin. Second, muscle mass is directly tied to metabolism: the more muscle we have, the faster our metabolism goes. Every time our body loses muscle mass, our metabolism slows. Over time, this decrease in metabolism can lead to an increase in body fat if we don't compensate by eating less food. Lastly, a decrease in muscle tissue also leads to a decrease in strength and functionality of the body.

These challenges associated with glucose, insulin, and muscle mass are especially troubling for Jeff because of his type 2 diabetes. The condition developed later in his life due to his diet, excess body fat, and lack of exercise. The repeated bouts of stress and accompanying hormone release make his problematic health condition even worse.

That's not all. Without a chance to Play It Out, the increased blood pressure from a stressful event damages Jeff's blood vessels in the coronary arteries. The walls of healthy arteries are normally flexible and elastic. But too much pressure can make them thick and stiff, restricting blood flow to our organs and tissues. In addition, each time the blood vessel walls are damaged, tiny scars form. The body sends out cholesterol plaque that attaches to these scarred and damaged sites, resulting in what's known as atherosclerosis. This plaque formation grows over time, and arteries become narrow or blocked, preventing blood flow. This can cause chest pain or even a heart attack. If the artery damage happens in our brain, it can result in a stroke.

In yet another negative side effect, blood diverting to the arms and legs means less blood going to activities such as food intake, digestion, and reproduction. Sneaky Pete knows focusing energy on these activities could be potentially life threatening in a fight-or-flight situation. Adrenaline relaxes the muscles of the stomach and intestine, slowing or stopping digestion completely. That's why Jeff began feeling sick to his stomach anticipating the stress of the meeting. This decrease in digestion not only leads to an upset stomach, but it can also result in digestion issues and irritable bowel syndrome.

After the Meeting

You've just learned how incredibly powerful stress chemicals are—and we haven't even gotten into what cortisol made Jeff's body do in the several hours *after* the meeting. To get a good understanding of how cortisol works, let's go back to Jeff and find out what happens after his meeting is over.

Jeff has to document the details of the meeting and file all the associated paperwork, so he sits at his desk for the hour immediately afterward. He then sits in several other meetings throughout the afternoon.

While he's in one of these meetings, Jeff realizes how hungry he is. In fact, he's *starving*. Luckily there's a tray of giant cookies in the room. Before he knows it, he has eaten two of them. At about 6:30 p.m., he leaves the office and drives home through rush hour traffic. The freeway is a parking lot. There's an accident, and cars are backed up for what looks like miles.

He just wants to get home and forget about the day he's had. And he's hungry again, as those cookies didn't last him as long as he thought they would. The stress gets to him again; he comes unglued and pounds on the steering wheel, using a few of his favorite expletives. He decides to get off the freeway at the next exit and make his way home via the side streets, driving like a maniac through a maze the entire way.

He walks in the door, and the first thing he does is grab a beer. After the day he's had, he feels he's surely earned one. The first one goes down fast, and he grabs another while he and his wife make dinner. While they're cooking, Jeff grabs a bag of chips to try sating his hunger until the meal is ready.

While in the kitchen, his wife mentions they need to make a decision about the remodeling project they've been contemplating. They've gotten several bids and need to choose a contractor. Jeff becomes very frustrated and angry about how much it's going to cost, not to mention the inconvenience of it all. He blows up at his wife, yelling about cancelling the whole idea.

It's close to 8:00 p.m. by the time they eat. Jeff fills and cleans his plate two times. He's painfully full, but it tastes so good, and this is the first time he's had to relax all day. After dinner, all he wants to do is veg out and disconnect from his day. He watches TV for a while, then decides to also get on his laptop to do a bit of work. Even though he had a big meal not long ago, he's feeling a bit snacky for some reason. He grabs a bag of candy from the pantry and eats while he's working in his home office.

It's late and he's physically exhausted, but he's still feeling a bit wired. He has another beer to relax and unwind. It's almost always hard for him to fall asleep. He also wakes up several times throughout the night and has a hard time getting back to sleep. He feels as if his brain does not have a shutoff button.

Cortisol was responsible for many of the actions Jeff took after the meeting was over as well as throughout the evening, especially the ones related to hunger, food, and sleep. The fact that he stimulated the stress response several more times and never got to Play It Out made matters even worse.

Cortisol—The Bad News

The first wave of the stress response kicked things off with adrenaline and noradrenaline. It was swift and effective at initiating action. In the second wave, the HPA axis released cortisol. Its main function is to return the body to a state of balance after the stressful event is over. Let's talk about the good news before we get to the not-so-good news.

Cortisol is the heavy hitter that backs up many of the functions of adrenaline and noradrenaline for a longer period of time. It effectively prepares the body for the next time it has to fight or flee. Glucocorticoids, such as cortisol, rapidly increase blood glucose levels, providing the muscles with a burst of energy. It also helps reset the body and return energy levels to a state of balance by regulating hunger, feeding behavior, and energy utilization and storage.

Cortisol plays a very important role in stress, and we wouldn't want to live without it. By design, cortisol doesn't need to know if Jeff fought, fled, or played it out in the moment of stress. Cortisol just does its job regardless of what does or does not happen. It assumes Jeff had followed through with some burst of activity so his body would have properly used up the cortisol in the energy expenditure.

But unfortunately, Jeff just sat there like a log—he didn't hold up his end of the stress response design. He didn't use up the cortisol at all. And when cortisol is frequently released and not utilized, it continues to circulate through the system. Things turn *nasty* when levels are continuously elevated, when it has more time to exert deleterious effects on many parts of the body and brain.

Cortisol prolongs the elevation of blood glucose for several hours.[7] As explained above, more glucose requires more insulin to be produced to remove it from the bloodstream. Jeff's pancreas not only has to work harder, it also has to work longer. This places undue stress on the organ, and this continued high exposure to insulin also decreases his body's sensitivity to it. And much of the glucose insulin removes from his bloodstream gets stored in his fat cells.

To make matters worse, inactivity and lack of energy expenditure create a situation where cortisol blocks the action of insulin to take up glucose from Jeff's bloodstream. This results in a combination of high levels of insulin and glucose, which increases the storage of fat on the body—particularly in the abdominal region—as well as the formation of plaque in Jeff's arteries.[8] Similar to adrenaline and noradrenaline, cortisol also promotes the loss of protein from muscle mass by converting it to glucose. This further decreases insulin sensitivity, metabolism, muscle strength, and functionality.

Cortisol also makes Jeff hungrier in order to replace the energy it assumes he burned while fighting or fleeing. However, cortisol has no idea Jeff never had the opportunity to move a muscle, didn't burn any extra calories, and doesn't need the extra energy. This increase in hunger and appetite can be stimulated not only just after the stressful event, but also over the course of several *days*.[9]

Research reveals that two-thirds of people eat more when they're stressed and one third eat less.[10] One possible reason for the different eating habits is that stress affects our appetite in different ways. Adrenaline and noradrenaline initially suppress appetite, while cortisol increases it. This means during the stressful event, we typically don't feel like eating, then many minutes to hours later, we start feeling hungry again. Another explanation for the research finding is that our stress-related eating habits depend on the *type* of stress we experience. When stress includes a threat to one's ego or self-esteem, such as being publicly embarrassed or experiencing failure, it stimulates more eating, while stress occurring from a challenging event decreases it.[11]

In more bad news, elevated cortisol levels are making Jeff more susceptible to illnesses or diseases that make him sick. It's important to point out that cortisol doesn't directly make Jeff sick. Rather, it suppresses his long-term immune system[12] in order to shunt resources to short-term immunity, which deals with immediate injury potentially sustained while fighting or fleeing. The hit to his long-term immunity makes him less able to fight off illness.

Every year, salmon make their journey upstream to return to their spawning grounds to mate and lay eggs. The journey is stressful, arduous, and long—traveling as far as a thousand miles. After they mate and pass on their DNA, they die. I always thought their death was a result of how their lifecycle is programmed. However, the truth is that by the time they have reached their destination, their energy supply is low, and prolonged high levels of cortisol have devastated their immune systems. They get sick and they die.[13] Research also shows that coronary arteriosclerosis (a hardening of the arteries and a buildup of plaque) develops during this time, and it happens most when upstream migration conditions are particularly severe.[14] Arteriosclerosis is typically a function of age, so the stress of migration makes them age prematurely.

In a similar situation, the male marsupial mouse dies after mating due to excessive stress that suppresses his immune system.[15] Mating only happens once per year. The competition for a female mouse is incredibly fierce—many males have only one shot at passing on their DNA. And did I mention that when they find a female, they mate for up to twelve hours at a go? That would be enough to kill anyone.

Stress also decreases the secretion of estrogen, progesterone, and testosterone. This results in a decrease of sex drive and sexual function, and an increase in reproductive issues.[16] Hormones related to growth are also affected during stress. In the short term, these hormones help cell division and bone growth. But prolonged activation of the HPA axis suppresses growth hormone secretion and insulin-like growth factor,[17] affecting growth over the long term. These are but more examples of how the body adapts to dealing with short-term stressors. It focuses energy on immediate survival instead of worrying about future concerns such as reproduction and growth when it's not sure there will be a tomorrow or next week.

Cortisol and Sleep

If you recall, Jeff consistently has trouble falling asleep and staying asleep. Much of this is cortisol's fault. Let's explore the connection between cortisol and sleep in detail.

Cortisol levels have a natural ebb and flow throughout the day. Under normal circumstances, cortisol levels rise during the early morning hours and are highest between 7:00 and 8:00 a.m., and this is what actually wakes us up and gets us out of bed.

Cortisol spikes about an hour before we wake up because the first

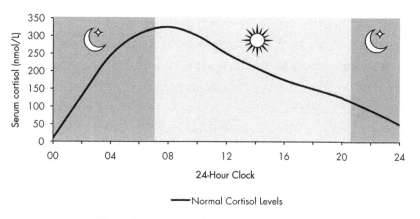

—Normal Cortisol Levels

Normal cortisol levels throughout the day

major stressful event of the day is actually the process of waking up. We all know from experience just how difficult this simple process can actually be! We go from lying down, to sitting, and then to standing. Then it's getting in the shower, fighting morning traffic, meeting the challenges of work or school, and so on. . . . Granted, these things may not be major stressors, but they still place demand on the body and brain. The spike in cortisol before waking is the body's way to prep us for it. The stress response prepares us to adapt by increasing cortisol levels.

Cortisol levels then ebb throughout the afternoon. They reach their lowest point in the evening and during the early phase of sleep.

INCREASE IN CORTISOL = WAKE UP
DECREASE IN CORTISOL = GO TO SLEEP

Here's an interesting study that shows how powerfully cortisol affects our sleep-awake cycle: a group of volunteers was allowed to sleep for as long as they each wanted, which turned out to be around 9:00 a.m. As would be expected, their stress hormones began to rise around 8:00 a.m. They had enough sleep, their brains knew it, and the body started secreting hormones to prepare to end the sleep cycle.

A second group of volunteers went to sleep at the same time, but were told they would be woken up at 6:00 a.m. *At 5:00 a.m., their stress hormones began to rise.* Did their stress hormone levels rise three hours earlier than the other group's because they needed three hours less sleep? The rise wasn't about them feeling rejuvenated—it was about the *stressful anticipation* of being woken up earlier. Their brains were feeling anticipatory stress while sleeping.[18]

I'll bet something similar has happened to you: you know you have to wake up at a certain time, and you "somehow" manage to wake up a few minutes before the alarm goes off. Or you wake up several times during the night to check the time to make sure you haven't overslept. We can't even catch a break from stress while being asleep!

DEAR GOD . . . WE'RE EVEN STRESSED WHILE WE'RE SLEEPING.

Cortisol ebbs and flows in the normal course of a day. But let's go back to our caveman ancestors for a moment to see what happens when stress is introduced.

Several cavemen are in a hunting party on the savannah, far from their village. It gets to be late night—it's dark. They've made a camp, they're bedding down, and suddenly they hear a pride of lions nearby. As long as they can stay awake to protect themselves, they can stay alive. It's critical they do not let their defenses down, drift off to sleep, and compromise their safety. How do they do this? The stress hormones adrenaline and noradrenaline are released to stimulate wakefulness[19] and cortisol backs up this heightened arousal for several hours.

It's the same for us today. Every time we're exposed to stress, cortisol is released. Everyday life is full of discreet stressful moments all day long. We feel we recover in between them, but cortisol's effects are long lasting. It takes quite a while for cortisol to dissipate in the body. The half-life of moderate amounts of cortisol in the circulation is approximately ninety minutes.[20] However, with large amounts, the half-life increases to 120 minutes.[21] This means that two hours after a major stressor, the body still has elevated levels of cortisol and will for many hours afterward.

Let's look at a typical day to see how this works. You wake up, open your eyes, and can't believe how well rested you feel. You haven't felt this refreshed in a long time. This is going to be a good day. You slowly roll over, look at the alarm clock, and realize you have overslept. *SQUIRT!* There goes some cortisol.

You're running around the house like a mad person, trying to get yourself ready. You wake the kids to get them off to school, but they're completely uncooperative and cranky. *SQUIRT!* There goes some more cortisol.

You finally get the kids off to the bus and yourself out of the house. You jump in your car and make a mad dash for the freeway. As you're pulling on, you see traffic is bumper to bumper and moving at a snail's pace. You are going to be *so* late for work. *SQUIRRRRT!* More cortisol.

You finally get to the office. As long as you can quickly sneak to your desk, perhaps no one will notice you're roughly an hour and a half late. As you're heading down the hallway and round the corner, you run right into your boss. It's obvious you're just arriving to work. *SQUIRT! SQUIRT!*

You get to your desk, turn on your computer, and think the worst is over. As your calendar opens up, you come to the stark realization the meeting you're facilitating starts in ten minutes. You had planned on coming in early to prepare. *SSSSQUIRT* goes more cortisol.

You've been awake for two whole hours, and you've already secreted stress hormones five times. God only knows what the rest of the day has in store for you!

As you can see, it's not so much that we're under long-term stressors (most of the time), but rather that we're exposed to frequent bouts of stress all day long. When we pair this with no opportunity to Play It Out, it's no wonder we suffer the negative consequences of stress, including with our sleep.

Because of these repeated episodes of stress throughout the day, cortisol levels often do not decrease as normally expected as the day goes on. Elevated levels of cortisol in the evening are a sign of stress.[22] And poor sleepers tend to have higher levels of glucocorticoids in their bloodstream.[23] In addition, researchers compared patients with insomnia to those without sleep disturbances. They found that "insomniacs with the highest degree of sleep disturbance secreted the highest amount of cortisol, particularly in the evening and nighttime hour," which suggests chronic insomnia is a disorder of sustained hyperarousal of the body's stress response system.[24]

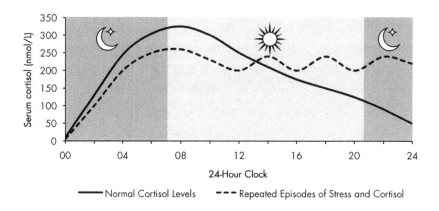

Cortisol levels when exposed to repeated episodes of stress throughout the day

The National Sleep Foundation reports that 74 percent of adults in the United States experience a sleeping problem a few nights a week or more, and about 75 percent of insomnia cases are triggered by some major stressor.[25] The effects of sleep deprivation are thought to cost US businesses more than $100 billion a year.[26]

Poor sleep can also lead to a vicious cycle. Stressing out about sleep leads to more stress, more cortisol release, and even worse bouts of insomnia. Sleep deprivation even increases activity of the sympathetic nervous system (the gas pedal) and makes the parasympathetic nervous system (the brake) less effective.[27]

There are several other pieces of bad news about not getting enough sleep. First, a consistent lack of sleep increases body fat levels, specifically visceral fat around the midsection. A study that tracked more than 68,000 women found that those who slept fewer than five hours per night were 32 percent more likely to gain roughly *thirty pounds* over the next sixteen years than those who slept for at least seven hours a night.[28]

Also, when we're tired, it means we lack energy. To get more energy, the body alters hormones that make us hungry, and we end up eating more calories. Specifically, we eat calories high in simple carbohydrates—such as pretzels, chips, crackers, popcorn, muffins, cookies, ice cream, and candy—because they're quick sources of glucose.[29] Unfortunately, this spike in blood glucose is followed by a crash that leaves us exhausted and craving more sweets and chips. In addition, sleep debt makes it harder for the body to handle that glucose spike. Poor sleep reduces glucose clearance from the bloodstream and increases insulin resistance.[30]

Overall, insufficient sleep is directly linked to poor health, with new research suggesting it increases the risk of diabetes, heart disease, obesity, and even premature death. Even a few nights of bad sleep can be detrimental.[31] A study of almost a million people over age thirty found that men who usually slept less than four hours a day were nearly three times as likely to die within six years compared to men who said they averaged seven to eight hours of sleep.[32]

Cortisol—The Ugly News

We've discussed the bad news about cortisol, and we've explored its negative effect on sleep. As if all that weren't enough for you, there's some *ugly* news. In a nutshell, consistently high levels of cortisol are a continual punch in the face when it comes to overeating and storing fat. It affects not only how much fat we store, but *where* we store it, raising our risk of many serious diseases. It also makes us ridiculously hungry for high-fat, high-sugar foods in order to supply these fat stores.

Cortisol's job is to replace lost energy during the fight-or-flight process, and it means business. It wants to do it in the most efficient and effective way possible. It makes us seek out the most energy-rich sources of food: **sugar** and **fat**. The reason we crave "comfort foods" such as chips, cookies, fast food, burgers, pizza, and chocolate when we're stressed out is that Sneaky Pete is on the hunt for calorie-rich foods.

Remember how and what Jeff ate after his stressful meeting and once he got home? He got really hungry, ate two cookies in an afternoon meeting, scarfed a bunch of chips before dinner was ready, overate at dinner, then felt snacky again later in the evening and ate candy. It's not so much that Jeff lacks self-discipline or willpower when it comes to eating. It's more so that the consistently high levels of cortisol make him seek out fatty, sugary foods. Cortisol wants to replace the resources it thinks he burned so he's ready for his next stressful encounter. If Jeff would have had the opportunity to Play It Out with a short burst of intense physical activity after his high-stress meeting, the increase in food intake would have been warranted instead of detrimental, and using the cortisol would have diminished his strong cravings for junk food.

We eat large amounts of high-fat, high-sugar foods in an attempt to comfort ourselves, but the double-edged sword is that they ultimately add *more* stress to the system in several ways. First, eating excessive amounts of food results in excessive amounts of glucose, especially when the food is high in sugar. And in turn, excessive amounts of glucose require excessive amounts of insulin to get blood glucose levels back down into the ideal range. And you know what happens next—insulin sensitivity decreases and more stress is placed on the pancreas.

To add insult to injury, much of this excess glucose is processed and stored away as fat around the abdominal region. Excess fat—particularly around the midsection—also places more stress on the body's joints and systems.

Eating high amounts of unhealthy dietary fats places further stress on the body, increases cortisol release, and is one of the major risk factors for heart disease.[33] A diet high in saturated fat results in a cholesterol buildup in the arteries, causing them to harden and narrow. This then increases pressure in the arteries as well as strain on the heart to maintain adequate blood flow throughout the body. Dietary fat has a high-calorie content, with nine calories per gram compared to protein and carbohydrates, which have only four. For this reason, too much dietary fat further elevates the risk of heart disease as it increases the likelihood of obesity. Obesity is another risk factor for heart disease.

Cushing's syndrome is a hormonal disorder brought on by prolonged exposure to cortisol, either from a disease that creates excess cortisol production or from taking glucocorticoid drugs. Symptoms of Cushing's syndrome include upper-body obesity; increased fat around the face, neck, and shoulders; severe fatigue and muscle weakness; insomnia; memory and attention dysfunction; high blood pressure; and elevated blood glucose. It affects an estimated ten to fifteen million people each year.[34]

Cortisol and Your Fight-or-Flight Fuel Allocation Station

Cortisol "restocks the shelves" after the stress response by storing energy as fat. It does so on two very specific sites of the body: on the blood vessel walls and in and around the abdominal region. Fat in the arteries is obviously a bad thing. But when fat is also found deep within the midsection, it becomes very dangerous, as this combination raises the risk of heart disease, type 2 diabetes, and death.[35]

Most of us are genetically predisposed to be shaped like one of two fruits when it comes to where we store fat on the body. Some of us have a natural tendency to gain weight around the hips, butt, and thighs, creating more of a pear-shape body fat distribution. Others are more prone to storing it around the waist, resulting in an apple shape.

However, in addition to genetics, stress also plays a role in where we store fat. Apple-shaped body fat distribution may be a sign of stress, as cortisol makes us deposit more fat in and around the abdominal area. If you just can't seem to lose weight—especially around your middle—no

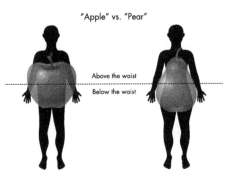

"Apple" vs. "Pear"

Above the waist

Below the waist

Apple and pear body fat distribution

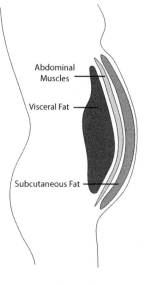

Abdominal Muscles

Visceral Fat

Subcutaneous Fat

Visceral fat

matter what you do, it's important to consider the level of stress in your life and what you're doing to cope with it.

As described earlier, the fat stored deep within the midsection around our internal organs is called visceral, or central, body fat. It's very different from the subcutaneous fat stored just under our skin. Visceral fat has much greater blood flow as well as more cortisol receptors, so it's very easy for fat to be stored here. In fact, we have 400 percent more cortisol receptors in visceral fat than in subcutaneous fat.[36] Visceral fat is less sensitive to insulin, and it actually generates its own cortisol. This creates an unfortunate effect, where cortisol results in more visceral fat, and more visceral fat results in more cortisol being released in the body.

INCREASED FAT AROUND YOUR MIDSECTION MAY BE A SIGN OF STRESS.

This fat is also metabolically active tissue, sending and receiving signals from other organs that can increase inflammation in the body. Obesity has been described as an "unconventional type of persistent, generalized, low grade inflammatory state."[37] Visceral fat also releases fatty acids and hormones that ultimately lead to increased low-density lipoprotein cholesterol, triglycerides, blood glucose, and blood pressure.[38] In other words, it's much more dangerous to our health to be apple shaped.

I like to refer to that spare tire or muffin top we may have because of stress as the "fight-or-flight fuel allocation station." This fat is invaluable for the stress response. Visceral fat is closer to the portal vein of the liver. That means it can quickly be converted into glucose and then released into the bloodstream to provide much-needed energy for fighting or fleeing. Convenient, right?

Waist-to-Hip Ratio

How do you know how much of your fat is visceral? To accurately ascertain levels of visceral fat, you need a CT scan, MRI, or other imaging technique. However, measuring the circumference of your waist is an alternative method because more belly fat usually means large deposits of both visceral and subcutaneous fat. An effective way to measure visceral obesity without a medical imaging technique is to compare your waist circumference to your hip circumference—what's known as the waist-to-hip ratio, or WHR.

Knowing your waist-to-hip ratio is important in understanding how your body is dealing with stress. It's hypothesized that increased WHR is a symptom of chronic hypothalamic arousal due to stress.[39] Meaning, the "gas pedal" of the sympathetic nervous system is punched to the floor more often than not, and cortisol secretion is increased.

Another important factor WHR brings to light is the increased risk of disease regardless of total body fat, because it focuses instead on *where* fat is stored. The Nurses' Health Study, one of the largest and longest studies to date that has measured abdominal obesity, found that women at "normal weight" were at higher risk of death from cancer or other causes if they were carrying more of that weight around their waist than other areas.[40] In another study, WHR showed a significant positive association with heart attack, chest pain, stroke, and death. And these findings were *independent* of age, body mass index, smoking habit, serum cholesterol concentration, serum triglyceride concentration, and systolic blood pressure.[41]

Waist circumference alone can also be a good indicator for risk of cardiovascular disease. Women with a waist bigger than 35 inches and men with a waist bigger than 40 inches have a higher risk of heart disease and diabetes.[42]

EVEN IF YOU'RE NOT OVERWEIGHT, HAVING A LARGE WAIST PUTS YOU AT A HIGHER RISK OF SERIOUS HEALTH PROBLEMS THAN SOMEONE WITH A SMALLER WAIST.

How to Measure Your Waist-to-Hip Ratio

To measure your waist, place a tape measure around your abdomen, at the midpoint between your lowest, last rib and the top of your iliac crest (hip bone). Be sure the tape is snug but not compressing your skin, and keep it parallel to the floor. Take the measurement at the end of a natural exhale. For hip measurement, place the tape measure around your hips, and align it with the point of greatest protrusion (where your buttocks stick out the most).

How to Calculate Your Waist-to-Hip Ratio

Divide your waist measurement by your hip measurement, then reference the chart below. For men, the ideal ratio is less than 0.9, and for women, it is less than 0.8.

Waist-to-hip Ratio (WHR) Norms				
Gender	Excellent	Good	Average	At Risk
Males	<0.85	0.85-0.89	0.90-0.95	≥0.95
Females	<0.75	0.75-0.79	0.80-0.86	≥0.86

Bray, G.A. & Gray, D.S. (1988). Obesity: Part 1: Pathogenesis. *Western Journal of Medicine*, 149, 429-441.

Waist-to-hip ratio norms

You Still Have the Brain of a Caveman

Let's switch gears for a bit. Throughout this chapter, you've learned how stress affects the chemistry of the brain. But there's more: it also changes the brain's physical structure. Before we tackle that idea, let's start with the basics of how our brain is designed.

Saying you have the brain of a caveman is not meant to be an insult. It's a biological truth. We may think we've evolved far past our distant ancestors with our advances in technology, feats of engineering, space travel, and the creation of the cronut. But we still carry around a primitive, rudimental brain in our head, and it's very much affected by stress.

Over thousands and thousands of years, our brain has continued to develop, evolve, and grow. Lucky for us, our cranial operating systems have gotten continuous upgrades along the way. As the changes and improvements occurred, however, we didn't get rid of the older versions of our brain: the newer ones were simply added on top.

There are three major portions of the brain, beginning from inside to outside:

1) Reptilian

2) Limbic

3) Neocortex

Even though they are different parts of the brain, they are not separate in terms of operating independently of one another. Many interconnections allow them to operate as one, but with vastly different responsibilities.

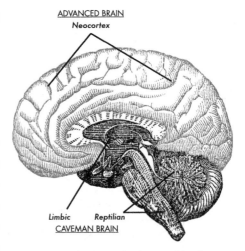

ADVANCED BRAIN
Neocortex

Limbic   Reptilian
CAVEMAN BRAIN

Caveman brain and advanced brain

The reptilian and limbic parts of the brain are what I refer to as our "caveman brain," aka Sneaky Pete. They are the most ancient and elemental portions dealing with the basics of survival. The newest, outer portion I call our "advanced brain." It evolved much later and deals with what we think of as intelligence, complex thought, and higher reasoning.

Reptilian: Instinct

The oldest of the three portions is known as the reptilian, or lizard, brain. It's located in the deepest part. It's basically the brain stem. We share this portion of our brain with reptiles and birds. When you think about their cognitive ability, it becomes obvious this part of the brain is all about instinct and survival. The reptilian brain does not have the capacity to think or feel; its job is to take *action*.

THE REPTILIAN BRAIN IS INSTINCTIVE; ITS JOB IS TO **ACT**.

This earliest part of our brain is the most animalistic and instinctive, responsible for the three Fs: fight, flight, and fornication. (And here you thought there were only two.) It also regulates survival functions such as heart rate, breathing, and body temperature as well as establishes dominance and defends territory.

A typical day for a lizard is to evade predators, fight to establish dominion and province, have sex with good-looking female lizards, and eat. Too bad there's no beer for them, or it truly would be the perfect day.

Limbic: Emotion

The limbic system was the next portion to evolve. It's layered right over the top of the reptilian brain. It first emerged in mammals and is therefore sometimes also referred to as our mammalian brain. It's responsible for emotion, mood, memory, behavior, olfaction, and hormone control.

Whereas the reptilian brain contains the circuitry for fight-or-flight, the limbic brain *manages* these circuits and is hardwired to protect us. It makes very quick and strong value judgments based on emotion, which exert a powerful influence on our behavior. The two major emotions that drive the limbic system are pleasure and pain. At a very basic Sneaky Pete level, we are all driven and motivated to seek things that make us feel good and to avoid things that make us feel bad.

THE LIMBIC BRAIN IS ALL ABOUT PLEASURE AND PAIN; ITS JOB IS TO **FEEL**.

There are two important structures within the limbic system: the amygdala and hippocampus. The amygdala is critical in the formation and storage of memories associated with notably emotional events. It pairs an event with a feeling, and this connection is infinitely long lasting, stored away in our long-term memory.

The stress hormones, in combination with the amygdala, create "flash bulb moments," where we remember exactly where we were and what we were doing when we learned a piece of highly emotional news. For instance, I remember precisely where I was and what I was doing when I learned of the attempted assassination of President Reagan when I was nine years old. In fact, I even recall what I was wearing on 9/11 (not that it was relevant), and that was over twelve years ago. Pair this up against the fact I can't remember where I set my phone down, and it's pretty amazing.

These imprinted memories are not just associated with negative events. They also take place when something wonderful or positive happens. Perhaps you can recall the tiniest details surrounding a job offer or promotion, your engagement proposal, or the birth of a child.

It also happens with our sense of smell. You can be walking down a busy street, get a whiff of something, and have the smell instantly take you back to your grandmother's basement when you were a small child or the vacation you took to Martinique in your twenties. Objectively speaking, the smell of a new car is not necessarily the most beautiful aroma—it smells like synthetic petroleum products—but most of us think it's a great odor. The amygdala has associated it with the positive emotions of buying a new car.

The second structure, the hippocampus, works in conjunction with the amygdala to form short- and long-term memories of these highly emotional events to be filed away for later use. Our cavemen ancestors had to remember what led to potentially stressful or dangerous situations so they could avoid them in the future. They also needed to recall what things led to pleasurable events so they could repeat them.

All right, it's time for the memory association game to help remember the functions of the amygdala and hippocampus. If you're a fan* of *Star Wars*, you're familiar with Queen Amidala, who was Luke Skywalker's mother and the secret wife of Anakin Skywalker, who later became Darth Vader. When she learned of Anakin's fall to the dark side, she died of a broken heart—a huge emotional response. *Emotional* Queen Amidala = Amygdala.

Here's another one. In 2011, I had the privilege of going on safari in Africa. While I was there, I learned the most dangerous animal to humans is not a lion, a poisonous snake, or a crocodile, but the hippopotamus! The hippopotamus is responsible for more human fatalities in Africa than any other large animal. So it's important to remember the hippopotamus is very dangerous. *Remember* the hippopotamus = hippocampus and memory.

*I feel it's important to defend and clarify: I am not a *Star Wars* nerd. I simply live with two of them.

Neocortex: Reasoning

The newest portion of the brain is the neocortex. This outermost layer (*neo* meaning "new" and *cortex* referring to the outer portion of an organ) finally assumed prominence in primates. It's our "gray matter" and what I refer to as our advanced brain. It's responsible for the higher functions of conscious thought, language, complex social interaction, sensory perception, generation of motor commands, and spatial reasoning.

An important region of this part of the brain is the prefrontal cortex, which is involved with working memory, judgment, planning, abstract reasoning, sequencing of activity, and dividing attention. In a nutshell, the prefrontal cortex controls executive function and all the things we need to excel in our professional careers and personal lives.

It's here that we orchestrate our thoughts and actions in accordance with internal goals. We have to rely heavily on the prefrontal cortex when we're trying to exercise regularly or eat healthy. We'll use this portion of the brain when forming strategies and planning.

The prefrontal cortex also helps us predict the possible outcomes of actions or events as well as identify future consequences of current activities. When we contemplate dessert after dinner (Sneaky Pete *really* wants us to eat it) and choose to forgo it because we want to eat in a way that improves our health, that reasoning all takes place here.

We use the prefrontal cortex for social control, our ability to suppress urges that could lead to socially unacceptable outcomes. Holding our tongues when we disagree with something during a meeting or not making a snide remark to a coworker is thanks to the prefrontal cortex. Speaking of control, it also helps control impulsive behavior. When you're out shopping and see something expensive you really want, caveman brain tells you to buy it, while advanced brain thinks about paying the credit card bill later on. It also allows us to differentiate among conflicting thoughts to determine good and bad, better and best, same and different.

THE NEOCORTEX IS RESPONSIBLE FOR
COMPLEX REASONING AND EXECUTIVE
FUNCTION; ITS JOB IS TO **THINK**.

This Is Your Brain on Stress

The activities of the advanced brain are all very rational. Because we're such rational creatures, we live with the belief that our advanced brain runs the show and is stronger than our caveman brain. For the most part, this is true—when everything in our lives is running smoothly, we're not trying to make change, and we have no stress.

However, when we're exposed to stress, the *caveman brain quickly and completely overrides the advanced brain*. We are instantly transformed into Sneaky Pete the moment our brain registers a potential threat. We're hardwired to immediately default to survival mode.

If advanced brain was running the show during life-threatening stress, we'd be analyzing the data to determine whether this was a truly life-threatening situation, making a list of possible actions to take, and consulting a spreadsheet to help predict the outcomes of said possible scenarios. In the meantime, we died twenty minutes ago. Caveman brain senses danger and acts before our advanced brain even has time to register what just happened. It's Sneaky Pete to the rescue. Hooray for caveman brain!

STRESS STIMULATES
YOUR CAVEMAN BRAIN.

Here's the chemistry of how caveman brain leapfrogs our advanced brain: Remember the HPA (hypothalamic-pituitary-adrenal) axis that perceives danger and stimulates the pituitary gland to tell the adrenal glands to produce the hormones adrenaline, noradrenaline, and cortisol? The hypothalamus is located in the limbic portion of the brain.

When the limbic system senses fear, the automated technology network of the HPA axis sends these chemical signals to the body and brain. The amygdala and hippocampus have high concentrations of adrenaline, noradrenaline, and cortisol receptors,[43] which make them the primary targets of stress. They immediately jump online. Queen Amidala and the hippopotamus give control over to Sneaky Pete. (Who knew you had so many characters living in your head?)

Jeff has to fire many people, and their reactions are a great example of how quickly and completely Sneaky Pete can take over. Executives in leadership positions have to think clearly under pressure, control their emotions, and consider long-term consequences of immediate decisions. Unfortunately, all that goes out the window when faced with the profound stress of losing their jobs.

When Sneaky Pete takes over, it reduces resources and access to the frontal cortex. We will fall victim to "negativity bias," which means we prioritize negative information over positive. From an evolutionary perspective, cavemen were better off quickly assuming something was threatening or dangerous. That sound in the woods? It's better to assume the worst—that it's a predator—than take the chance it was just the wind. Our brain errs on the side of caution to maximize survival. But this also leads to us continually assuming the worst when confronted with something potentially stressful.

When Sneaky Pete takes over, we also experience perceptual narrowing of many of our senses. For example, time distortion during stress is very common. While experiencing a highly stressful situation, we may feel as though things were moving in slow motion. It may seem we have loads of time to assess what's going on and decide on the right action to take. Or it may seem as though things were running at very high speed and we were struggling to keep up. We may experience tunnel vision, seeing things only directly in front of us and not noticing things in the background or our periphery. Auditory exclusion is also common, where we may not hear someone shouting or offering information. It's our body's way of trying not to overload the brain with too much information while it focuses on survival.

In these situations, our reactions become automatic. If you've ever been startled by someone, then reached out and smacked him a good one, you know there wasn't any rational or conscious thought behind punching. You just did it. Or perhaps you've blamed people for something you know they weren't responsible for or said something very hurtful to someone you love—you blurted these things out before thinking about the potential consequences.

When Sneaky Pete's in control, we also lock in more fear-conditioned responses and memories. An example of a fear-conditioned response would be the feeling most of us get when we go to the doctor. Because something negative may have happened there in the past—we got a shot when we were kids or we got socked with a huge medical bill as adults—we automatically assume something painful or bad is going to happen when we go again. We arrive at the doctor's office in full-on fight-or-flight mode even before anything negative or stressful has happened. Just thinking about going to the doctor can cause our breathing and heart rate to increase and our palms to become sweaty. We may experience many similar responses when going into meetings with our bosses, when heading to the airport (missed flight, anyone?), or when our significant others ask us if they can have "a word" in the kitchen.

Our buttons are easily pushed, and we become defensive and negative. It becomes very difficult to see the upside to the situation, and we take things very personally. We no longer have the ability to be objective. The hippocampus is less able to perform its usual role of processing objective and neutral information. Instead, it's transformed into playing more of an amygdala-like role.

Caveman brain also increases our confidence that we're right. We lose the capacity to see alternative options or other people's point of view. Sneaky Pete can have a one-track mind, becoming very obstinate and stubborn. Why would he want to switch tack or strategy when he's already invested precious energy in a way of thinking or doing? In addition, stopping to ask himself whether a scenario is truly dangerous for his long-term future could mean injury or death while he's pondering alternatives. (Remember that sound in the woods?)

Stress also decreases our working memory, the cognitive mechanism that allows us to keep a small amount of information active for a limited period of time. We may find ourselves becoming forgetful or easily distracted in the throes of stress.

STRESS HIJACKS OUR ADVANCED BRAIN.

Most scuba diving accidents take place in relatively shallow water, or even on the surface of the water. When something goes wrong with a diver's air regulator, caveman brain comes online. The brain experiences perceptual narrowing, short-term memory is wiped out, and the brain refuses to evaluate all the information available. The diver may attempt to grab the regulator out of a diving partner's mouth or forget he has a backup regulator as he shoots up too quickly the surface. The diver's thought process is reduced to one motive: get air. Once at the surface, he will rip off his facemask in order to breathe and fight to stay afloat. He doesn't think to drop his weights or anything he's holding, and he doesn't realize he could inflate his buoyancy compensator. Logic goes out the window. Survival is driving every (re)action, even if to detrimental consequences.

If you've ever had—or been—a toddler or teenager, then you know what caveman-brain-takeover is like. At either age, they can be completely crazy. They are irrational, impulsive, highly emotional, combative, and make stupid decisions. Part of the reason for this behavior is that the prefrontal cortex of the advanced brain doesn't fully form until the age of about twenty-five.

Teenagers take dumb risks because advanced brain can't yet do a very good job of putting the brake on caveman brain's crazy ideas. (Car insurance companies know it's not a good idea to give a car to someone under the age of twenty-five.) Teenagers can be highly overreactive and emotional, as caveman brain is all about acting and feeling, and advanced brain can't override those emotions yet.

Toddlers can also be extremely difficult to deal with because they don't respond to rational conversations. We can use logic to argue with them all day to put on warm clothes when it's cold out or not to drink out of the dog's water bowl, but it won't work. At that age, their brains are not optimized for logic, and they have zero ability to reason. Without a developed prefrontal cortex, they live in the present moment, are completely irrational, and want to act on every impulse. It's impossible to get them to understand they can't have a cookie right now but can have one later. They literally can't think that way. Without a fully developed prefrontal cortex, they can't understand that restraining impulses is a good thing, that if they wait now they'll be rewarded later. They freak out and throw a tantrum. (Another fine example of no impulse control.)

Now think about us adults. You're trying to plan your day and your life. You've got to get things done, follow through with responsibilities and deadlines, achieve personal goals—and then you encounter something stressful. Sneaky Pete hijacks advanced brain and makes you think and act like a toddler or teenager. (Or perhaps you've witnessed your coworker or boss have this transformation.) Sneaky Pete says screw it, screw you, and let's go screw off.

Put into a professional context, it's obvious this is *not* the part of the brain you want managing a team, leading people in an organization, or making important business decisions. On a personal level too, you don't want Sneaky Pete to be driving the bus when it comes to courting your spouse, raising your children, or interacting with anyone important in your life.

WHEN YOU'RE STRESSED OUT, YOU *LITERALLY* LOSE YOUR MIND

Let's put this all together now—combining what we know about the structure of the brain plus the chemistry of stress. Chemicals like cortisol are neurotoxic and known to reduce brain volume. You read that right: *stress shrinks our brain.*

Not only do stress hormones affect brain function, memory, and learning, they also *change the physical structure* of our brain. These influences and changes can have significant consequences on the way we interact with coworkers and clients, what decisions we make, whether we can accomplish long-term goals, and our ability to deal with daily challenges.

Cortisol can kill and shrink nerve cells in the hippocampus as well as halt the creation of new hippocampal neurons. Because the hippocampus is critical for memory, these changes are associated with aging and memory problems.

The hippocampus also plays a role in shutting off the HPA axis after stress is over. Damage or shrinking of the hippocampus hinders that shutoff, which leads to a longer HPA response to psychological stressors.[44] Cortisol is also believed to forge a pathway between the hippocampus and amygdala, which predisposes us to be in a constant state of fight-or-flight.

Chronic stress shrinks the medial prefrontal cortex.[45] This negatively affects decision making, working memory, and control of impulsive behavior. Stress also has the ability to affect stem cells, turning them into a type of cell that inhibits access to the prefrontal cortex. Without access to advanced brain, Sneaky Pete is allowed to run wild without any supervision. The result is a brain that is less capable of learning and memory but more prone to anxiety and depression.

To make matters worse, our amygdala grows larger under stress, in addition to becoming more active.[46] This growth and activity increases negative emotions such as fear, anxiety, and aggression. These brain changes diminish our ability to learn, remember, and make decisions. In addition, they also make it more difficult to successfully manage stressful situations in the future, leading to a vicious cycle.

YOUR HIPPOPOTAMUS SHRINKS AND YOUR QUEEN AMIDALA GROWS.

Finally—The Good News

The stress response is one of many amazing systems in the body. It's simultaneously complex and simple: there are a multitude of steps, hormones, and responses, but it all happens quickly, and we don't have to think about it.

Unfortunately, the world we're now living in is short-circuiting the system, and we *do* need to start thinking about it. We have to Play It Out in order to avoid the negative side effects and garner the benefits.

Now that you've got the background on Sneaky Pete and the stress response, the next section of the book will reacquaint you with the innate wisdom and design of your body as well as teach you a few things you may not know.

You're going to start using stress to your advantage. Not only will you avoid the negative side effects of stress, you'll also build your resiliency and enjoy some new side effects: better health, body fat levels, sleep, and mental function.

To learn more about the stress response and how it affects you, visit www.ph-performance.com/chemistry

Success Story

ERIN

Erin's Story

When major companies have an IT project too ambitious to handle in-house, they call Erin, the manager of a growing team of technology consultants. She explains, "Every day and every client is different. We are often brought in to help with projects that companies can't take on themselves, and they want them done *quickly*."

Erin typically works fifty hours or more per week, not including a commute of one to two hours. Her responsibilities include hiring, firing, and professional development, as well as client communication and project management.

At thirty-five years old, Erin is married and has two children, ages one and three. Her husband's job is also demanding, and both of them struggle at times to recover from work stress and reset for quality family time. "We are both *very* busy with work," she says. "With a job that requires many hours, and then a long commute, then we come home to play with our kids . . . it's tough to get it all in."

With her work commitments, she finds herself eating out for one or more meals each day—sometimes all three—and she knows she doesn't always make sensible choices from the menu. The intense schedule and frequent high-energy engagements with clients leave her feeling exhausted. She has little time for physical exercise.

Erin's rEvolution

With no two days the same, and every hour at the gym one less to spend with her family, Erin takes to Hit the Deck (which you're about to learn about) right off the bat. "It's something quick," she says, "and I have no excuse *not* to do it." The super-flexible workout guidelines—with no need for equipment or even gym clothes in a pinch—make it ideal not only for fitting exercise into her day, but also for recovering from individual stress events as they occur.

After sixty days of resiliency training, Erin notices a significant improvement in sleep quality and feels more energetic during the day. By paying more attention to eating regularly, she has cut down her midday cravings for sweets and dropped almost ten pounds of body fat—weight that had frustrated her since her last pregnancy.

She reports the strongest improvement in perceived stress, noting that she feels less anxiety and is less distracted by stress during work. It gives her better resources for supporting her team and meeting customers' high expectations.

ERIN AFTER SIXTY DAYS OF RESILIENCY TRAINING

- 25 percent decrease in perceived stress

- 19 percent increase in energy

- 10 percent improvement in quality of sleep

- Lost 9.7 pounds (4 percent) of body fat

- Gained 1.7 pounds of muscle

- Lost 5 inches

Chapter 3

PLAY IT OUT

The previous chapter may have seemed like quite a bit of bad news about stress. So if you're still with me and haven't thrown the book down in a fit of despair, you're about to learn some very, very positive news: Sneaky Pete does not have to control your life, *and it's only going to take you thirty to sixty seconds to fix it.* That's all it takes to Play It Out—the cornerstone of the Resiliency rEvolution.

But that's not the only good news in this chapter. You'll also learn how playing it out goes hand in hand with cardiovascular interval training as well as resistance training for overall fitness. Whether you move your body for thirty seconds or three ten-minute bouts, exercise builds the resiliency you need and remedies the negative consequences of stress.

As senior marketing manager of a global communications company, Angela is at her desk trying to get through some emails. She opens a message that tells her the company is restructuring her department and that she'll need to move to Nashville, Tennessee, if she wants to keep her position.

Her stomach drops, her heart hammers in her chest, and she starts to panic. Because of her job, she's moved her husband and two children twice within the past ten years, and she was *sure* the previous move would be the last. The kids love their current school and friends, and she couldn't possibly ask her husband to find another job again.

She immediately gets very angry. Why does this department need to get restructured? It's running just fine. If the team had stronger leadership, this move could have been fought. She's given so much of her life to this company, and this is what she gets in return? Another upheaval to her life?

She reaches for the phone to call her boss and tell her just how she feels about this move—it's unfair, it's unwarranted, and she doesn't want to do it. As she's about to dial the last number, she freezes. She recognizes Sneaky Pete is making decisions that may not be good for the longevity of her career.

Angela knows exactly what to do. She pushes her chair back, stands up, and walks out of her office. She strides purposefully down the hallway and throws open the door to the stairwell. She takes Sneaky Pete by the hand and sprints up two flights of steps, going as fast as she can. When she reaches the last step, she's breathing fast and her heart is beating double time. She turns around and walks back down. When she gets to the bottom, her heart rate and breathing have slowed, then she turns around and does the two flights one more time.

As she's standing at the bottom of the steps again, catching her breath, she starts thinking about why the department move could be necessary for the success of the company. She still doesn't want to move, but she's feeling capable of having a rational conversation with her boss to find out more information. Angela makes her way back to her desk, sits down, and calmly calls her boss to learn more about the email.

The Short Burst Short-Circuit

If you recall from this flow chart in chapter one, the key to restoring balance after the stress response has been stimulated is to fight or flee—or more realistically in today's environment, to Play It Out with a short burst of vigorous physical activity.

One of the biggest problems we face today is that most of us are exposed to frequent bouts of stress all day long, but we don't have the opportunity to duke it out, run in the opposite direction, or even Play It Out. We have mainly sedentary jobs, we use an endless array of labor-saving devices, and we live in environments where little to no movement is necessary.

STRESS
↓
STRESS HORMONES
↓
ENERGY
↓
FIGHT OR FLEE
(PLAY IT OUT)
↓
BLISS MOLECULES
↓
BALANCE RESTORED

The stress response

If we don't Play It Out, it means we're stuck marinating in a riptide of stress hormones. Without this bout of high-intensity exercise, cortisol continues to circulate, which results in the negative consequences to the brain and body you just learned about in chapter two.

LACK OF MOVEMENT IS SHORT-CIRCUITING THE SYSTEM!

But there's more. By not playing it out, we not only create negative side effects; we also miss out on positive side effects. *Great* side effects, actually. This lack of movement also means we miss out on the release of the amazing bliss molecules that restore balance, make us feel happy and calm, increase brain volume, and boost immunity. Just minimizing the damage of the stress hormones is only half the equation. To fully take part in the rEvolution, it's critical we also get the release of bliss molecules to neutralize, restore, and enhance our body and brain.

We've got to Play It Out all the way to the end.

You're Thirty to Sixty Seconds Away from Feeling Better

I made the connection between fight-or-flight and stress hormones after seeing the caveman billboard I told you about earlier. Once I learned that intense movement triggers this release of feel-good hormones, I was very curious to learn *exactly* how to get them. How much exercise is necessary? How many minutes does it take? What kind of exercise is best? How hard must I work? Like you, I don't have time to waste. I wanted to know the most efficient and effective way to get this dose of bliss.

I spent weeks poring over research journals, and here's what I found: the body releases endorphins after exercising a minimum of fifteen to twenty minutes at 70 to 80 percent of our VO_2 max.[1, 2, 3] The VO_2 max is the greatest amount of oxygen that can be used during intense or maximal exercise. To simplify things, think about this as working at 70 to 80 percent of your maximum ability.

I was a bit disheartened by this information. You mean we need to work out for *at least* fifteen minutes before we even get a droplet of feel-good hormones? In some studies, it was sixty minutes![4]

As I continued my research, though, I learned something incredible: the body also releases the bliss molecules after thirty to sixty *seconds* of intense physical activity.[5, 6, 7, 8, 9] If you think about the time frame of thirty to sixty seconds, this makes complete sense. Historically, the fight-or-flight response was intense and short lived. You either escaped or you were eaten, and either way, it was over in less than sixty seconds! You played it out. It all goes back to the body's brilliant evolutionary design.

....

THIRTY TO SIXTY SECONDS OF INTENSE PHYSICAL ACTIVITY RELEASES THE BLISS MOLECULES AND RESTORES BALANCE!

....

Your Pharmacy for Stress

When we Play It Out with a short burst of intense physical activity, the parasympathetic nervous system (the brake) releases chemical neurotransmitters. These are very powerful chemicals that neutralize the stress response. They calm us down, make us feel good, minimize pain, boost immunity, and enhance our health and sleep. These neurotransmitters work in opposition to the sympathetic nervous system (the gas pedal) to create balance.

Remember how stress shrinks the brain? When we Play It Out, we also release substances that counteract the shrinkage. These substances create new neurons in the brain as well as promote growth throughout the body and brain.

PLAYING IT OUT HELPS PUT THE BRAKES ON THE STRESS RESPONSE.

From an evolutionary perspective, these natural pain-killers evolved to help us deal with the inevitable pain of strained muscles and joints from fighting or fleeing, and they helped us keep going after we sustained an injury. When our lives were on the line or our clans were starving, we had to escape or make the kill no matter the circumstances. These substances helped us do just that.

You know that "runner's high" we sometimes get from exercise? It may be our caveman brain trying to make sense of our modern activity. The high may be the brain's last-ditch attempt to keep the body moving in what it can only perceive to be a life-threatening situation. The notion of running for "exercise" makes no sense to the caveman brain. It most likely assumes we've already walked twelve miles that day, as cavemen historically did.

Playing it out is like unlocking our own pharmacy to help us with stress. What's even more brilliant about this internal pharmacy is that it's accessible at any time. All we have to do is stimulate it, and it doesn't take long!

After you Play It Out for thirty to sixty seconds, the body releases endorphins and endocannabinoids to help restore balance after the stress response. But that's not all. Several other beneficial hormones are also released in response to exercise in general: dopamine, serotonin, brain-derived neurotrophic factor, and human growth hormones.

Let's take a closer look at these feel-good substances we have right at our own disposal.

Endorphins

The word *endorphin* (it's also sometimes referred to as *beta endorphin*) is a shortened form of "endogenous morphine." That literally means it's a morphine-like substance produced naturally in the body. If you're unfamiliar with morphine, it's a powerful narcotic derived from opium. In the medical industry, it's often considered the gold standard for pain relief.

Endorphins give us a feeling of well-being, enhance immune response, slow the heart rate, and are known to alleviate anxiety and depression.[10] Some researches refer to these neurotransmitters as the "bliss molecules." They are released in response to strenuous exercise, pain, excitement, or orgasm. (In this book, we'll focus on getting the release from exercise and save the other three for another time.)

Any drug that works in your body does so because you already have the receptors you produced yourself. It's little surprise the binding sites for these neurotransmitters are very densely found in the amygdala and hypothalamus, right where they need to be to counterbalance the stress response.

Endocannabinoids

During speaking engagements, I often ask my live audiences to raise their hands if they know what endocannabinoids are or if they've ever heard of them. Usually only one or two uncertain hands go up. I then ask the question, "How many of you can make an educated guess as to what these chemicals are all about?" At this time, they start making the connection to the word *cannabis*, and laughter breaks out.

Discovered in the early 1990s, endocannabinoids are a class of neurotransmitters that block activation of the HPA axis,[11] blunt pain, reduce anxiety, and produce all the euphoric feelings of marijuana. Our brain is a sponge for endocannabinoids, with ten times more receptors than we have for endorphins. If that's not enough, exercise expands these receptors and increases our body's ability to produce even more of them. *The harder we work out, the more endocannabinoids we produce*[12] *and the more receptors we have to suck them up.*

This feedback loop, paired with the addictive nature of these neurochemicals, means we can get addicted to exercise. It turns it into something we seek out on a regular basis, rather than feeling like a form of punishment.

> The first endocannabinoid to be discovered was anandamide, named from the Sanskrit word meaning "ultimate bliss." It's been the focus of much research to learn exactly how it affects pain, depression, appetite, memory, and fertility.

ENDORPHINS AND ENDOCANNABINOIDS ARE RELEASED IN RESPONSE TO EXERCISE AND ARE POWERFUL NEUTRALIZERS OF THE STRESS RESPONSE.

Dopamine

Dopamine is a neurotransmitter often referred to as "the reward molecule." It facilitates motivation, goal-oriented behavior, and achievement. When we do something that provides a reward, such as exercise, we get a release of dopamine, which increases our drive or motivation for the reward. For instance, when you set a goal and achieve it, dopamine is released. It's that little rush of pleasure we get when crossing something off our to-do list or following through on a commitment.

Dopamine creates a cycle of pleasure. First we get a rush when we perform the rewarding action. Then pretty soon, the sensation of pleasure comes from just *thinking* about performing the action, not just from the actual performing of it. For this reason, it's also known to increase desire, making us crave that behavior even more. If you've ever had your eyes roll back in your head while thinking about your favorite ice cream, and then soon found yourself reaching into the freezer for it, you know how this works.

It's easy to see why dopamine has been associated with addiction and addictive behaviors. Sex, food, cocaine, and gambling all play on our dopamine systems, creating desire for the good feeling we can get from these substances or activities. If you've ever met someone who seems "addicted" to exercise or eating healthy, dopamine is at work there too.

You're going to be learning a lot more about dopamine when you create your action plan in chapter six. It'll be an important tool to create the desire to perform some healthy new behaviors in your life. And soon you'll be able to put it to work for you, too.

Serotonin

Serotonin affects mood, anxiety, sleep, appetite, memory, and learning, as well as sexual desire and function. Almost any kind of exercise releases serotonin, which makes exercise an effective tool to manage depression and cope with stress.[13] Increasing serotonin receptivity is very often involved in the treatment of depression, as many who suffer from it have decreased levels of serotonin. Many antidepressants function by enhancing serotonin activity in the brain. (Note: discontinuing use of antidepressants should only occur after close consultation with your physician.)

Brain-Derived Neurotrophic Factor

This one is a mouthful, but boy, will you sound super-smart when you drop it into your next conversation. Brain-derived neurotrophic factor (BDNF) helps in the development of healthy brain tissue and reverses the negative effects of stress. Think of it as fertilizer for certain neurons in the brain—many of them found in the hippocampus. It helps keep existing neurons vital and healthy and also encourages the growth of new neurons (neurogenesis). The more we exercise, the more BDNF we create.

Human Growth Hormone

Human growth hormone (HGH) is vital to the growth and development of all brain and body cells. It's primarily produced in response to exercise and sleep. It controls fuel allocation, burns belly fat, increases muscle mass, pumps up brain volume, increases bone density, increases exercise capacity, and counteracts the natural cellular atrophy of aging.[14]

A single bout of sprinting for thirty seconds can generate a sixfold increase in HGH, with levels peaking two hours later.[15] In a nutshell, HGH is pretty awesome, and interval training is a great way to get it.

Stressproof Your Brain

As you learned in the previous chapter, stress has many negative side effects on the brain. Stress shrinks the hippocampus—a part of the brain associated with learning, memory, and emotional regulation. And it increases the size of the amygdala, creating more emotional fear responses. It can also turn off the gene that produces BDNF,[16] an important substance that keeps neurons alive and growing.

Exercise is the key to reversing these side effects. The brain responds to exercise similar to the way muscles do: it gets bigger and stronger. Exercise spurs neurogenesis, or neuron regrowth, *particularly in the hip-*

pocampus. In a randomized controlled trial of 120 older adults, aerobic training was found to increase hippocampal volume by 2 percent. Adults who train aerobically have also been found to have greater increases in brain activity in the frontal cortex—the advanced part of our brain critical for important tasks such as attention and conflict resolution.[17]

If you remember from earlier, Sneaky Pete hijacks the advanced brain during the stress response. The good news is, exercise helps your advanced brain take back control. Exercise improves the following mental tasks, most of them controlled by the advanced brain: executive control processes; planning; scheduling; working memory; coordination of people, places, and events; reaction time; perception and interpretation of visual images; inhibition; and the ability to block out unnecessary distractions.[18]

Exercise also fuels the brain, instantly improving cognitive performance. Exercise elevates heart rate, which increases blood circulation, which delivers more glucose, oxygen, and energy to the brain. Even a single bout of exercise can improve brain function for several hours.

EXERCISE CAN BUILD A STRESS-RESISTANT BRAIN.

If you're coming up on an important meeting, presentation, or interview, one of the best things you can do to improve your performance is to get in a quick bout of cardiovascular exercise. It's also a great way to get over a creative block or productivity hump. When you step away from a project for a short burst of activity, you'll not only get mental distance and recovery, but you'll also superfuel your brain. Some of my best ideas come when I'm exercising. I've left myself a multitude of gasping voice memos on my phone.

EXERCISE INCREASES COGNITIVE
FUNCTION AND BRAIN SIZE.

Motion Changes Emotion

In addition to releasing the feel-good hormones that reset the system and restore balance, exercise has several other beneficial ways it helps us deal with stress. First off, it's a healthy response to stress, especially compared to going to the vending machine, stepping outside for a cigarette, or downing a cocktail. It's also more constructive than standing at someone's cubicle or getting on the phone to vent and complain. And it sure beats mentally checking out by surfing the Internet or vegging in front of the television for hours on end.

Studies have shown exercise to be one of the most reliable long-term mood boosters on the planet. A review of more than fifty studies confirmed evidence that even a *single bout* of physical activity can improve mood. In addition, people who are more physically active rate their mental well-being more positively.[19] Another review of more than eighty studies concluded that exercise compares favorably with standard psychotherapy for clinical depression and has also proven to be effective to nonclinical cases as well.[20] It's also been shown to decrease anxiety, as even short five-minute bursts of cardiovascular activity stimulate anti-anxiety effects.[21]

Exercise also gives us the opportunity to physically remove ourselves from stressful situations. When we gain distance, we often gain perspective and insight. We move the focus away from the stressor and place it onto something else—repetitive movement, breathing, or application of skill. These actions are like meditation in motion that can calm and refocus our brain.

At one of my speaking engagements, a woman who worked at a multinational telecommunications corporation piped up and shared this story: she recently faced the biggest problem of her twenty-one years with the organization. At the time, she knew how she handled this urgent challenge would strongly influence the direction of her career. Though she was tempted to jump in and respond immediately (with Sneaky Pete in charge), she stepped away from her desk and took some time for an intense workout. She said it was the best thing she could have ever done, both for herself and her career.

Exercise has many benefits when it comes to stress. Next we're going to explore what is perhaps the best benefit of all.

Building Your Resiliency

We've discussed how exercise gives us the feel-good chemicals we need to recover from stress and how it's a healthy response. As if that weren't enough, here's the real kicker: exercise can actually make us more resilient to stress.

According to *Merriam-Webster*, the definition of *resilient* is 1) the ability to become strong, healthy, or successful again after something bad happens; and 2) the ability of something to return to its original shape after it has been pulled, stretched, pressed, bent, etc. What does that mean when it comes to stress? We're inundated with continuous stressors all day long, and there's nothing we can do to prevent the vast majority of them. Stress is a part of our jobs and daily experiences as humans. The goal of resiliency training is to recover faster from these stresses, return to a state of balance, and prepare for the next stressor that's coming. The more resilient we are, the better our performance becomes.

This improvement happens in the short term, helping you immediately restore balance after a stressful event. But it also adds up to sustainable performance over the long run. When we're resilient to stress, we can be better leaders, parents, significant others, and friends over the span of our lives, without having to cut corners or make sacrifices in order to do so. When we use the fight-or-flight response the way it was designed to function—with a burst of exercise after a stress event—we can leave our body in a stronger state and improve our health. That's right: we can strategically *use* stress and the stress response to expand our capacity, as well as to make us stronger and healthier in the process.

BEING RESILIENT TO STRESS MEANS WE CAN RECOVER FROM IT QUICKLY AND EFFICIENTLY AS WELL AS INCREASE OUR CAPACITY FOR IT.

Resiliency is directly connected to fitness, and we can learn a lot about both by looking at the heart. We determine someone's fitness level by measuring how quickly the heart rate drops after the stress of exercise. The faster the heart rate drops, the higher the level of fitness.

A FASTER DROP IN HEART RATE AFTER EXERCISE = IMPROVED FITNESS

We learned in chapters one and two that heart rate also increases dramatically in response to stress. The sooner we can get the heart rate to slow back down, the sooner the body recovers from the stressor. A faster drop in heart rate means a faster recovery, which also means improved resiliency. (We'll discuss this in more detail in the next section.)

A FASTER DROP IN HEART RATE AFTER STRESS = IMPROVED RESILIENCY

Interval Training and Stress

One of the *best* ways to improve fitness is with cardiovascular interval training: short bursts of high-intensity work followed by short periods of recovery. This pattern is suspiciously similar to the stress response: short periods of increased heart rate, breathing, and muscle use, followed by recovery. (Resistance training is another great way to improve fitness, and we'll discuss that later in the chapter.)

There is a *direct connection* between training the heart rate to drop and recover after the stress of exercise and getting it to drop and recover after the stress of everyday life. Training the body to recover from *any* type of stress—physical, mental, or emotional—improves the body's resiliency. Cardiovascular interval training trains your body to better recover from stress.

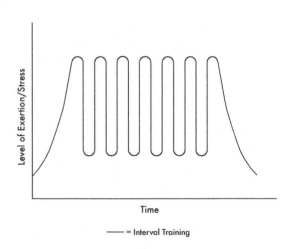

= Interval Training

Short bursts of high-intensity work/stress followed by short periods of recovery teach your body to recover from stress more quickly and efficiently. This improves your resiliency.

Researchers note that exercise also plays a preventative role, rather than just a corrective one, with stress. Cardiovascular interval training raises the trigger point at which our body decides something is stressful. This means it trains the body to handle more stress before it trips the stress response. Our threshold for stress increases, and we can handle more before we freak out.

Studies have concluded that people with higher levels of fitness are capable of managing stress more effectively than those who are less fit. The data suggest an inverse relationship: the higher the level of physical fitness, the lower the levels of stress.[22, 23]

An interesting—and fairly diabolical—study exposed two groups of men to a psychosocial laboratory stressor. One group was made up of elite athletes, and the other was untrained. In the study, the participants learned they had ten minutes to prepare before they'd have to give a speech and perform complex math calculations—all in front of a live audience. (It's important to note public speaking is most people's number one fear.) To make matters more stressful, the audience was instructed not to smile, to be very short and curt, and to give the participants the stink eye.

Results of the experiment showed that elite athletes had significantly lower cortisol and heart rate and reported less anxiety responses than untrained subjects.[24] This means the things that make the athletes fit also make them better able to handle stress.

Heart Rate Variability and Stress

Now that you have a general sense of how heart rate is related to stress, let's dig deeper. One of the best biological indicators of stress resilience is something called heart rate variability (HRV). HRV doesn't really relate to how our heart rate speeds up or slows down with our level of activity. Instead, it's the variation in the time interval between heart beats as we breathe. HRV can tell us a lot about our resiliency to stress.

If you recall from chapter two, heart rate is affected by the sympathetic and parasympathetic nervous systems (the gas pedal and the brake). When the systems are balanced, HRV coordinates with your breath: your heart rate speeds up slightly when you inhale, then slows when you exhale. HRV is also known as your autonomic resilience.

The more your heart rate varies—speeds up then slows down—with each breath, the higher your HRV level. And a high level of HRV is good. The speeding up and slowing down indicates the sympathetic and parasympathetic systems are balancing each other out. In other words, it means your body is not stuck in chronic fight-or-flight mode—the gas pedal is not permanently pressed to the floor. As you may have guessed, high HRV is also a measurement of overall cardiovascular health.

HIGH HRV IS GOOD.

When we experience stress, our heart rate speeds up, but unfortunately our HRV goes down. Keep in mind that when the HRV level is down, it means the heart rate is actually up. It means the gas pedal of the sympathetic nervous system is stuck, which makes the heart beat at a higher rate with no slowing between breaths. This creates the pounding chest and feelings of anxiety that go with stress. The sympathetic nervous system is dominating, and Sneaky Pete is in control.

LOW HRV IS BAD.

Researchers have found that people with a higher resting HRV respond better to stress than those with a lower HRV.[25] They also adapt more quickly to stressful environments; cope better with mental, emotional, and social stress; and recover more quickly from stressful experiences.[26] In short, HRV is a resiliency reserve that helps buffer against the effects of stress.

HRV is also a critical factor when making lifestyle change and implementing the training techniques you're learning in this book. We'll be revisiting the power of HRV in chapter six, when we put together your resiliency training action plan.

HRV is highly influenced by cardiovascular exercise—both interval and endurance training. Medical researchers have begun to make HRV training a primary focus in treating stress-related diseases, and exercise is a proven method for doing so. It's been shown to improve HRV in many different populations, including healthy adults,[28, 28] children,[29] the elderly,[30] as well as those recovering from coronary problems.[31, 32] Next we're going to discuss how you too can increase your HRV to reap the benefit of resiliency.

EXERCISE IMPROVES HRV AND RESILIENCY.

Your Resiliency Training Program

By now, you're understanding more about the rEvolution and the many reasons it's critical you work with, not against, your body's design in response to stress. You also see why playing it out with a short burst of cardiovascular exercise is the best way to do just that. You know the goal is to become more resilient to stress.

For cavemen, that short burst of exercise literally meant fighting or fleeing. Today, we can't *actually* fight or flee at work, on the freeway, or in the living room. We have to come up with a scenario in order to achieve the same outcome. That's why we Play It Out.

Now it's time to take that understanding and turn it into action.

Your Resiliency Training Program will re-create the fight-or-flight response with thirty to sixty seconds of high-intensity interval training.

The Play It Out pattern improves resiliency in many ways. First, high-intensity interval training quickly improves heart rate recovery time. This is good news. It means it trains the body to recover from the stress of exercise more quickly and efficiently, which in turn means we can recover from any type of stress more quickly and efficiently. We hit the reset button faster. Improved heart rate recovery also means improved overall fitness.

Second, it increases insulin sensitivity, which helps control blood glucose levels more effectively.[33] As you're about to learn in the upcoming chapter on nutrition and stress, becoming insensitive to insulin places undue stress on the organs and body. When the body is more sensitive to insulin, the pancreas gets away with not having to work as hard. It can produce smaller amounts of insulin and still do its job well. Having a higher level of fitness is associated with an increased number of insulin receptors as well as improved insulin binding,[34] which increases the body's sensitivity to insulin.[35] This improved sensitivity also reduces our risk for metabolic disorders such as diabetes.[36] And while poor glucose tolerance is associated with cognitive impairments such as decreased verbal memory,[37] people with higher glucose tolerance perform better in cognitive tests such as working memory and selective attention.[38]

Last, interval training enhances glucose metabolism.[39] This means the body can more efficiently transport glucose into the cells of muscle and brain tissue, providing consistent levels of energy for sustained mental and physical performance. When glucose levels build up in the blood, the pancreas must produce large amounts of insulin to remove it, and much of the excess gets stored as fat on the body. High-intensity interval training has been shown to reduce spikes of blood glucose after meals, in addition to lowering twenty-four-hour blood glucose concentrations in diabetics—all after just six training sessions over two weeks.[40]

PowerHouse Hit the Deck

Absolutely any activity can be made into interval training for improved resiliency. All you have to do is increase the speed, intensity, or resistance for thirty to sixty seconds, and then reduce the speed, intensity, or resistance for as long (or short) as it takes for you to be ready to do your next thirty-to-sixty-second interval.

But in order to make it easy and convenient for you to Play It Out, I've developed a resiliency training tool that tells you exactly what to do, how to do it, and for how long. It's literally like having me as a coach

PowerHouse Hit the Deck

in a box. It also doesn't require any equipment, so you can do it anytime, anywhere. If you're in your office or traveling for work, if you don't have access to equipment, or if you just need something convenient, this is for you. You can purchase Hit the Deck at www.ph-performance.com.

POWERHOUSE HIT THE DECK IS YOUR FIGHT-OR-FLIGHT TRAINING TOOL.

PowerHouse Hit the Deck consists of thirty-five cards along with a programmable interval timer. Each card features one exercise activity. The goal is to draw a card and do as many repetitions as possible of that exercise during the time set on the timer—**ideally thirty to sixty seconds**. The designated exercise will both elevate your heart rate as well as challenge your muscles: the very same actions as fighting or fleeing. This is how you Play It Out!

If you have time for only one card, that's fine. The short burst will use the stress hormones as they were intended, and you'll get your bliss molecules. If you've got time for more, then stop the timer, draw another card, and turn the timer back on when you're ready to go. Do as many repetitions as possible of that exercise until the timer beeps. Do a series of cards if you can. The recurring intervals will train your body to recover from stress as quickly as possible, and continuing to push yourself raises your threshold for stress.

One of my favorite things to tell audiences about Hit the Deck is this:

if you've got your body with you, and gravity is turned on, you're good to go! The body is a brilliant piece of training equipment. It doesn't take up extra space, you don't have to travel to use it, and it's available anytime. Whether you're on the road, in your office, or in your living room, you always have everything you need.

When Should I Do It?

Ideally, you should Hit the Deck or do any type of short-burst interval training to Play It Out the moment you realize the stress response has been triggered. Say you open your email and see that your project specs changed yet again. Step away and do thirty to sixty seconds of one or two Hit the Deck cards. Or do some other form of intense movement, such as shadowboxing, jumping rope with no rope (it still gets your heart rate up), or sprinting up some stairs. Play It Out immediately. If you get another nasty email in the afternoon, Play It Out again. Do that short burst of activity each time the stress response is triggered, if possible.

But of course, that's not possible in many situations. The reality is, you can't stand up in the middle of a tense negotiation or meeting and start doing squat jumps. (Though it could be just the tension breaker everyone needs.) Or maybe you played it out once at the office, but now there's no way you can pull over on the freeway during rush hour, get out of your car, and do burpees. *Get the short burst of physical movement as soon as you possibly can after a stress event, and if you get only one chance to Play It Out, that's better than nothing.* Remember that adrenaline and noradrenaline burn off fairly quickly in the first wave of the stress tsunami, but cortisol's effects linger in the body for much longer. If you can't hit that reset button until you get home from work, it's still better than not doing it at all.

You may want to plan a Play It Out time at work every day. After a speaking engagement in my hometown of Minneapolis, a woman came up to me and told me the managers in her Fortune 100 organization routinely walk around cubicle land with Hit the Deck. They had heard me speak at a different event, and now they do regular resiliency breaks for everyone. They get people up for a minute or two to do a few cards, burn off stress, get a dose of the feel-good hormones, and increase everyone's energy levels.

It's important to Play It Out during the day so your cortisol levels diminish by the evening, leading to a better night's sleep. More importantly, training during the day on a regular basis will build your threshold for stress. This means you'll be less likely to trigger the stress response at any time.

But what if the stress response happens late at night? You may suddenly find yourself staring up at the ceiling worrying about how you'll finish that report or pay that bill. I typically recommend people don't Play It Out or exercise late in the evening because it may hinder their sleep. As we'll discuss later in the chapter, exercise speeds up our metabolism, and this increase in energy can last a few hours if we work out really hard. This can make it hard to fall asleep.

There is a difference, though, if you weren't stressed when you went to bed, then you suddenly remembered something that triggered the stress response. If the stressor is serious enough that it could keep you awake for hours, it may make sense to get up and do some short bursts of activity. Otherwise, if the stressor is minor, a psychological technique such as writing, meditating, or reading may be a better option.

Benefits of Interval Training for Fitness

We just discussed the many benefits of interval training, such as Hit the Deck, for improving resiliency to stress. It's the perfect way to Play It Out.

As you can imagine, there are also many benefits to interval training for fitness. When I do follow-up programs or reconnect with clients, one of the things they share is how much of a difference interval training has made not only for their resilience, but also for their fitness, body fat, enjoyment, and consistency of exercise.

Interval training drops us into this beautiful wormhole where time goes by more quickly. We're so focused on these small, manageable bits of exercise, we don't notice how long we're working out in total. In contrast, steady-state, continuous training (sustaining the same heart rate while exercising) typically drops us into a wormhole where time slows down to exercise dog years: every one minute feels like at least seven.

The physical benefits of interval training are plentiful. We exercise physiologists have known for many years it's a superior way of exercising. In many cases, it offers greater benefits than long, sometimes tedious bouts of steady-state exercise.[41, 42] Numerous studies have shown that in terms of fitness-related gains, body fat, and weight loss, people doing short bursts of activity for short periods of time achieve more benefits than endurance-trained subjects, despite that the overall training time was much less.[43]

Interval training gives us a wide range of physiological gains in less time than does continuous exercise. This is partially because it allows us to do a greater volume of work.[44, 45] We get more work done in the same or shorter amount of time because we're able to work at greater intensity levels.

During steady-state training, it's impossible to sustain a high level of intensity for an extended period. We have to lower the intensity in order to last the entire duration of the workout. In contrast, interval training allows us to work very hard for a short period of time, get a few seconds or minutes of recovery, and then perform another hard-work interval. Despite the frequent breaks, when we add up all the high-intensity intervals, our overall production (calories burned) is greater than with steady-state training.

A study conducted by Martin Gibala, PhD—chairman of the Department of Kinesiology at McMaster University in Ontario, Canada—pitted two groups of exercisers against each other. Group one did steady-state exercise for 90 to 120 minutes, three times per week. Group

two did four bouts of 20- to 30-second intervals at the highest intensity they could stand, and they were working out for no more than three
minutes per day. At the end of two weeks, both groups showed *almost
identical* increases in their endurance, though the first group exercised
for up to two hours per day and the second group exercised for only up
to three minutes per day. The author stated: "Sprint interval training is
a time-efficient strategy to induce rapid adaptations in skeletal muscle and exercise performance that are comparable to endurance training."[46]

Another study had one group of children exercise with a series of
30-second sprints and another group doing 20 minutes of continuous
exercise. The 30-second-sprints group exercised a total of 63 minutes and burned 907 calories, and the continuous exercisers did 420
minutes and burned 4,410 calories. Both groups showed significant
improvements in cardiorespiratory fitness, blood pressure, body composition, and insulin resistance. But the high-intensity sprinting group
achieved the benefits with *only 15 percent of the exercise time* as the steady
state group.[47]

Interval training has also been shown to burn more body fat.[48, 49, 50, 51]
This is important because stress and cortisol make us deposit more fat
on the body, and short-burst interval training is a great way to get rid of
it. Researchers have found that high-intensity interval training produces a
ninefold reduction in body fat compared to endurance training.[52] It significantly increases muscle oxidative capacity, which is associated with
an improved ability to oxidize fats, or burn fat as fuel.[53] One study found
high-intensity interval training increases fat use by 36 percent.[54] It not
only increases fat burning during exercise, but for several hours to days
afterward.

Interval training also improves our level of fitness very quickly because it produces a dramatic improvement in exercise tolerance, typically
in just a couple weeks.[55] Interestingly, it's also been shown to increase

cardiovascular endurance.[56] Even though exercise bouts are short, they improve our endurance to do longer sessions without the long time commitment of endurance training.

This is because interval training increases mitochondria density.[57] Mitochondria are involved in manufacturing energy for muscle cells. A higher density means more energy for our working muscles so we can work harder for longer. These improvements in fitness allow us to work at a higher intensity during our workouts. And in turn, this increased performance means more work is accomplished and more calories are burned during an exercise session. In addition, it improves VO_2 max (which we discussed earlier) and cardiovascular function.[58]

Your Interval Training Bonus Prize

You reap many benefits while you interval train. But you also reap them when you're done and no longer working out. Interval training increases the number of calories you burn *after you're done exercising.* That's right—while you're back at your desk going about your business or while you're spending time with family, your body continues to expend higher levels of energy. And the even better news is, your body takes much of this energy from your fat cells.

When we exercise, our metabolism and heart rate speed up. When we're done exercising, however, our metabolism doesn't drop back down to a resting state, like our heart rate does.

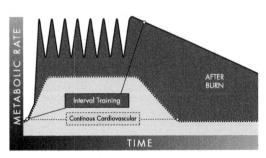

Excess post-exercise oxygen consumption (EPOC) elevates metabolism

There's a period of time after exercise called excess post-exercise oxygen consumption (EPOC), where our metabolism stays elevated and then very gradually slows back down.

During this time, our working muscle cells restore physiological and metabolic factors to pre-exercise levels. I like to call this our "after burn," where we burn more fat and calories by doing nothing. It's free calories being burned! Depending on the type and intensity of the cardiovascular exercise we do, EPOC can last up to forty-eight hours.[59]

WE BURN FAT AND CALORIES NOT ONLY *WHILE* WE'RE EXERCISING, BUT FOR MANY HOURS AFTERWARD.

Here's what we know influences EPOC:

- **Intensity matters**: The harder we work, the higher our EPOC will be.

- **Type matters**: Interval training produces a much higher EPOC than steady-state training does. In order to maximize EPOC, sixty-second high-intensity intervals are optimal.[60]

- **Time matters**: The longer we work out, the higher our EPOC will be.

- **Splitting matters**: Doing two or three shorter workouts during the day makes our EPOC higher than doing one longer workout. (More on this below.)

- **Resistance matters**: Resistance training actually drives a higher EPOC level than cardiovascular does. (More about this later, too.)

Using Hit the Deck for Fitness

You've already learned how PowerHouse Hit the Deck works as a fight-or-flight training tool. Its most important goal is building resiliency to all the stress you face so you can perform to your absolute best both at work and at home.

However, you may be overjoyed to learn it also has many other positive side effects—the biggest being it can be used as an interval training tool. As we just discussed above, interval training improves health and fitness as well as reduces body fat. Again, these are *side effects* of resiliency training and Hit the Deck, not the primary focus. But because resiliency and fitness are directly connected, these side effects enhance the primary goal.

When you use Hit the Deck as part of a regular exercise routine, it can:

- Help you lose weight, burn fat, and add muscle

- Improve your overall levels of fitness and wellness

- Improve your muscular strength and endurance

- Increase your cardiovascular capacity

- Improve the quality of your sleep

- Increase your energy levels

Here's how it works. The length of your workout will be determined by how much time you set on the programmable interval timer and how many cards you perform in that time. I recommended you begin with thirty-second intervals and gradually work your way up to sixty. However, if thirty seconds is too long, start with a shorter duration until you build up your capacity.

After setting the timer, perform the five Warm Up and Cool Down cards for one minute each. Or you can do each card for thirty seconds, then repeat them all.

After the warm-up, you're ready to jump into the heart of your workout. Draw your first exercise card, hit start on the timer, and do as many repetitions as you can during the interval. When the timer beeps, hit stop, catch your breath for a moment, and draw your next card. Then hit start on the timer and get going on your next exercise. Move from one card to the next as quickly as possible and continue on until you are out of cards or have repeated the cycle as many times as desired.

Finish with the five Warm Up and Cool Down cards, and you are done. BOOM! You just hit the reset button and got a great workout, and now it's time to bask in your bliss molecules!

Hit the Deck is a very efficient and effective way to exercise. There's no need to squeeze in time for a cardiovascular workout plus another time for resistance training. You're doing both simultaneously. (We'll learn more about resistance training later in the chapter.)

It's also a very flexible tool. Your workout can be as long or short as you want. If you've got only a few minutes, do a few cards. If you have more time, do more cards or repeat the ones you've chosen. You can also alter how much time you spend on each interval, making it shorter or longer as needed.

For those who get bored with workouts, Hit the Deck offers an endless amount of variety. You can do the same cards for a couple weeks and then change them up, or you can shuffle the deck each time for a completely different workout every day. You can also custom arrange the cards in any order or combination.

Hit the Deck will also meet you wherever you are on your fitness journey. Depending on your current fitness level, there are three different intensity categories you can work from: "No Sweat" if you're just starting out, "I'm Glistening" if you've been exercising for a while, and "Sweating Buckets" if you're ready to kick it up a notch. If you're just starting out, choose the "No Sweat" cards and do them for a shorter period of time. As your body successfully adapts to the stress of exercise and your fitness improves, you can choose more challenging cards and add more time to the timer.

It's also a great way to cross-train if you're looking for something new and different. Each intensity category has ten cards that work all your major muscle groups. The variety of movements and exercises means you don't do any one thing for too long to get overtrained.

And did I mention it's an excellent workout with no fitness equipment? No weights, mats, machines, benches, or gadgets needed. You could even do the workout with no shoes if you had to. (I know from personal experience when traveling, there's only so much room in the suitcase. If it comes down to packing a pair of sassy shoes or workout sneakers, it's not even a fair competition.)

Here are some other ways to use PowerHouse Hit the Deck:

- **Alternate Colors:** First card is blue, second card is green, third is red, fourth is blue, fifth is green, etc.
- **1–30:** See if you can complete the whole deck!
- **Shuffle the Whole Deck:** What you draw is what you do.
- **Build Your Capacity:** Stick with the same cards for a short period of time, and keep track of how many repetitions of each you can do. See if you can increase the number of repetitions within the same time.
- **Muscle Group Workout:** Do all the cards that work the legs. The next day, do all the cards that work the chest, and so on.
- **Move It, Then Hit It:** Sprinkle some cards into a cardiovascular workout. Walk for five minutes, do five cards, walk for another five minutes, etc.
- **Energy Burst:** Do a few cards midmorning and midafternoon for a quick energy pick-me-up.
- **Partner Workout:** Take turns doing cards, or see who can do the most repetitions during each interval.
- **Group Workout:** Grab your coworkers or friends. Everyone takes turns leading the workout by drawing cards, or one person is designated the group leader.
- **Kids' Game:** Work out with your kids. If they are very young, they can be in charge of pushing the buttons on the timer and drawing the cards. If they are older, have them join in. See who can do the most repetitions of each exercise in the designated time.

• **Stretching**: After your workout, use the timer to make sure you are holding each stretch for fifteen to thirty seconds.

Other Interval Training Workouts

You don't necessarily need a tool such as Hit the Deck to get an interval training workout. Many sports—such as basketball, racquetball, and tennis—are interval in nature. They automatically follow the work/rest formula. In truth, we're only limited by our creativity.

There's a hill about a mile from my house that makes a phenomenal interval workout. I jog to the hill as my warm-up, then sprint up the hill as fast as I can. It takes me about thirty seconds to reach the top, and by the time I get there, the exertion has pushed me into a serious state of physical discomfort. Once I pass a designated tree at the top of the path, I switch to a very slow jog (to be truthful, it's more of a shuffle) and gradually make my way back down the hill. About forty-eight seconds pass while I make my way to the bottom, catch my breath, feel good again—then turn around to sprint up the hill another time. I repeat this process about a dozen times, then jog back home as my cool-down. Check out my PowerHousePerform YouTube channel to see the video of my "Running the Hill" workout.

I've also done what I call Instagram Interval Workouts. I typically carry my phone to listen to music or keep time on runs, and I've put the camera app to good use many times. The assignment is to run until I find something interesting to photograph. When I spot it, I stop and snap a picture. The few seconds it takes me to get the photo are my recovery intervals, then I get back to running. It's a great way for workouts to go by more quickly. I focus on looking around my environment to see things in a new way, instead of thinking about how out of breath I am or how long the workout is taking. I've also gotten some great photos along the way!

Music also makes a great interval training tool. Find a song you really enjoy, one that gets you moving, and make the song's chorus and verse patterns your work and recovery intervals. Exercise as hard as you can during the verses, then reduce your intensity whenever you hear the chorus. When the song is over, start shuffling through your playlist until you find the next song that will motivate you to power through another series of work/rest intervals.

I came upon a great example of creative interval training a few years ago when I was traveling to a speaking engagement for a large technology company in San Jose, California. As I was walking out of the airport to find the driver who would take me to my hotel, I spotted something out of the corner of my eye. Across the pickup lane by a shuttle van was an older gentleman jumping rope in his dress shirt and khaki pants.

This was not something you see every day. I was curious enough to walk over, introduce myself, and ask him what he was doing. His name was Ali. He looked to be in his mid-sixties, and he was a hotel shuttle driver. Whenever he waited to pick up guests, he grabbed his jump rope, got out on the sidewalk, and did a few minutes of jumping. *I loved it!* I asked him if I could video him, and he happily obliged. Check out my PowerHousePerform YouTube channel to see Ali doing his thing in "The Real Ali of San Jose."

Ali's job was to *sit in a van* for his entire shift, driving through the crazy, stressful traffic around the airport. However, he recognized that he had a few minutes here and there to squeeze in some short-burst interval training to burn off his stress and stay fit. He didn't worry about changing his clothes. He was just exercising for a few minutes at a time, which didn't work up much of a sweat. (I'm guessing not too many people would have wanted to get into a van with a stranger who was breathing heavy and sweating.)

This was a great way for Ali to fit regular workouts into a busy schedule. If you think about how many minutes of exercise he managed to accumulate throughout the span of his workday, he probably got around forty to sixty minutes of exercise. And he did it all while working his sedentary job!

Muscle Mass: The Other Piece of Play It Out

As you've seen so far in this chapter, cardiovascular interval exercise is a key component of resiliency training and overall fitness. Whether you Play It Out for thirty seconds or run hill intervals for ten minutes, it's great to get your heart pumping.

Pumping your muscles is also a great way to improve your resiliency. We're going to learn about how to put your muscles to work with resistance training. But first, let's explore why muscle mass is a critical piece of resiliency and health.

Think about it: the actions of fighting and fleeing involved more than our cardiovascular system. Fighting called on plenty of muscular strength and endurance. When fleeing, we may have had to use muscles to jump over boulders or downed trees, push things out of our way to escape, or pull ourselves up to safety.

Working our muscles accomplishes many of the same effects as working our cardiovascular system. When we call on the major muscles of the body, the demand for oxygen increases in order to supply the muscles with energy. The body adapts to this increased need for oxygen by speeding up our breathing in addition to our heart rate in order to pump this oxygenated blood to all the muscles that need it.

Here's a quick experiment. Stand up with your feet spaced hip-width apart. Lower yourself into a squat position, making sure your knees do not extend past your toes and keeping your weight shifted back on your heels. Now rise up and lower down as quickly as you can for sixty seconds. Ready, go!

Once you finish, quickly place two fingers on the carotid artery in your neck to feel your pulse—or simply notice how fast you're breathing. It wasn't a traditional cardiovascular exercise, but your pulse is quick and you're breathing fast, right? The large muscles of your hamstrings, quadriceps, and gluteus demanded a lot of energy and oxygen, so your heart rate and breathing increased to meet the greater demand.

Our muscle mass is clearly an important component of our resiliency, so let's take a look as to why we need to use it—or lose it.

Muscle Mass: Use It or Lose It

Our ancestors spent large amounts of energy working, fighting, fleeing, and reproducing. A high proportion of muscle mass made it possible. Muscle tissue composes up to 40 percent of the body's total weight. Because it is metabolically active, it requires close to a quarter of our daily energy intake.[61] But this metabolic cost was a bit of a catch-22 for our ancestors: the more muscle mass they had, the more work they could do; but that also meant they had to find more food to sustain it.

We were constantly living on the margins of energy balance. So in order to survive, we developed the ability to alter our metabolism, to either speed up or slow down the rate at which our body required energy.

Our ancestors' metabolic rate plugged along just fine when they were active every day and when food was available to supply the energy for that daily activity. However, when food became scarce, the body was able to slow down the metabolic rate. And if the food shortage persisted, the body would break down muscle tissue and use it for life-sustaining energy. It was a necessary balance when food was hard to come by—with less muscle mass, the body didn't require as many calories in a twenty-four-hour period.

Remember that our genetics haven't changed much in the last ten thousand years. The human genome is still programmed to expect daily, regular physical activity. Sitting used to be a break in the day; now it's how we spend the majority of it. We're pretty motionless for hours on end. If we're lucky, we move about like mad for thirty minutes to burn 250 calories, then return to low activity levels. This is certainly *not* how we're designed to function.

Even though food shortage is no longer a problem for many of us, our body is still diligent about monitoring energy balance. We often don't utilize our muscles to a large degree, so maintaining a large amount of energy-expensive muscle mass doesn't make sense to our energy-conserving body. We're better off not having so much muscle mass that's going unused, so the body does us a favor by getting rid of it. If we don't use it, we lose it.

Think of it as having an expensive membership to a gym or golf course. As much as you love the idea of going to the gym or playing golf regularly, you come to the realization you don't use it very often. It's ridiculous to keep paying that much for something so costly you never use, so you cancel your membership. This membership is like muscle mass on the body: it's metabolically expensive to sustain, and if it's not being used regularly, the body "does you a favor" and gets rid of it.

What Happens When You Lose It

A loss of muscle mass is unfortunate for many reasons, including from a resiliency perspective. It decreases insulin and glucose sensitivity, which results in more stress on the body. This is something you learned in chapter two and will be exploring more in the next chapter on nutrition.

When we're less sensitive to insulin, the pancreas has to work harder and harder to produce progressively higher amounts insulin to manage our blood glucose levels. This increased workload places stress on the pancreas to the point where it can eventually burn out the cells that produce insulin.

When the body cannot properly utilize glucose, the cells don't get the energy they need. This can cause extreme fatigue, thirst, and urination; cognitive difficulties, and blurred vision. It also creates chronically high levels of glucose in the bloodstream, which can damage blood vessels, nerves, and organs and can eventually lead to a coma. A decrease in glucose sensitivity, or glucose intolerance, is often referred to as prediabetes and can lead to many chronic conditions such as full-blown diabetes, heart disease, and stroke.

A decrease in muscle mass also means a decrease in metabolism. Less muscle requires fewer calories, but we typically don't realize we've lost muscle, so we don't eat less. When we couple this with daily repeated releases of cortisol, we begin to store more fat on the body, particularly around the waist. As you learned earlier, this raises our risk for many health problems and diseases that cause large amounts of physical and psychological stress.

It's a vicious cycle: excess fat on the body further decreases sensitivity to insulin and glucose, causing more stress on the body, including more pressure on the joints. To make the cycle even more vicious, chronic exposure to cortisol is catabolic, meaning it breaks down muscle mass. As researchers at the University of Texas have shown, not only does inactivity lead to muscle loss, but high levels of stress and cortisol accelerate that loss.[62]

What Happens When You Use It

Being physically inactive is abnormal behavior for how we're designed to function. In addition to decreasing muscle mass, it's leading to many serious metabolic dysfunctions. Being sedentary rapidly results in insulin resistance in our muscles.[63]

However, physical exercise is an effective antidote. It very quickly increases our muscles' sensitivity and responsiveness to insulin. Staying physically active—and in a way that maintains or even increases muscle mass—means our body can operate optimally on many levels: metabolically, hormonally, functionally, and even psychologically. If you want to use, not lose, your muscle mass, resistance training is the way to go.

The goal of resistance training is to increase stress on the muscles in order to decrease stress on many physiological systems in the body. It pays off in dividends. The more muscle mass we have, the more sensitive we are to insulin. Each 10 percent increase in muscle mass results in an 11 percent decrease in the risk of insulin resistance. In addition, each 10 percent increase also reduces the risk of developing prediabetes or full-blown diabetes—major stressors on the body.[64] When the body is more sensitive to insulin, the pancreas isn't under the sustained stress of producing large amounts of it to regulate our blood glucose levels.

Glucose metabolism also improves with resistance training.[65, 66] In people with type 2 diabetes, combined aerobic and resistance training has been shown to be superior to cardiovascular training alone for improving glycemic control.[67] Better usage of glucose means levels are more often within the ideal range and less insulin is required to metabolize it. This improvement in metabolism decreases the risk of coronary heart disease, stroke, and diabetes.

BETTER INSULIN SENSITIVITY AND GLUCOSE METABOLISM DECREASE STRESS ON THE BODY.

Resistance training plays an important role in increasing metabolism as well as muscle mass, which helps decrease the percentage of body fat. A high level of body fat places excess stress on the joints, which can lead to pain in many areas, including the low back, knees, and feet. This sustained stress causes damage to the joints and increases the risk of arthritis. As we discussed, excess body fat also interferes with insulin's ability to remove glucose from the bloodstream, forcing the pancreas to work harder. In addition, when body fat levels are high, the heart has to work much harder to pump blood throughout the body. Heart function can become impaired.

LESS BODY FAT TRANSLATES TO LESS STRESS ON JOINTS AND ORGANS.

The good news continues. Resistance training is also proven to decrease psychological stress. A review of multiple resistance training studies concluded that resistance training is a meaningful intervention for people suffering from anxiety.[68] Several studies have also shown it can have positive effects on depression, fatigue, sleep, and self-esteem.[69]

RESISTANCE TRAINING IMPROVES MOOD AND MENTAL HEALTH.

Not only does resistance training increase the size of our muscles, it also increases the size of our brain. If you recall, stress shrinks brain cells in the hippocampus, which negatively affects important cognitive functions such as memory and recall. In contrast, resistance training improves many aspects of cognition in healthy adults. One of the most profound changes involves improved memory and memory-related tasks as well as enhanced executive function (being able to use our advanced brain).[70] It is speculated that resistance training improves cognition because it generates new nerve cells in the brain, more neurotransmitters (substances that send nerve impulses in the brain), and more blood cells, which all improve oxygen delivery and waste removal in the brain.[71]

RESISTANCE TRAINING IMPROVES COGNITION AND EXECUTIVE FUNCTION.

What Counts as Resistance?

Are you ready to put those muscles to work with some resistance training? It's easier than you think. The purpose is to contract your muscles against some form of resistance, of which there are many.

Resistance training doesn't only happen in a gym with heavy weights and fancy machines. As stated earlier in the chapter, you have all the exercise equipment you need: your body and gravity. Our distant ancestors had high proportions of muscle mass despite the fact they didn't have any kettlebells or barbells. Your body is a legitimate and effective piece of resistance training equipment. Depending on the position you place your body in and how the force of gravity pulls down on it, you can do some very challenging moves.

IF IT CHALLENGES YOUR MUSCLES, IT COUNTS AS RESISTANCE TRAINING.

For example, pushups are a very effective form of resistance training. They not only work the chest, but also the shoulders, triceps, and core. Different body positions allow different levels of challenge. Keeping your knees on the floor makes it easier. Placing your feet on a chair or other raised surface makes it much more challenging. Changing the position of your hands mixes up how the muscles are used. You can keep your hands out wide in the traditional stance; place your hands closer together and keep your elbows alongside your body; or put your hands close together to form a triangle, which makes the triceps work harder.

Other common resistance exercises include lunges, squats, and crunches. Really, there's an endless array of resistance exercises that can be done in different ways, simply by changing position, speed, range of motion, number of repetitions, and level of impact. For example, move through a full range of motion quickly versus taking four counts to lower down and four counts to press up. You can hold a challenging position for a period of time or do a series of small pulses. These all challenge the body in different ways.

Like cardiovascular training, resistance training lends itself well to the interval format. An intense burst of resistance-based movement, followed by a recovery period, is a great way to get those muscles working.

Our hunter-gatherer ancestors did short bursts of higher intensity hunting, fighting, and fleeing. In comparison, our farming ancestors performed "continuous workouts." They worked very long hours each day, but at a moderate intensity. The fact that hunter-gatherers were much stronger and more muscular than farmers suggests the *intensity* of intermittent exercise is more important to muscular development than the *duration*.[72]

Combining Cardiovascular and Resistance Training

After everything you've learned in this chapter, I bet Sneaky Pete is whispering in your ear right now: there's *no way* you have time to do cardiovascular *and* resistance training. It's hard enough to squeeze in one workout that gets your heart rate up, let alone to add another workout for increasing muscle mass. He's saying you don't have the time or equipment to get it done and this book is asking too much of you.

The good news is, you don't have to do two separate workouts—you can combine them in one. It's more than just a time saver. It's the best of both worlds when you want to Play It Out for resiliency as well as when you want to work out for fitness.

Cardiovascular activity alone does not produce the increase in heart rate we experience when we add some form of muscular resistance to the movement. Stressing our muscles during short-burst cardiovascular activities helps create an even higher heart rate in a shorter period of time. This increases the efficiency and effectiveness of a fitness workout. More importantly, it's precisely what we're trying to accomplish in our resiliency training program.

ADDING RESISTANCE TRAINING TO SHORT BURSTS OF PHYSICAL ACTIVITY INCREASES EFFICIENCY AND EFFECTIVENESS.

As discussed earlier in the chapter, high-intensity interval training is one of the best ways to elevate our resting metabolic rate (the number of calories we burn while at rest). This benefit is even greater, however, when we add resistance training to the aerobic intervals. Exercises that build muscle mass significantly increase resting metabolic rate. Resistance training also increases our EPOC. Remember that from earlier in the chapter? It's the "after burn." Resistance training actually drives a higher EPOC level than cardiovascular interval training does.[73] When we combine the two, it's even more pronounced.

This not only means we burn more calories in a twenty-four-hour period, it also means we generate more energy in those twenty-four hours. Who among us doesn't need more energy to meet the many demands of our lives? Being more productive and checking more things off our to-do lists decreases the stress of deadlines and responsibilities. It also means we have more energy for things outside of our jobs, such as family, friends, community, or leisure-time pursuits that make us feel happy and fulfilled.

The PowerHouse Hit the Deck cards combine both resistance and cardiovascular training exercises in short bursts, but any type of interval activity that challenges your muscles as well as raises your heart rate will do the same. Consider moves such as pushups, lunges, and squats. If you want these exercises to really elevate your heart rate, get creative and play with body position, speed, impact level (high versus low), amount of movement, or combining exercises. Taking a pushup to the next level could mean starting in a standing position, then squatting down and placing your hands by the feet, jumping your feet back and landing in a pushup position, performing one pushup, jumping your feet back by your hands, then standing or jumping up. It increases the heart rate and overall challenge level of the exercise.

For squats, you can add a jump straight up or move forward or backward. You can add leg raises with or without rotation. For lunges, you can move forward or backward or jump up in the air between lunges to switch which leg is in front.

There are many benefits to blending your cardiovascular and resistance training. It's a more efficient and effective way to exercise, and it literally slashes your fitness time commitment in half. And as we'll discuss next, that time commitment is not as long—or hard—as you may think.

10/10/10

You know it takes only thirty to sixty seconds to Play It Out for resiliency training. That's easy, right? But after reading all this information about cardiovascular and resistance training for improved fitness, you're probably wondering how long *that* takes.

Many people assume exercise is something we must do in large spans of time, all in one session—thirty, forty-five, or sixty minutes. Who has such large chunks of time to set aside? So most of us don't do anything at all.

Let me tell you, 10/10/10 is the most beautiful number combination you'll ever lay eyes on. The good news is, research shows that physical activity accumulated throughout the day in three ten-minute bouts can be just as effective for improving fitness and decreasing body fat as exercising once for thirty minutes straight.

Experiments have compared groups of people who either exercised for thirty consecutive minutes or achieved thirty minutes of exercise through three ten-minute bouts throughout the day. At the conclusions of the studies, results for both groups were similar, if not better in the 10/10/10 group.[74, 75]

There are several benefits to breaking our workouts into 10/10/10 instead of exercising for thirty consecutive minutes. First, instead of getting only one EPOC after burn, we get three. This means we boost our metabolism three times during the day, plus we enjoy not one but three opportunities to burn extra fat and calories after we work out.

Second, "exercise snacks"—multiple brief bouts—can control blood glucose levels better than a single continuous workout. In chapter four, you'll learn about the importance of food snacking throughout the day to be resilient. But it's just as important to "snack" on short bursts of physical activity.

A recent study had participants do high-intensity cardiovascular intervals, alternating one minute of work and one minute of recovery for a total of twelve minutes. On a different day, the participants did one minute of high-intensity cardiovascular work followed by one minute of resistance training for a total of another twelve minutes. Then on another day, they did one continuous moderate workout for thirty minutes.

The results were striking: each of the exercise snacks lowered and regulated the participants' blood glucose levels during the workouts, and then the beneficial effects lasted roughly twenty-four hours. From just twelve-minute bouts of work![76] The participants not only saw better results from the exercise snacks than the continuous training, but they also enjoyed the snack format more than the longer sustained workout.

Third, we're more likely to get consistent, regular exercise if we break it into the 10/10/10 format.[77] We should approach a regular exercise routine with the mindset that every little bit counts and that we'll get it where and when we can. We'll accumulate more minutes of exercise over the long run. Ten minutes here, ten minutes there, done consistently on a daily basis, really adds up over time. Obviously, this can be useful when trying to fit resiliency training or physical activity into a busy schedule!

Fourth, 10/10/10 gives us an opportunity to burn more fat and calories. If I asked you to exercise for thirty minutes without stopping, you'd pace yourself and work at a moderate intensity to make sure you'd last the full thirty minutes. But if I asked you to work out for just ten minutes without stopping, you'd work much harder. You'd know it was a short period of time, so you could give it all you've got. And then if I asked you to do three of these ten-minute bouts while working really hard, it'd add up to more fat and calories burned than one thirty-minute session at moderate intensity.

10/10/10 IS A GREAT WAY TO FIT IN EXERCISE AND HAS SEVERAL ADVANTAGES OVER LONGER WORKOUTS.

Fifth, 10/10/10 not only provides better fitness results, but it's also good for your overall health. In 2004 the American College of Sports Medicine (ACSM) issued a news release stating that "accumulated short bouts of exercise are more effective than continuous exercise for lowering fat and triglyceride levels in the bloodstream after eating."[78] Researchers believe this is because each short exercise bout may provide a slight increase in metabolism.[79] The ACSM went on to say that intermittent exercise consisting of multiple ten-minute bouts that accumulate to at least thirty minutes on most, if not all, days of the week is an effective way to reduce the risk of heart disease.[80]

Robert Gerszten—the director of clinical and translational medicine at Massachusetts General Hospital's cardiology division and an associate professor of medicine—found that more than twenty different metabolites change during exercise. These metabolites are compounds involved in burning calories and fat, in addition to improving blood glucose control. He found these changes begin after just ten minutes of exercise and are still measurable for sixty minutes afterward.[81]

Finally, short bouts of exercise go hand in hand with resiliency training. The best way to Play It Out is with a short burst of intense activity, so the 10/10/10 format gives you three quick opportunities to build resiliency and fitness. Fight some bad traffic on the way to work? Close your office door and do as many Hit the Deck cards as you can in ten minutes. You just hit the reset button, but you also just finished a third of your daily workout! In particular, short exercise bouts are immediate stress-busters. A 2010 analysis of ten studies found that five-minute doses of exercise have the biggest effect on enhancing mood and combating stress.[82]

Yeah, But . . .

I get it—there's a battle going on in your head right now. As wonderful as the information in this chapter about exercise may seem to your advanced brain, Sneaky Pete is saying, "Yeah, but . . ."

In the last two chapters, we'll thoroughly address how to successfully implement the training techniques you're learning in this book. But right now, it's important to address some of the things Sneaky Pete might be whispering in your ear about what you've read so far. He may be saying you don't have time, it will be too hard, you've got personal commitments in addition to job responsibilities, or any number of excuses. Let's address each one and set him straight.

This Is All Great, But I Don't Have Time to Exercise

I literally meet thousands of people each year, and the number one obstacle they tell me is that they don't have time to exercise. There is both reality and excuse in this statement. The reality piece we'll tackle now, and the excuse part we'll deal with in chapter six.

It's true we've got a lot on our plates with work, home, and personal commitments. You literally may not have a thirty-, forty-five-, or sixty-minute chunk of time available for exercise during the day. But with the 10/10/10 strategy, fitting exercise into your day is merely a matter of finding a couple ten-minute windows. It's safe to say we can all clear out ten minutes a few times a day. Instead of flipping through channels or poking at apps for ten minutes, why not do a couple Hit the Deck cards?

Also, a tool like Hit the Deck or any other body-weight circuit allows to you maximize your time in many ways. As we've discussed, doing an exercise session like Hit the Deck combines your cardiovascular *and* resistance training workouts—you're pumping your heart and your muscles at the same time.

I Have a Family to Take Care of, and Exercise Means Even More Time Away from Them

Many of us immediately think exercise is something that takes time away from family or friends. Who says? I'm going to challenge you to rethink what exercise is.

Exercise is not something you have to do alone or schedule separate time for. Why not make Hit the Deck or a body-weight-circuit session a family game? If you have kids, have them exercise along with you. Or perhaps do some of their activities along with them. If you're going to the park, don't just sit on the bench, head bent over your phone. Come up with a creative obstacle course or game and run it with them. What better example can we set as parents than to mirror the behaviors we want to see in our children? They learn more by watching us than listening to us.

On cold Minnesota winter days, I used to take my young daughter down to the basement to play "The Game." It consisted of me coming up with a move we would both do for sixty seconds. Then it would be her turn, and she would come up with some crazy ideas. However, after each sixty-second interval, our heart rates were up and some muscle group somewhere was burning. As we continued on, things would quickly escalate as we tried to outdo each other with outlandish moves—and the laughing made it all the more challenging.

Also, a significant other can make a great workout partner. Think of exercise as a way to spend quality time together without all the distractions of technology and daily life. Maybe date night is a game of tennis, a dance class, or rollerblading. Perhaps it's a walk around the neighborhood. Perhaps have fun doing ten minutes of Hit the Deck cards, then think of ways to put the feel-good hormones to work.

The same thing goes with friends. Be honest and finish this sentence: You call a friend and say, "Hey! Let's get together and _____." Most of us fill in the blank with "grab a bite to eat" or "get a drink or coffee." For some reason, the go-to social activity is usually sedentary and involves food. Why not mix things up and find something active to do? You don't have to choose between a social life and exercise if you simply combine them.

Wait a Minute—Isn't Exercise Stress?

Now Sneaky Pete is really pulling out the stops. He's making an "intellectual" appeal to your advanced brain, claiming that exercise is actually a stressor in and of itself. He's saying it defeats the whole purpose of resetting the stress response. Let's get the facts straight.

It's true that cortisol is released during cardiovascular and resistance training, but in proportion to the intensity and duration of the exercise. The concern over negative effects is more so related to long sessions of endurance training and intense athletic activity.

During long periods of endurance exercise, blood glucose levels can become very low. In turn, cortisol secretion switches the energy source from glucose to stored protein from the muscles as well as fatty acids. You'll be learning more about this in the nutrition chapter, but using stored protein breaks down hard-earned muscle mass that's essential to a strong metabolism.

However, when an exercise session is short (less than forty-five minutes), cortisol release is thought to be irrelevant in negatively affecting muscle-protein balance. When blood glucose levels are maintained during shorter bouts of exercise, there is less need for the body to secrete cortisol. Plus, the release of human growth hormone and other beneficial hormones counterbalances any increase in cortisol during short-session exercise.

In addition, it's true that exercise can create byproducts that can be harmful to the body, such as free radicals. But under normal circumstances, exercise also stimulates repair mechanisms in the body that actually leave cells stronger for future stress. Things in the cells are broken down and built up much like muscles. Stressing them makes them stronger in the long run.

So, it's clear the type of exercise recommended in this book, such as the 10/10/10 format, doesn't add more "stress" as Sneaky Pete claims. However, exercise can be a stressor when taken to the extreme. Intense athletic training elevates the sympathetic nervous system (the gas pedal) and HPA axis activity.

Remember the fight-or-flight fuel allocation station from chapter two? You might notice how some fanatical runners are quite thin, but what little body fat they do have is typically centered around the midsection and not the butt or thighs. That's a sign of stress.

In addition, marathon runners' immune systems have been studied extensively, and data reveals the stress of extreme training can compromise immunity.[83] Research shows that in contrast to intense endurance training, regular moderate physical activity can improve immune response.[84, 85]

Or perhaps it's not the physiological effects of stress you're worried about. Maybe you're not sure you can emotionally handle the "stress" your body goes through with physical activity. You may fear it'll be torture. But keep in mind that the physical stress of exercise is predictable and controllable because you're initiating the action. A sense of predictability and control is key to our perception of stress. You won't see it as stress because it's not something *being done to you*; it's something *you are doing*.

Start Where You Are

The last thing I want to do is add more stress to your life.

This book is not about telling you you're not doing enough or that you've got to pack more into an already busy day. I can't tell you how important it is to simply start where you are and don't beat yourself up.

If you manage to squeeze in one Hit the Deck card, or if you decide to shoot up a flight of stairs instead of taking the elevator, awesome. If instead of going to a friend's cubicle to complain about your boss, you grab that friend and walk quickly around the building (okay, maybe while venting), you've made a great decision. If you've always just done steady-state exercising, sprinkle a couple intervals into your routine. If you do a few pushups (even if you have to keep your knees on the floor), it's worth all the effort. If you even manage once or twice to add some aerobic moves to those pushups, all the better.

Remember that every little bit counts. With each step, you're on your way to improved resiliency. And I'm not going to leave you hanging after I explain all the science behind the Resiliency rEvolution. Chapters five and six will address how to successfully implement the tools you're learning. So tell Sneaky Pete to relax—we're going to make this unquestionably doable.

This chapter has covered quite a bit of information, discussing how the purpose of the stress response is to turn on the body for a sudden explosion of muscular activity, and how easy it can be. Most importantly, we've explored how a sedentary life means stewing in your stress hormones, while a physically active life allows the stress hormones and bliss molecules to work the way they were designed.

When you feel yourself experiencing the stress response, stop and ask this question: *What would a caveman do?* Surf the Internet or spend hours on Facebook? Eat too much? Smoke? Drink? Bury himself in work so he doesn't have to deal with his problems? No. He would Play It Out. As this chapter shows, playing it out not only builds your resiliency, it also improves fitness, health, and body fat.

And in the next chapter, we'll discuss another critical step: how stress affects the foods you eat, and how the foods you eat affect your stress.

To gain further understanding of how short bursts of physical activity build resiliency and to purchase PowerHouse Hit the Deck, go to www.ph-performance.com/playitout

Success Story

PAUL

Paul's Story

At forty-one years old, Paul realizes his persistent insomnia and increasing pain-management issues are a crucial wake-up call. As the vice president of human resources for a global financial services company, he leads business-partner teams on major projects in addition to directing employee relations and HR compliance.

"It's intense," he explains. "There are multiple, competing priorities in employee relations, and lots of travel. The 24/7 nature of the job means there's trouble with life-work balance. A lot of the work stress comes home."

Paul's husband is extremely supportive of his career, but at times that makes it too easy for Paul to work long hours without a break.

Paul realizes stress is taking over his life. He's unhappy with his health and eating habits, and he worries it's getting too easy to unwind with a few cocktails. He has tried a variety of fitness programs, but finds it hard to stick to a diet and exercise regime while traveling constantly. When he's home, it's easier to choose TV time on the couch with his husband or to go out to a nice restaurant as an antidote to stress, rather than exercise.

Paul's rEvolution

However, he says, "PowerHouse gave me an excellent and easy way to incorporate movement into my life, no matter where in the world I might be." Because Hit the Deck simplifies exercise choices and fits any amount of time, he sticks to it at home and away. He has also started thinking about food ahead of time in order to make sensible, manageable changes in his eating habits.

Compared to other programs, he says, "This works well for balance, for long-term change management, and for overall wellness. It's a holistic approach that is easy to follow." Paul makes accountability a major part of his plan and requests extra coaching via phone when he needs encouragement.

After sixty days of resiliency training, Paul has lost a few pounds. He's also seen dramatic improvements in ease and quality of sleep, which helps him feel more energetic each day. He describes these improvements as "life-changing."

He feels less anxiety about job demands and his capacity to handle challenges, leaving him free to do his best work. And more and more, he's able to leave work *at* work, bringing new balance between nutrition, movement, rest, and relationships into his life.

Looking back on his progress, Paul remains dedicated to his life changes. "I will not let anything get in the way of me being the best and healthiest me I can be. I am forty-one years old, and I plan on living at least another forty-one years. I need to make sure that my body is cared for to last, that my mind is focused and happy, and that I have peace and balance overall in life."

PAUL AFTER SIXTY DAYS OF RESILIENCY TRAINING

44 percent decrease in perceived stress

50 percent increase in energy

40 percent improvement in quality of sleep

30 percent improvement in ability to fall asleep

Lost 5 pounds (2 percent) of body fat

Chapter 4

PLATE IT OUT

Eating is something we all have to do on a regular basis, multiple times each day. But if we're not careful, the wrong choices can take a toll on our ability to handle stress and perform well at work and at home. Many of us inadvertently add more stress to our brain and body with our daily food decisions.

We may not realize that going too long without eating adds stress. We might be unaware that eating too much places stress on the body. Reaching for sweets, alcohol, caffeine, or nicotine in an attempt to reduce stress does the opposite—they actually heighten our stress levels. Dieting or restricting what we eat places tremendous stress on the brain and body.

In the previous chapter, you learned how physical activity can expand your resiliency for stress, helping you recover from it more quickly and effectively. In this chapter, we'll be learning how our eating habits affect our levels of stress and how our levels of stress affect our eating habits. There's real potential for our food choices to increase our stress. And when stress increases, the resulting hormones make us choose and eat foods that add even more stress. This feedback loop can have serious consequences on our resilience, performance, and health. You'll learn how to break this cycle as well as how to avoid it in the first place.

WHAT AND HOW YOU EAT CAN INCREASE YOUR STRESS. STRESS CAN INCREASE WHAT AND HOW YOU EAT.

This big chapter is full of strategies and information about making better choices with eating. That's great news . . . but it may also seem a little overwhelming. Keep in mind as you read that you're not expected to change everything in your life all at once. If you tried that, Sneaky Pete would freak out, and he'd thwart your efforts.

As I've said before, the last thing I want to do is add more stress to your life. Instead, your goal will be to focus on one or two basic, effective nutrition strategies at a time. Once those first changes are a part of your daily routine, you can keep coming back to this chapter to look for your next moves. (You'll learn more about how to do this in the chapter on change.)

In the exercise chapter, you learned it was possible to Play It Out sixty seconds at a time. This strategy worked with both the biology and psychology of Sneaky Pete because it wasn't a time-consuming, complex, or overwhelming request. It was quick and simple. In a similar way, Sneaky Pete also often tells us we don't have time to eat healthy. In stressful situations, when energy and effort are maxed out, he tells us to grab that candy instead of something that would properly fuel our body and brain. But in this chapter you'll learn how to create sixty-second strategies for eating in a way that keeps Sneaky Pete happy as well as builds resiliency. Though these choices and changes will be simple, their effects will be exponential.

You'll also be happy to hear we're going to give you a lot of choice as to how you use this nutrition information in your life. There is no boilerplate, unrealistic meal plan to follow. Sneaky Pete doesn't like to feel like his options are limited. You'll have a lot of autonomy to make choices that work for you, based on your preferences, beliefs, time, and food availability. Being a part of the rEvolution means you need strategies that are sustainable over the course of your life—not just for a few weeks. If you're a road warrior who travels a lot for work, you'll still be able to succeed. If you don't like to cook, that's not a deal breaker. If you're busy, you'll have choices that are quick and easy.

Let's get started, as usual, by looking back at our cavemen counterparts. Our body may not have changed in ten thousand years, but how and what we eat has certainly dEvolved in many ways.

The dEvolution of Food

Sneaky Pete and his friends were hunter-gatherers. They ate the game they captured or killed as well as the plants they were able to find. It's hard to know for sure, but it is estimated that about two-thirds of their diet came from animal foods (including fish and seafood) and about one-third from plant foods.

Although their consumption of protein was likely higher than ours, the fat in those meats was mainly unsaturated (which is the healthier type of fat) because the animals were wild—they foraged and did not consume manufactured feed. These animals were also very lean, so cavemen consumed a lower total amount of fat than we do today.

Hunter-gatherers ate carbohydrates mainly from fruits, vegetables, and roots rather than processed grains or cereals. Their carbohydrates were very high in fiber and nutrients. Eventually grains and legumes became a larger portion of the human diet as we established more of an agrarian way of life. Our ancestors began farming around 9,500 BCE, during the Neolithic Period (considered the last part of the Stone Age).

The grains they ate were a bit different than the ones we eat today, mainly because of the way they were processed. Our ancestors had to process the grains by grinding them between stones. The resulting flours had large particles, which slowed the rate of digestion and glucose release. This prevented large surges and crashes in blood glucose. (We'll get into this topic later.)

With the industrial revolution, we developed the technology to grind flours. We don't have to spend hours grinding wheat into flour to make bread from scratch in our hearths. We don't have to grind corn to cook tortillas over an open fire or form the components necessary to make our own cereals. We've developed ways to grind flours more and more finely as well as separate the bran completely from white flour. Flour today is so finely ground, it's similar in texture to talcum powder.

There's no doubt many of the foods in our modern world are faster and easier to prepare than foods in any other time in history. From a labor-saving perspective, these advances in food technology are beneficial for sure. However, several aspects of the food "dEvolution" have resulted in negative consequences for our performance, health, and stress load. For instance, though very fine flour makes soft, delicious breads and light, airy baked goods, it speeds up the rate of glucose released into the bloodstream. Also, quick-cooking or "instant" convenience foods are processed and stripped of fiber. They're fast to cook and eat, but unfortunately fast to digest, and therefore they affect blood glucose.

A major difference between us and our ancestors is the amount and type of sugar and fat we consume. Our ancestors were—and we are still today—genetically hard-wired to crave foods high in sugar and fat. This was beneficial to our ancestors' survival because those foods are also high in energy. Taking into consideration the amount of energy they burned each day, on top of the fact that food was often scarce, they needed to eat large amounts of high-calorie food when it was available. Storing fat on the body was a critical advantage. (It was the primitive pantry.)

However, even though we're programmed to crave large amounts of sugar, our body is actually designed to get by on very little of it. We cannot process large amounts of sugar on a regular basis. While that wasn't a problem for our ancestors, it's a major problem for us.

For Sneaky Pete, simple sugars were limited to foods such as wild fruit (which was not as sweet as many of our hybrids today) and honey (which was scarce). But our world is now flooded with sugars and sweeteners. Even our beverages are full of them. When Sneaky Pete was thirsty, he drank water. Today we have a dizzying amount of beverages that supply large amounts of sugars, empty calories and spike our blood glucose levels.

An example of how we cannot process sweets is what happens when we consume large amounts of high fructose corn syrup. We're now producing so much corn, we've had to invent other ways to use it. High fructose corn syrup is added to many food products—from processed snacks to soda, juices, breads, yogurt, cereals, sauces, and even ketchup.

This manmade sweetener is a combination of approximately half glucose and half fructose. As we know, glucose is metabolized by cells all throughout our body. Fructose, on the other hand, is a form of sugar mainly processed by the liver. If we consume large amounts of fructose, the liver transforms it into triglycerides, a form of fat. Much of this fat is released into the bloodstream, but some of it stays in the liver. The fat in the liver can build up to dangerous amounts that eventually lead to fatty liver disease and cirrhosis. High triglyceride levels in the bloodstream contribute to the hardening and thickening of the arteries, which increases our risk of stroke, heart attack, and heart disease—all physiological and psychologically stressful events, to say the least.

Even though our body cannot process high amounts of sugars and fats, we still crave them in a way that's hard to fathom. We've all been completely full from a delicious meal, couldn't possibly eat another bite, and are ready to leave the table—when suddenly dessert appears. Somehow we magically find room for another serving of food. The desire to taste and feel that delicious flourless chocolate cake in our mouths completely overrides the body's satiety cues. Our hardwiring for sugars and fats is still so powerful, an injection of sugar into the bloodstream stimulates the same pleasure centers of the brain that light up from heroin and cocaine. If you've heard people jokingly refer to themselves as "sugar addicts," little do they know they're not kidding.

From an evolutionary perspective, however, this actually makes sense. Our ancestors were not concerned about suppressing appetite, but about getting enough food to survive during lean times. As we've said before, food was often hard to come by, yet they needed a lot to meet their energy needs. Those who ate as much as they could whenever they could had a higher rate of survival. In this context, it's easy to understand how the caveman brain can view overeating high-calorie foods as a good thing. It doesn't realize food is far from scarce now or that our mostly sedentary lives don't require as many calories. And when our body is under stress, that caveman brain completely takes over, telling us to eat as much high-sugar and high-fat foods as we can.

To make matters even more difficult, food companies are well aware of our evolutionary programming. Many of our modern processed foods are scientifically designed in laboratories to be fiercely appetizing and to seduce as many of our senses as possible. They are full of fats and sugars that trigger the addictive pleasure centers of the brain. Food companies know we'll get hooked and buy more of their products to sate our desires.

When you add these modern foods with our deep-seated desire to eat them in excessive amounts, it's easy to see how we're placing chronic stress on our body. And a great deal of that stress falls on the pancreas, which must work intensely to produce enough insulin to return levels back into the body's optimal range. Let's look at this more closely.

The Temperate Zone

Remember what you learned in chapter two about glucose, insulin, cortisol, and so on? That information is coming full circle now as we explore how our eating habits can add or reduce stress on our brain and body.

For example, you'll recall that your body has a perfectly designed glucose-insulin regulatory system. Think of it like your home's programmable heating and cooling system: you set your thermostat for an ideal, comfortable temperature, and depending on external factors (the weather), your heating and cooling system does whatever it takes to keep the temperature where it's supposed to be.

When it gets too hot, the air conditioner kicks in to lower the temperature. Think of the air conditioner as insulin, which lowers blood glucose levels when they get too high. When it gets too cold, the furnace comes online to raise the temperature. Think of the furnace as glucagon, which stimulates the increase of blood glucose levels. Because the pancreas produces these two hormones, it's the key to regulating the "glucose temperature" in our body.

··

OUR PANCREAS RUNS BOTH THE "FURNACE" AND THE "AIR CONDITIONER."

··

When the temperature is constantly bouncing around, or when there's extreme heat or extreme cold, it places more stress on your heating and cooling system. It has to work harder to do its job. Your utility bill is very expensive, not to mention that your furnace and air conditioner both burn out quickly.

Your body is very similar when it comes to managing blood glucose levels. The more you can keep blood glucose levels within the ideal range, the less stress you place on your body. But external factors—such as going too long without eating, overeating, or eating the wrong foods—can make our body work a lot harder to maintain an ideal range. Our organs wear out, and it's a dear price we end up paying.

Instead, we should be eating in a way that keeps our "glucose temperature" within the ideal range. We don't want to put in too much glucose to raise levels, nor do we want to go too long without putting in glucose, which decreases levels. We're better off when we add small amounts of glucose frequently throughout the day, staying in the temperate zone so the furnace and air conditioner don't have to work as hard.

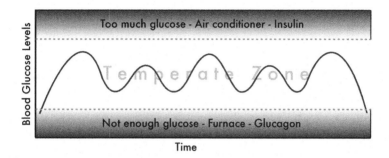

Eating in the Temperate Zone keeps blood glucose levels within the ideal range

STAY IN THE TEMPERATE ZONE WHEN EATING.

The Stress of the Highs and Lows

When we stay in the temperate zone and glucose levels are adequate, we don't add stress to the body and brain. The brain and muscle cells can function optimally. But let's look at two common habits that make our glucose levels too low or too high: going too long without eating as well as eating too much.

When we skip meals or go too long without eating, glucose levels get low. When there's not enough energy for all the cells to function optimally, the body thinks a famine is occurring. A perceived famine is a threat to our existence, so the stress response is stimulated, and the body secretes adrenaline and cortisol.

Cortisol puts us into food-seeking mode to get much-needed glucose and energy into the body. Cortisol is very specific about getting energy in the form of sugar and fat because, as we discussed earlier, these two substances have a lot of calories. Cortisol also makes us eat large amounts of food and stores much of this extra energy away in our fat cells for the next famine.

Besides these negative physiological effects, low blood sugar also diminishes our ability to perform to our absolute best at work as well as at home. Our cognitive function is impaired, it's hard to focus and concentrate, and we can become highly emotional, impatient, and irrational. We are in survival mode—and that means Sneaky Pete is in charge.

GOING TOO LONG WITHOUT EATING INCREASES STRESS.

At the other end of the spectrum, eating a large amount of food—with much of it being high fat and high sugar—often makes blood glucose levels too high. You learned in chapter two that insulin is necessary to facilitate the transport of glucose from the bloodstream into the cells of the brain, muscles, and organs. When a large amount of glucose needs to be moved, a large amount of insulin must be produced; it's a linear relationship. Continually needing to produce large amounts of insulin puts undue stress on the pancreas. The cells eventually wear out, and we are unable to produce enough insulin.

In the short term, too much glucose in the bloodstream can make us feel tired and weak, and we experience headaches, blurred vision, and difficulty concentrating. It also damages blood vessels that supply blood to vital organs, which increases our risk of heart disease, stroke, kidney disease, and nerve and vision problems. Over the long term, high blood glucose can also cause high blood pressure, diabetes, blindness, and amputation of limbs. All chronic stressors, to say the least.

EATING TOO MUCH INCREASES STRESS.

As you'll remember from chapter two, this is a vicious cycle. When glucose levels are high, insulin stores much of it as fat on the body as well as in the blood vessel walls. And when cortisol is released during the stress response, it ensures much of this fat will be stored primarily around the midsection. To make matters worse, more fat in this "fight-or-flight fuel allocation station" increases stress, further diminishes insulin sensitivity, and raises our risk of many diseases. Stress pushes us ever closer to insulin resistance with each event.

The good news is, eating habits that regulate blood glucose levels can minimize stress on the body. By not going too long without eating and by not overeating, we can avoid piling more stress on top of the already high amounts we experience from our daily demands. Plus, when you start training to become more resilient with the tools in this book, you'll gain muscle mass and lose body fat, which will increase your insulin sensitivity. It's like getting an upgrade to a high-efficiency heating and cooling system!

ONE OF THE MOST IMPORTANT WAYS WE CAN MINIMIZE STRESS IS TO KEEP BLOOD GLUCOSE LEVELS WITHIN THE IDEAL RANGE.

Insulin Resistance and the Stress of Diabetes

As we discussed before, if we're frequently exposed to large amounts of insulin over time, we become less sensitive to its effects. It's similar to building up a resistance to caffeine or alcohol over time. The pancreas must work progressively harder each day, each year, to produce ever-greater amounts of insulin—even just to regulate normal levels of blood glucose. This places additional strain on the organ.

What many of us don't realize is that insulin resistance can affect different parts of the body in different ways. It doesn't just happen to the entire body all at the same time or in the same way. When the brain becomes insulin resistant, it has difficulty suppressing hunger, and we feel hungrier more of the time. When our muscles become resistant, we experience muscle loss, less fuel getting into the muscle cells, and decreased performance. If the liver becomes insulin resistant, there's an increase in glycogen breakdown and glucose production, which raises blood glucose levels. It also reduces our capacity to burn fat and sugar and our ability to feel full after eating. In fact, many people who are obese and insulin resistant are hungry much of the time, yet they can be malnourished because the glucose can't get into the cells.

At a certain point, we can develop what's commonly known as type 2 diabetes. This happens when the body becomes resistant to the effects of insulin and/or the cells in the pancreas wear out and cannot produce enough of it. The incidence of type 2 diabetes used to be relatively rare. It used to be called adult-onset diabetes. But the name change was necessary because it's become far too common in children and young people, affecting one in ten Americans.[1]

This medical condition is becoming a worldwide problem. Diseases such as type 2 diabetes increase dramatically as developing nations establish more of a middle-class society and westernize their eating and physical activity habits. As India's middle class explodes, for instance, the number of people with diabetes is skyrocketing. In 2010, it was up to fifty million, and this number is expected to grow to more than one hundred million by 2030.[2] Interestingly, the number of people who live in India's rural areas—who labor more intensely and don't have access to large amounts of processed food—have one-third the rate of diabetes of those living in urban centers.[3]

Diabetes also stresses the brain. People with type 2 diabetes have an up to 1.5 times greater chance of decreased cognitive function, in addition to a 1.6 times increase of future dementia.[4] Diabetes also stresses the organs, eyes, and extremities. It increases blood pressure, which damages blood vessels that supply oxygen and nutrients to the kidneys and eyes, as well as nerves in the arms and legs. That's not to mention it's a *huge* stress on the pocketbook. People with diabetes incur medical expenses of close to $14,000 per year.[5] As an annual cost, this really adds up over a lifetime.

Julianna's Story

In addition to being head of information technology at a major consumer goods company, Julianna is a single mother of two children, ages five and seven. She has a lot on her plate with the long daily commute to and from her job; the amount of work that needs to be done at the office; her kids' extracurricular activities; and the fact she's the only one who cleans, cooks, and grocery shops.

Mornings are always chaotic. It's a mad dash to get the kids dressed, fed, and to school on time plus get herself to work by 8:30 a.m. In the process, there's a lot of yelling. Julianna hates how impatient she is with her children, but they've got to get moving, and there is no time for dawdling.

The only thing Julianna has time to make for herself in the morning is coffee. She has a cup or two at home, then pours the remaining three or so cups of the pot into a thermos and drinks it during her long drive into the office. She also has one or two cigarettes on the way.

She typically works diligently through the first couple hours of the morning, as it's her most productive time of day. She can't stand being interrupted during this time and is very impatient when someone comes into her office to ask a question or make a request. There are always one or two meetings before lunch, and by the time the last one gets started, she's so hungry it's hard to concentrate. She often finds herself drifting off to plan what fast-food restaurant she'll swing through for lunch, or she becomes very critical and negative about ideas shared in the meeting.

By the time she leaves for lunch, it's typically after 1:00 p.m. She is *starving* as she hasn't had anything other than caffeine and nicotine. Luckily there are several convenient fast-food drive-throughs near the office, and today she decides on a burger place. She orders a cheeseburger, fries, and soda. The clerk asks if she would like to upsize her order to a large for just fifty cents more... Sneaky Pete's ears perk up. She's really hungry and has no idea when she'll have a chance to eat anything the rest of the day, so Julianna opts for the larger portion. Besides, more food for just a few cents is a great value.

She eats it all on the way back to the office. She's really stuffed, but doesn't feel too bad about it because she didn't eat breakfast, and this meal has to last her for the rest of the day. She returns to work and now has an afternoon of back-to-back meetings. During the first meeting, all she can think about is how full and uncomfortable she is. It's hard to breathe, and she's kicking herself for not wearing pants with an elastic waistband. She's also feeling tired and sluggish, and she's having a hard time staying engaged during the meeting. That big meal has put her right into a food coma.

After several hours, she starts to get hungry again, but doesn't have any snacks with her. She and Sneaky Pete go on a hunting and foraging expedition to see if anyone's got any candy at their desks. She manages to find a large handful of licorice. She eats it and perks up for a bit, but about thirty minutes later, Julianna is feeling tired and hungry again. She decides to have more coffee to tamp down her hunger and help get her through the afternoon.

By the time she leaves the office and starts her long drive home, she's famished. She picks the kids up from after-school day care, gives them a small snack, and heads into the kitchen. The Dinner Fairy missed bringing dinner to her house again, so she pours herself a glass of wine and grabs a bag of chips and a block of cheese to tide her over while she finds something to make for dinner. She refills her wine glass another time or two while cooking and eating. It helps her relax and takes the edge off both her hunger and her mood.

Dinner is finally ready, and to be honest, she's not all that hungry after the wine, chips, and cheese. But because she went to the trouble to make it, she feels she should eat it. Not to mention it's important family time. This is the first opportunity she's had to relax all day.

The food tastes really good, so she ends up eating a full plate even though she intended to eat only a little bit. She's feeling bloated and tired again. While she struggles to motivate herself to clean up, the kids ask her to play with them. She convinces them to play what she secretly refers to as "floor games": things that allow her to lie down and exert as little effort as possible.

Julianna had planned on doing a load of laundry and a bit of work on her laptop after getting the kids into bed. But the only thing she can motivate herself to do is find the couch and the remote control.

Julianna doesn't realize it, but many of the nutrition choices she made during the day layered more stress on top of the stress she already has. It diminished her cognitive performance, productivity, energy, and engagement, as well as her body composition and health.

If you recall from chapter two, stress is a chemistry problem. Anything we put into our body alters the system's chemical makeup. In addition, anything we *don't* put in that's necessary will also shift our chemistry.

I gave you the simple definition of stress: anything that pushes the body out of balance. This explanation becomes vitally important as it relates to the way we eat. As you just learned, **keeping blood glucose levels balanced in an ideal range is one of the most important factors in minimizing stress and keeping the body and brain running as smoothly as possible.**

In the next several sections, we're going to revisit Julianna's day of eating (and not eating) to understand how her choices affected her stress and performance. More importantly, we'll also look at better, healthier choices that can help you build your resiliency against stress.

Julianna Skips Breakfast

When Julianna wakes up in the morning, her blood glucose levels are very low because she hasn't eaten since the night before. Then she skips breakfast. (We haven't yet developed the ability to survive on caffeine alone.) This sends a signal to her body that no food is available. Her advanced brain understands that food is abundant and available in her environment; Julianna has simply chosen to skip breakfast. Sneaky Pete, on the other hand, has no clue. He thinks there's a famine.

Lack of food—even by choice—is a serious stressor and threat to our body because survival depends on having adequate fuel. The lack of adequate glucose has stimulated Julianna's fight-or-flight response; her body is in survival mode, and caveman brain is now in charge. It's no wonder she's impatient and snappy with her kids.

Jumping right out of bed and darting around the house to get herself and her kids ready further increases her body's need for energy it doesn't have. When you add in her frustration that her kids aren't moving as fast as she wants them to, the stress response has been triggered multiple times. The stress tsunami has her swimming in adrenaline, noradrenaline, and cortisol.

If you recall, one of cortisol's main functions is to make us hungry, especially for energy-rich foods high in fat and sugar. It also puts the body into fat-storage mode to replace all the energy theoretically used during fight-or-flight.

....

STRESS = SURVIVAL MODE
= FAT-STORAGE MODE

....

There's no getting around the fact her body needs energy to function. She hasn't consumed any glucose, and that stress has altered her chemistry dramatically. Julianna's body needs to find an internal energy source, seeing as food is presumably not available.

Cortisol makes us store fat on the body, so that's off-limits. The body hoards it, doesn't let it go, and in fact wants to *increase* its reserve. As a result, one of the only sources of stored energy left to utilize is protein from her muscle tissue.[6] Her body starts breaking down muscle mass into amino acids, which are then transformed into a form of glucose through gluconeogenesis. Muscle becomes a usable fuel for the brain and body.

As we discussed in the last chapter, this decrease in muscle mass will have long-term consequences on her metabolism and energy needs. Each and every time we go too long without eating, the body catabolizes valuable muscle mass, which ends up slowing our metabolism. Less muscle mass means we need less food. But if Julianna doesn't decrease the amount of food she eats in response to the diminished need for energy, her body will start to store the excess in her fat cells. Cortisol ensures a good amount of that fat will be around her waist. The loss of muscle mass will also affect her body's ability to effectively respond to insulin and use glucose. This decrease in efficacy results in even more fat being deposited on her body.

How many of us make this same mistake as Julianna? I, for one, used to think skipping breakfast gave me a jump start on my diet for the day. Look at me! I just woke up, and I'm already ahead of the game because I created a calorie deficit by not eating! Little did I know skipping breakfast was one of the (many) reasons things were backfiring in my face. The cortisol from lack of glucose made me store fat, the loss of muscle mass and metabolism made me store fat, and the decreased sensitivity to insulin and glucose made me store fat. No wonder I was so hungry, frustrated, and stressed all the time.

What to Do: Start the Day with Food—Especially Protein

Try to put some glucose into your bloodstream first thing in the morning, ideally within an hour of waking up. The sooner you can get your glucose levels in the ideal range, the less stress you'll place on the system, and the more your brain and body will be fueled to function well for your busy morning. If you go longer than an hour without eating, the body goes into survival mode and starts secreting stress hormones.

Protein is an important element of any meal (we'll discuss this more below), but it's especially important at breakfast. Foods that contain protein slow down the release of glucose. They keep us from having big spikes that require the pancreas to secrete large amounts of insulin (the air conditioner) to lower levels back into the ideal range. A slower, gradual release of glucose over time adds less stress to the body and requires smaller amounts of insulin. Lack of protein can start the day with a spike in blood glucose that leads to a roller coaster of spikes, crashes, cravings, and stress that can last the entire day.

EATING AN IDEAL BREAKFAST PREVENTS THE RELEASE OF STRESS HORMONES.

Protein also increases our feelings of being satisfied or full after eating. Research has shown that people who eat more protein at breakfast feel fuller for longer and consume less food at the midday meal. It also decreases their drive to eat later on in the day, and they are less likely to snack on high-fat, high-sugar foods in the evening. Interestingly, this same study also showed that a high-protein breakfast reduces activation of the hippocampus and amygdala[7]—if you remember, the parts of our caveman brain associated with the stress response.

Finally, consuming a low-glycemic breakfast (we'll discuss this later) has been shown to result in better cognitive performance throughout the morning.[8] That's critical for the amount of important work we need to get done before breaking for lunch.

Many people claim they don't feel hungry first thing in the morning or that they don't have time to make breakfast. The good news is, it does not have to be a full breakfast if you're not very hungry. Instead of having breakfast and then a midmorning snack (more on this below), you can reverse it with a snack first and then breakfast midmorning. Your prebreakfast snack could be a hard-boiled egg, a few spoonfuls of yogurt, a piece of cheese, several nuts, a glass of milk or soy milk, or some nut butter on a small piece of bread. It also doesn't have to take a lot of time to prepare as these options are quick and easy to eat.

If you're up for a full breakfast meal first thing, let's discuss what your plate should look like. In fact, this is what your plate should look like for *all* major meals of the day: breakfast, lunch, and dinner.

Plate It Out

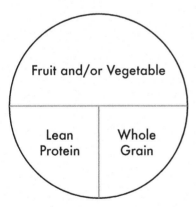

The T Plate for meals

For each stressful event you experience, I've suggested you Play It Out. For each meal event, I'm going to ask you to *Plate* It Out. At every major meal, you'll want to create what I call the T Plate. (You can see the food proportions make a T shape.) In approximate terms, one quarter of your plate needs to be a source of lean protein, one quarter should be a source of whole grains, and the remaining half should consist of fruits and/or vegetables. By hitting this 25/25/50 ratio at every meal, you provide your body with the wide variety of nutrients, vitamins, and minerals each day to function optimally and be well.

Remember the definition of stress we're working with: anything that pushes the body out of balance. If we're missing certain elements or nutrients, we can stress the body in many different ways. If we eat too much or not enough, we push the body out of balance. In each instance, the body and brain are forced to function at suboptimal levels, cognitive performance declines, and the continuous release of stress hormones can lead to several negative states of health.

It's important to emphasize that the T Plate is a meal-by-meal recommendation, not a *daily* one. The goal isn't to end each day with some combination of lean protein, whole grains, and fruits and vegetables. Instead, you want to make sure you have *each* element, at *each* major meal, in the recommended proportions. If you miss an element at a meal, you throw things out of balance. You cannot "make it up" later by eating two meals' worth of fruit in a smoothie, for instance. Your body can only process so much of any one thing at a time before it gets stored as fat.

T Plate Breakfast Examples

Grain, Protein, Fruit and/or Vegetable

Whole grain toast, eggs or egg whites, spinach and mushrooms
Steel-cut oatmeal, nuts, dried fruit
Muesli, milk/soy milk/yogurt, banana
Tortilla, beans or eggs, tomato
Rice, fish, seaweed
Paratha, paneer, chutney
Noodles, egg, pickles
Croissant, cold cuts, fresh fruit
Whole grain toast, beans, tomato
Porridge, milk/soy milk, apple

According to the National Weight Control Registry, which tracks more than five thousand people who have successfully maintained long-term weight loss, 78 percent of these successful "losers" eat breakfast every day. This makes a lot of sense when you think about the physiology of breakfast and what it does for them. They start the day off with their blood glucose levels within the ideal range, they avoid the cortisol release that would make them overeat later, the body is *not* in fat-storage mode, and it is not catabolizing muscle mass.

Sixty-Second Solutions for an Ideal Breakfast

When you're in a high-stress situation with a lot of demand on your time and energy, it may not be possible to sit down to an intricately made meal. When you need a stress solution, these quick-and-easy breakfast ideas will do the trick.

High-fiber, high-protein cereal with milk and fresh berries
Whole grain toast with nut butter and sliced banana on top
Nutrition bar and apple
Cottage cheese, whole grain crackers or bread, and cherry tomatoes
Yogurt, granola, and fruit
Fruit-and-yogurt smoothie with granola on top
Snack mix of nuts, dried fruit, and whole grain cereal
Cheese, piece of fruit or vegetable, and nuts
Whole grain bagel, nut butter, raisins on top

Julianna Ingests Caffeine and Nicotine Instead of Food

In order to get the energy boost she would have gotten from breakfast, Julianna has several cups of coffee to dull the hunger and get her going. Little does she know the coffee further exacerbates the stress response because caffeine stimulates the release of adrenaline and cortisol.[9] It also increases her blood pressure.

Caffeine at any time adds stress to the body, but morning is actually the worst time to ingest it. If you recall, cortisol levels naturally rise in the morning, and that's what wakes us up and gets us out of bed. The peak production of cortisol happens approximately an hour before we wake up. So, any intake of caffeine in the morning makes our cortisol levels rise even more above that natural peak. To make matters worse, caffeine has been shown to exacerbate mental stress to further increase cortisol levels.[10] That's a one-two punch.

Caffeine is a stimulant that provides the chemical sensation of energy, but it does not provide any glucose for the body's cells. That means we don't get "real" energy from it, as we do from food. In addition, stimulants like caffeine can blunt the sensation of hunger. This is a problem because hunger cues are very important. They let us know the body needs glucose, in an attempt to prevent the stress of blood glucose levels getting too low. But if caffeine drowns out those helpful cues, we don't know we need to eat, and glucose levels plummet.

Like Julianna, many people use nicotine to manage stress and suppress hunger. However, nicotine stimulates the HPA axis and releases adrenaline and cortisol,[11] which can exacerbate the stress response. And like caffeine, nicotine tunes out hunger cues, which can cause glucose levels to drop too low without us realizing it. This increases stress on the body.

Julianna doesn't think she can function without coffee and cigarettes for "breakfast." But as we've just seen, these choices add a great deal of stress to her body before she even steps foot into the office.

What to Do: Keep Caffeine and Nicotine to a Minimum—or Cut Them Out Completely

From a stress perspective, cutting out all caffeine and nicotine is ideal. Why voluntarily pump more stress hormones into the body on top of the ones secreted by circadian rhythms and other daily difficulties? Caffeine and nicotine are some of the worst things to reach for when you're stressed—they just add to the toxic broth of dread.

Nicotine from cigarettes should be cut out completely. The additional stress it places on the respiratory and cardiovascular systems are very dangerous to health and longevity.

If you choose to consume caffeine, do so in small amounts and don't let it take the place of food. It would also be better to wait until late morning or early afternoon to have it. If you enjoy the taste of coffee, switch to decaffeinated. Choose teas that have little to no caffeine.

Drinking soda first thing in the morning is one of the worst things we can do. Not only do most sodas have caffeine, but they're also full of sugar. It will spike blood glucose, push us out of the temperate zone, and give us a front-row seat on the glucose rollercoaster. If you enjoy the carbonation of soda, think about making a switch to bubbly water, flavored or not. Switching to diet soda may sound like a good alternative, but the chemicals in a diet, caffeine-free soda are not something Sneaky Pete was designed to metabolize well.

Brain Function and Performance in the Morning

Julianna was up and awake for only a short time, but her lack of breakfast and intake of caffeine and nicotine put her in an elevated state of stress. Caffeine and nicotine as her first choices for energy stimulated the stress response. The "energy" she got was drug related. Caffeine and nicotine provide the chemical sensations of energy, but without real food, the brain and muscle cells have not been nourished.

She was in survival mode before she even got to work. Her impatience first with her kids then with her coworkers, as well as her inability to concentrate throughout the morning, are strongly connected to her lack of glucose.

The brain requires large amounts of glucose to function well. Increased mental activity—what we need at home and at work in the morning—requires increased glucose metabolism. But Julianna hasn't put any glucose in her body since the night before. Her brain has to put any available energy toward survival functions like breathing, heart rate, and other important autonomic functions keeping her alive. There's far less energy for advanced processes, such as staying patient with her kids and processing information relating to her work in information technology. Poor glucose regulation is associated with a decrease in volume of the hippocampus.[12] In particular, lack of breakfast has been found to have adverse effects on memory, performance, and learning.[13] Not ideal states for optimal performance at work or at home.

Julianna is negative and short with her coworkers because lack of glucose and the secretion of adrenaline and cortisol have put her in a fight-or-flight state. Sneaky Pete is running the show. As you'll recall, caveman brain gives us a negativity bias, where we become pessimistic and focus on adverse events. We lose the ability to be objective, and we feel increased confidence that our way is the only right way. Reactions become automatic—we snap at people, or do something rude or hurtful.

LACK OF GLUCOSE PUTS CAVEMAN BRAIN IN CHARGE.

Keep in mind these are all great traits for a caveman. Lack of patience is actually useful from a survival perspective. Urgency and aggression were assets to Sneaky Pete's hunting success.

But these behaviors are not so great for Julianna—or any of us in today's world. If we skipped breakfast every morning, think about the long-term consequences of our Sneaky Pete behaviors: Our coworkers would think we were bad-tempered, abrupt, intolerant, know-it-all jerks. They'd think we weren't focused or productive, that we couldn't meet the ever-increasing speed and demands of our jobs. Our loved ones would see us as inattentive, easily frustrated, angry, and highly emotional. They may interpret these behaviors to mean we didn't love or care about them.

In contrast, many studies have seen benefits to cognitive performance from eating breakfast and have seen that these improvements last for most of the morning.[14] Eating increases activation of the prefrontal cortex,[15] the advanced brain that allows us to be more patient and to control our impulses. It also allows us to make choices good for our long-term goals rather than short-sighted decisions that have negative consequences later on.

Julianna Overate at Lunch

As explained in chapter two, cortisol is responsible for getting and replacing the energy used during fighting or fleeing. It makes us hungry for fatty, sugary foods because they're energy dense. It also makes us deposit more fat on the body, specifically in our fight-or-flight fuel allocation station.

Julianna secreted cortisol multiple times throughout the morning: when she skipped breakfast, got angry at her children, drank caffeine, inhaled nicotine, became frustrated during her long drive through heavy traffic, and got irritated with coworkers interrupting her while she was trying to work. That's a lot of cortisol without ever playing it out.

Julianna's cortisol has built up to high levels. It's no wonder she starts fantasizing about lunch during her meetings, then chooses and eats a large version of a very high-fat, high-sugar meal. Her physiology is demanding it. Unfortunately, though, because her body released high levels of cortisol in response to the lack of food, a significant amount of the excess calories will be stored as fat, primarily around her midsection.

What to Do: Have a Small Midmorning Snack

To avoid overeating at lunch as Julianna did, make sure you have a small midmorning snack, even if you have breakfast. Actually, in order to prevent overeating at any meal, you need to keep blood glucose levels within the ideal range, which means you need to add glucose in moderate amounts several times throughout the day. The brain and body use energy all day long, so they need a steady supply of it.

Let's say we eat a reasonably sized breakfast at 7:00 a.m. By about 10:30 a.m., our body has likely utilized much of this energy, and our glucose levels are dangerously low. By eating a small snack, we give the glucose levels a little bump to stay within the ideal range until lunch.

By having a small amount of food midmorning, we're also less likely to overeat at lunch. We haven't stimulated the release of cortisol, and we're not starving from going too long without glucose. This also means we're less likely to crave large amounts of fat and sugar. We'll make healthier choices, eat a moderate amount of food, have a moderate amount of glucose in the system, secrete a moderate amount of insulin, and be in balance.

Eating frequently throughout the day may seem like a "new" concept, but it's one we've all experienced. As babies, we ate at very frequent intervals, typically eight to twelve times each day or about every two to three hours. We also didn't eat the exact same amount of food each day. It varied with our energy needs. We listened to our body to know when it was time to start or stop eating. During preschool and kindergarten, we still ate light and often, having a midmorning break of milk and cookies and then an after-school snack.

Over time, though, most of us were trained to eat fewer times each day, on a set schedule convenient for our parents and society—ignoring the fact that what's good for someone's schedule and what's good for his or her body may be two different things. We were also taught to ignore our body's hunger cues—being told to eat only at designated mealtimes, to not snack in between meals because it might "ruin dinner," and to clean our plates whether we were full or not. Sometimes we were even rewarded with something called dessert when we overate rather than listened to our body. Following the wisdom of our body was trained right out of us.

By eating several small meals and light snacks throughout the day, we keep blood glucose levels in the ideal range for most, if not all, of the day. In contrast, if we eat only one or two meals each day, it results in large spans of time between meals where glucose levels become too low. We're also likely to overeat each time. This puts very large amounts of glucose into the body, makes the pancreas work hard to push out large amounts of insulin, and places undo stress on the system.

Let's go back to the heating-and-cooling example: A thermostat tracks temperature changes even one degree different from our ideal setting. This allows the system to make small, quick, easy adjustments throughout the day to keep the temperature steady. It wouldn't make much sense for the thermostat to let the temperature get way above or below the ideal setting, then kick in only one or two times to work long and hard to right the temperature. The temperature in your house wouldn't feel comfortable, the furnace and air conditioner would have to work very hard with such large swings, and your energy bills would be huge.

So what counts as a "small" snack? Snacks aren't so much about adding more food to your day, but rather about spreading your total calorie intake throughout the day to stabilize blood glucose levels. Think about snacks as small, quick runs of the furnace or air conditioner to keep room temperature at the ideal setting.

It doesn't take a lot of food to increase blood glucose levels. Depending on the body's needs, it may be in the range of 50 to 150 calories. As you can see in the list below, these snacks take little to no time to prepare. Most can be tossed into a briefcase first thing in the morning or the night before work.

Small Snack Examples

- **50 calories:** Half a banana, seven to eight almonds, or a small hard-boiled egg

- **100 calories:** Half a cup of edamame, a small container of yogurt, or half of a typical nutrition bar

- **150 calories:** Three kiwi fruit, approximately forty pistachios, or a medium apple with one tablespoon of nut butter

What to Do: Make the Snack Low Glycemic

Not only should your snacks be small, but they should also be low glycemic. A food's glycemic index is a measure of how quickly it is broken down into glucose and released into the bloodstream. All foods are categorized as high, moderate, or low glycemic. A high-glycemic food causes a rapid flood of glucose to be released all at once, whereas a low-glycemic food is broken down into glucose and released more slowly over time. A moderate-glycemic food falls right in the middle. Using the glycemic index for snacks is a useful tool for minimizing stress. It helps us choose foods that keep blood glucose levels balanced.

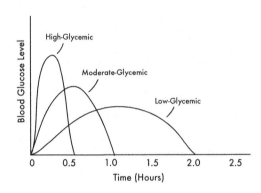

Blood glucose responses for high-, moderate- and low-glycemic foods

The massive spike in blood glucose from a high-glycemic food results in a correspondingly high output of insulin. Frequently consuming high-glycemic foods forces the pancreas to work hard to produce adequate amounts of insulin, placing undue stress on it. It's a bit like leaving the front door of our house open on a really hot or cold day, making the air conditioner or furnace run more often. To add insult to injury, continuously high levels of insulin make us less sensitive to its effects, and the pancreas has to work even harder to produce enough insulin to bring glucose levels back into the ideal range. Eventually this decreased sensitivity leads to insulin resistance and diabetes.

Spikes in blood glucose can also increase inflammation and oxidative stress. Oxidative stress is the burden placed on organisms by constant production of free radicals (molecules that trigger cellular injury) as well as by protein glycation (a process that produces substances that worsen many diseases). Both of these factors cause damage to the circulatory system over the long run.[16] They increase the risk of heart attack, stroke, aneurysm, and deep vein thrombosis. A high-glycemic diet can also exacerbate inflammation in the body, further increasing the risk of cardiovascular disease.[17]

A rebound effect also often happens when we consume high-glycemic foods. A large amount of insulin is needed to lower the glucose spike, but it can actually push levels down too far. When this happens, glucagon is released to stimulate the intake of more glucose. That means we end up craving another high-glycemic food to boost blood glucose levels back up. This results in a glucose roller coaster, where there's not enough glucose, then too much glucose, then too much insulin, then not enough glucose, then too much glucose, and so on. It's also like an endless cycle of the air conditioner working really hard to make it cold, then the furnace working really hard to make it hot.

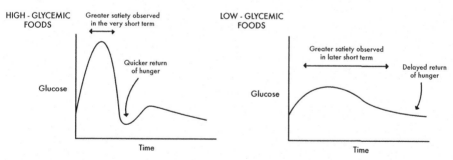

Consumption of high-glycemic foods seems to promote a more rapid return of hunger than the exact same calorie amount of low-glycemic foods. After consuming high-glycemic foods, there is a rapid decline in blood glucose from peak levels. This occurs because of the extreme counter-regulatory hormonal response set in motion to normalize high levels of circulating glucose.[18]

During these glucose spikes, our brain and muscle cells can take up only so much glucose, whereas our fat cells have an almost unlimited capacity to store energy. When there's a large amount of circulating glucose (from eating a high-glycemic snack or a large meal), insulin stimulates the fat cells to step up and store all the extra glucose. As we know, this further exacerbates stress on the body because extra body fat taxes our joints and increases our risk of many diseases.

GLUCOSE SPIKES AND CRASHES ADD STRESS AND BODY FAT.

The effects of glycemic index on metabolic changes can be seen more clearly in animal models because their diets can be more tightly controlled. After eighteen weeks, rats fed a high-glycemic diet, compared with those fed a low-glycemic diet, had approximately 40 percent more body fat and almost 10 percent less lean mass, despite having similar body weight and eating the same number of calories.[19]

While high-glycemic foods create glucose spikes, low-glycemic foods, on the other hand, release glucose into the bloodstream at a slower, steadier rate. There is no large spike, so less insulin is needed to remove the glucose from the bloodstream and put it in the brain and muscle cells. The pancreas can do its job with far less stress and strain. This slow stream of glucose is also less likely to be stored as fat because there's more time for the brain and muscle cells to use it.

Eating low-glycemic snacks and foods also make us feel fuller for longer, so the calories we consume go farther. For example, if we were to eat one hundred calories of a high-glycemic snack, the rapid rise and subsequent fall of blood glucose would leave us hungry again very soon. We would end up craving another high-glycemic food. We would eat more within a short time frame, and much of this glucose would be stored as fat. But if we were to eat one hundred calories of a low-glycemic food, it would have a higher satiety value. This would make us feel fuller for longer, and we would end up eating less food at subsequent meals.[20]

Research focusing on glycemic foods and obesity has shown that obese teenage boys will consume 81 percent more calories after eating a high-glycemic meal than after eating a low-glycemic one. In addition, when given the *same calorie amount* of oatmeal that was either high (instant) or low (steel cut) glycemic, the boys went on to eat 53 percent more after the high-glycemic version. [21]

Differences in glycemic index have also been shown to influence differences in fuel utilization both at rest as well as during exercise. This means consuming low-glycemic foods results in a greater amount of fat being used as energy during rest as well as during exercise. [22]

What Makes a Food Low Glycemic?

Three components of a food make it low glycemic: fiber, protein, and fat. The more fiber, protein, and fat a food has in it, the lower its glycemic index value. The majority of naturally occurring low-glycemic foods are some of the most nutritious in that they're loaded with fiber, vitamins, minerals, phytochemicals, and other disease-fighting compounds.

Fiber

Much of what Sneaky Pete ate was minimally processed and had more fiber, with large amounts of it coming from fresh fruits and vegetables. Today, much of our meager fiber intake comes from cereal grains that have been processed to remove the bran and endosperm. What's left of the grain is a poor source of fiber. Many of us also do not meet the minimum suggested intake of fresh fruits and vegetables each day.

There are two types of fiber: soluble and insoluble. Most natural foods contain both. Soluble fiber delays the emptying of our stomachs, which slows the release of glucose and increases insulin sensitivity, in addition to making us feel fuller for longer. Foods high in soluble fiber are fruits, vegetables, oats, lentils, nuts, seeds, beans, and peas. Insoluble fiber does not absorb water, so it passes through the digestive system mainly intact, creating bulk and speeding the passage of food and waste through the gut. Examples of foods that contain more insoluble fiber are whole wheat, whole grains, barley, couscous, brown rice, dark leafy greens, some fruits, and root vegetable skins.

We should be consuming 25 to 38 grams of fiber each day; however, the average American consumes only about 15 grams. A good strategy for finding foods high in fiber is to eat things as close to their whole, natural state as possible and to minimize the intake of anything processed. When deciding on what to eat for a snack, we're better off seeking types of food that Sneaky Pete would have had access to. The less humans have messed with it, changed it, processed it, or boxed it, the better. It's fairly safe to assume the more processed a food is, the higher its glycemic index will be.

With processed foods, it can be very difficult to tell how much fiber they have just by looking at them. Many have been colored to look dark and fiber filled in addition to having things like oats and seeds sprinkled on top, but the actual fiber content is very low to nonexistent. Some food manufacturers may add fiber supplements, such as inulin, but the only way to truly know how much fiber is in a processed food is to read the product label.

Protein

Protein has very little effect on increasing blood glucose levels. Why this happens is not completely understood. Some working theories include the following: a very slow conversion rate of protein to glucose, less protein being converted into glucose, glucose from protein synthesis being stored as glycogen, or glucogenesis from protein occurring over the course of several hours with ample time for the body to utilize it.

Protein can be found in anything an animal produces (meat, milk, eggs, etc.) as well as in many plants and grains, such as quinoa, beans, lentils, legumes, tofu and other soy products, nuts, seeds, tempeh, peas, and many leafy greens. If you're deciding on meat for protein, choose those that are low in saturated fat, such as poultry, fish, and pork.

Fat

Fat slows the rate of stomach emptying, which slows the release of glucose into the bloodstream. Choose unsaturated fats instead of saturated, as they are the healthier type we need. Unsaturated fats can be found in foods such as nuts, seeds, avocado, and olive oil, and in fish such as salmon.

Sixty-Second Solutions for Snacks

Again, during times of stress, the last thing you want is to sacrifice precious energy and thought on deciding what snack to eat. But instead of letting Sneaky Pete tell you to just forget the snack altogether, reach for one of these sixty-second solutions. Most of the low- and moderate-glycemic foods on this list require little to no time to prepare and can be quickly thrown in your bag each morning. Keep a stash in your desk drawer. They can also be found in airports, convenience stores, and gas stations when you're on the go.

GLYCEMIC INDEX VALUES

HIGH

Bagels	Donuts	Pretzels
Bread, white	English muffins	Rice, arborio and jasmine
Cake	French bread	
Carrots	Graham crackers	Rice cakes
Cereal, many*	Naan	Sports drinks
Chapati	Oatmeal, instant	Vanilla wafers
Cookies, many*	Peas	Waffles
Corn tortilla chips	Potatoes	Watermelon
		Yams

MODERATE

Apricots

Bananas

Blueberries

Cereal, some*

Cherries

Chocolate

Cola, regular

Cookies, some*

Corn

Couscous

Croissants

Dried fruit

Grapes

Honey

Ice cream

Kiwi

Muesli

Muffins

Orange juice

Pineapple

Pita bread

Popcorn

Potato chips

Raisins

Rice, brown and basmati

Strawberries

Sugar

Sweet potatoes

LOW

Apples

Beans

Beef

Bread, 100 percent whole grain

Cheese

Chicken

Chocolate-covered nuts

Corn tortillas

Dates

Edamame

Eggs

Fish

Grapefruit

Hummus

Lentils

Milk (including soy and almond)

Nut butters

Nutella

Nutrition bars, most*

Nuts

Oatmeal, steel cut or rolled

Oranges

Pasta

Peaches

Pears

Plums

Pork

Quinoa

Seeds

Tofu

Yogurt

*Obviously, not all of these food products are created equally. The more fat, fiber, and/or protein they contain, the lower their glycemic index value.

Julianna Ate Too Much Sugar and Fat at Lunch

Based on how much cortisol Julianna secretes during the morning, it's no surprise she eats a massive amount of high-fat, high-sugar food at lunch. It's what cortisol makes us do. The fight-or-flight response requires lots of energy to execute (even though Julianna never had a chance to Play It Out), and cortisol helps restock the energy shelves.

Millions of years of dietary insecurity—of not knowing if and when we'd have food—have resulted in a physiological design to find fat and sugar rewarding not only from a survival perspective, but from a neurochemical one as well. Fat and sugar make the pleasure centers in our brain light up like an entire neighborhood of Christmas lights. Not only do we love the flavor of fat, we also love the creamy, smooth, rich feel in our mouths.

Our ancestors had access to *either* high-sugar or high-fat foods, but rarely foods that had *both* of these highly addicting components. Today we have figured out endless ways to create foods that combine both of these stimulating tastes—things such as chips, donuts, French fries, pastries, and cakes.

In fact, fast-food and processed-food companies have scientists whose job it is to create products in a lab that hit as many of our pleasure buttons as possible to keep us coming back for more. A great look into their strategy can be seen in a 1960s television commercial for Lay's potato chips. An actor in a devil suit laughs diabolically and says, "Betcha can't eat just one!" Of course we can't—they've spent millions of dollars making sure.

In *Salt Sugar Fat: How the Food Giants Hooked Us*, Michael Moss refers to researchers finding the right "bliss point" for foods: too little fat, sugar, and salt is bland; too much of these is overwhelming; but the right combination gives us the most pleasure. Sneaky Pete *loves* pleasure!

Single ingredients alone can be attractive, but the countless combinations of sugar, fat, and salt we have available have tapped into the brain's reward centers and resulted in a feedback loop where we want more, even when we're full. Dr. David Kessler, former head of the Food and Drug Administration and author of *The End of Overeating: Taking Control of the Insatiable American Appetite,* talks about how "extraordinarily well engineered" a Snickers bar is. As we chew it, the sugar dissolves over our tongues, the fat melts in our mouth, and the caramel traps the peanuts so the entire combination of flavors is blissfully experienced in the mouth at the same time. (The simple act of just *writing* that last sentence has made my mouth water and my bliss center shoot off fireworks in hopeful anticipation.) Dr. Kessler argues that overeating is not due to an absence of willpower, but "conditioned hypereating" from the overstimulating food environment surrounding us.

Fast food is also designed to require very little chewing so it goes down fast and easy. It practically melts in our mouths. Think about how long it takes to chew a piece of steak versus a bite of fast-food burger— there's a big difference. When we eat quickly, we can completely miss the satiety signal our stomachs send to our brain, and we end up overeating. I don't know about you, but when I'm hungry, I can eat a *lot* of food in a short amount of time, especially when it's fast food.

Let's break down Julianna's lunch:

- Deluxe double burger with cheese: 990 calories; 65 grams of fat (24 grams saturated fat, 1.5 grams trans fats); 11 grams of sugar

- Large fries: 500 calories; 22 grams of fat (3.5 grams saturated fat)

- Large soda: 290 calories; 77 grams of sugar

Total: 1,780 calories, 87 grams of fat (27.5 grams saturated fat), 88 grams of sugar. [23]

For someone Julianna's size, this singular food event supplies roughly the total calories she needs for the *entire day*. Putting this large amount of food into the body at one time means there will be a substantial increase in blood glucose along with an equally large increase in insulin production—and a large amount of stress placed on the body.

Instead of overeating a high-fat, high-sugar lunch, Julianna should have made several other decisions. The next few sections will detail these better, less stress-inducing choices.

What to Do: Get Your Sources of Fat Primarily from Plants, Nuts, Seeds, Fish, and Liquid Oils

We've already discussed the amount of stress that results from too much sugar, but it's also important to understand how dietary fat adds stress to the body.

There are many types of fat, and the type we consume matters. Not all fat is bad, and we need an ideal amount of healthy fats in our diet each day. It's energy rich, an essential nutrient, and the right types of it are vital to our health and longevity.

An easy way to remember which fats to avoid and which ones to consume is the form they take when sitting on the kitchen counter. Unsaturated fats are liquid at room temperature, come from plant sources, and are better for our health. They benefit insulin levels and sensitivity, blood glucose control, and cholesterol, which decrease the risk of diabetes and heart disease. Polyunsaturated fats found in fish oil decrease inflammation in the body and can have beneficial effects on rheumatoid arthritis (inflammation of joints) as well as inflammatory bowel disease.[24]

As a general rule, saturated fats are solid at room temperature. They typically come from animal sources. They are found in full-fat dairy products, red meat, butter, lard, and coconut and palm oils. We should keep saturated fats to a minimum. A diet high in saturated fat increases cortisol secretion—a sign of stress. Julianna's total fat intake at lunch was almost 30 percent more than what's recommended for the entire day, not to mention that a large percentage of it came from saturated fat. These fats increase inflammation in the body[25] as well as cholesterol levels in the blood, which increase our risk of heart disease and stroke.

Trans fats are a type of saturated fat found in margarine, many processed snack and fast foods, and in some foods from animals. When reading ingredient labels, "hydrogenated" or "partially hydrogenated" indicate the use of trans fats. It is recommended that we not ingest any trans fats, as they contribute to insulin resistance, raise our bad levels of cholesterol, and lower our good cholesterol. They also stimulate inflammation and overactivity of the immune system, which has been implicated in heart disease, stroke, diabetes, and other chronic conditions. The US government is currently working on measures to ban the use of trans fats outright (see chapter five), which would make it easier to "meet" the daily recommendation of zero trans fats a day.

A simple way to choose the right types of fats is to steer clear of UFOs (unidentified fried objects) and instead consume more unsaturated fats such as MUFAs, PUFAs, and omega-3s. Sources of monounsaturated fats (MUFAs) are olive, peanut, and canola oils; avocado; poultry; nuts; and seeds. Polyunsaturated fats (PUFAs) are found in nut oils and vegetable oils such as safflower, corn, sunflower, and cottonseed. We can also get them from poultry, nuts, and seeds. Omega-3 fatty acids come from cold-water fish, such as salmon, mackerel, and herring, in addition to ground flaxseed, flax oil, and walnuts.

Keep total fat intake to 20 to 35 percent of total calories. If you have a general idea of the number of calories you eat each day, multiply your total calorie intake by 0.20 to 0.35 to determine the total percentage of calories needed from fat. Then divide this number by nine (fat has nine calories per gram) for total grams of fat per day. For example, let's figure how many fat grams to eat at a 20 percent ratio if you consume 2,500 calories in a day:

2,500 calories x 0.20 = 500
500 ÷ 9 = 55.5 grams of fat

What to Do: Eat a Moderate Amount of Food at Meals

Julianna simply could have eaten less at lunch. It may sound trite for me to prescribe "eating less" to you. But think about it: when we put it in the context of spreading total calorie intake throughout the day, and when we eat breakfast and then a small snack, we're not starving at lunch, so the odds of us overeating are greatly diminished. And by eating a moderate-sized lunch followed by a small afternoon snack, we're also far less likely to overeat at dinner. By minimizing the drops in blood glucose, we also minimize the spikes.

WHEN WE MINIMIZE THE SPIKES, WE MINIMIZE THE STRESS.
WHEN WE MINIMIZE THE DROPS, WE MINIMIZE THE STRESS.

Once we eat a meal, it takes about three to four hours for blood glucose to drop to fasting levels, which are below the ideal range. In order to prevent glucose levels from dropping too low and stimulating the stress response, we should eat about every three hours. This is why snacks between meals are so important.

Many books suggest a calorie range to shoot for. The problem with this strategy is that how many calories we need varies a tremendous amount day to day and from person to person. In addition, keeping track of calories increases stress—which we'll talk more about in a few pages.

The best strategy is to eat only the amount of food that will last you until your next food event, which will happen about three hours later. How much food this is will vary from meal to meal, day to day, so a strategy I suggest is the "virtual stomach scan." A few times while you're eating your meal, pause for a moment, assess how much food is in your stomach, and ask yourself this one question: *If I stop eating right now, will this amount of food satisfy me for the next three hours?* By "satisfy," the goal is to not feel stuffed (and have a glucose spike), but to have eaten enough food (and prevent a major glucose drop) to last until you eat next. If the answer is yes, you can stop eating. If the answer is no, you may need to eat a little bit more.

THE BEST AND MOST ACCURATE MEASURE OF HOW MUCH WE NEED TO EAT AT A MEAL IS TO TUNE IN TO HOW MUCH FOOD OUR STOMACHS ARE TELLING US TO EAT.

Virtual stomach scans are good before and after eating too. Do multiple scans during the course of a day and think about where you "score" on the Feast/Famine Scale. It ranges from being über-starved at level 1 to being über-stuffed at level 5, and it will tell you when you should both start and stop eating.

Feast/Famine Scale

1) **You're hangry. You're starving, irritable, and having a hard time focusing on anything other than hunting down something to eat. Cortisol is being released, and Sneaky Pete is telling you to find fast food ASAP—and to supersize it. Stress.**

2) **You're moderately hungry and want to eat. Blood glucose levels are getting low, but they're still within the ideal range. You should find food very soon.**

3) **You have eaten and you feel content—no longer hungry, but not full. You feel confident you won't need to eat again for about three hours.**

4) **You're definitely full, but not uncomfortable. You've eaten a bit more than you need for the next three hours.**

5) **You've eaten so much, you are painfully full and it's hard to**

breathe. Sneaky Pete wants you to crawl into your cave and sleep it off. Your pancreas is working hard to produce enough insulin to deal with the excess glucose in the bloodstream. Stress.

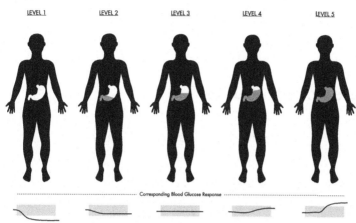

Amount of food in the stomach, corresponding feast/famine level, and how it affects blood glucose

Notice that our cue to *start* eating is a level 2. We're hungry, but not famished. If we eat at this point, we're less likely to overeat, because no cortisol has been released. If we let ourselves get down to a level 1, though, the stress response is stimulated, and Sneaky Pete will make sure we end up overeating high-fat, high-sugar food. Going to level 1 almost ensures we'll end up at level 5.

It's critical we do virtual stomach scans every time we eat a meal and then several times in between meals. Every day, every meal, our calorie needs are different, depending on how much energy we've spent. If after doing the virtual stomach scan you decide you've had enough to eat and there's still food on your plate, leave it. Your energy needs are not as high as you may have thought when you portioned your plate. Sneaky Pete may be telling you not to waste food, but eating too much will add to your stress. Or you may do the stomach scan and realize you need a bit more food, so help yourself to a few more bites. Every meal will be different.

The more you practice the virtual stomach scan, the more in tune you'll be with your body's true needs. You'll start to understand what it's like to be at level 3. You'll learn how much food gets you from eating event to eating event, with the goal of landing right at a level 2 each time you're ready to eat. At first, you might eat a bit too much or a bit too little at any given meal. But as long as the goal is to listen and learn from your body, you'll be well on your way.

T Plate Portion Guide

We've already talked about what meals should look like when we Plate It Out with the T Plate, but we haven't addressed *how much* food we should consume. Again, the point is not to count calories or set strict rules to follow every single meal. These are loose guidelines to help you get a sense of what might make you reach level 3 on the Feast/Famine Scale.

If you remember, the T Plate ratio is 25/25/50. An easy way to think of this is two to one: For every one bite of protein you take, you need to take two bites of fruit and/or vegetable. And for every one bite of whole grains you take, you need to take two bites of fruit and/or vegetable. Let's see how that roughly works out with portion sizes. Again, the goal at meals is to eat only enough food to last you about three hours, because you'll be having a small snack between each.

Start your meal by choosing your source of lean protein. A good way to estimate how much protein should be on your plate for each meal is to make it about the size of the "caveman" of electronics: the original iPod Classic, which is about four to five ounces. This is also about the size of a deck of playing cards or the size and thickness of your palm.

Though it's only about 25 percent of your T plate, protein is very powerful. Think of it as your "central side dish" because protein also contains fat and sometimes fiber, which are critical for slowing the release of glucose in the bloodstream. A slow glucose release means less of a spike, less stress on the body, and feeling fuller for longer. Protein is also a good source of the amino acids we need to build and maintain muscle mass. As you learned in chapter three, the more muscle mass we have, the more sensitive we are to insulin and glucose.

Keep in mind, however, that eating large amounts of protein will not translate into large amounts of muscle mass. The body can process only so much protein at a time, and anything over that amount is stored as fat. Excessive protein intake also stresses the kidneys, as they have to work very hard to filter and excrete byproducts related to metabolizing excess protein. Excess protein has also been shown to lead to greater loss of urinary calcium, which can increase the risk of osteoporosis.[26]

Animal proteins can be high in saturated fat, so if consuming animal products, choose those leaner, or lower, in fat. Plant proteins are naturally lower in fat and have the added benefit of fiber, which also helps with a lower and slower blood glucose effect.

Here are some examples of foods that are good sources of protein:

Amaranth	Greek yogurt	Seafood
Beans	Hummus	Seeds
Beef	Lentils	Seitan
Bulgur	Milk (including soy and almond)	Shrimp
Cheese		Soy
Chicken	Nut butters	Tempeh
Cottage cheese	Nuts	Tofu
Eggs	Pork	Turkey
Fish	Quinoa	Yogurt

Vegetables and fruits are your next priority. You should have between two to three fist-sized portions (two if you're smaller in size, three if you're bigger) at each meal. Again, these foods should take up approximately half of your plate. Fruits and vegetables are high in fiber, and fiber slows the release of glucose into the bloodstream.

Grains are the final piece of your ideal T Plate. As this will make up the final 25 percent of your meal, it will equate to one to two fistfuls (again, the number depending on your body size) after they have been cooked. Whenever possible, choose whole grains that have not been refined or processed. Whole grains are composed of the entire grain kernel (bran, germ, and endosperm) and contain more nutrients as well as fiber, which slows the glucose response. Refined flours and grains have been processed to remove the bran and germ, which lengthens the product's shelf life, but also reduces the amount of fiber, iron, and vitamins.

Cooking grains in their whole, natural state is ideal, but if you have to choose a grain that has been processed, read the label to choose the version that has the most fiber. Just because the package says "made with whole grains" or "whole wheat" does not mean it's going to be high in fiber, as it most likely contains a small amount of whole grain and a substantial amount of refined flours. Look for the words "100 percent whole grain" or "100 percent whole wheat."

Here are some examples of whole grains:

Amaranth	Corn	Quinoa
Barley	Farro	Whole oats
Brown rice	Freekeh	Wild rice
Buckwheat	Millet	100 percent whole wheat bread, pasta, or crackers
Bulgur (cracked wheat)	Oats	
	Popcorn	

Sixty-Second Solutions for Lunch

Just as with breakfast, you may not have a lot of time to prepare or eat your lunch. It would be fantastic if we all had time to stop our busy workdays and sit down to a leisurely meal. The reality is that many of us need something fast and easy. Here are some stress solutions for a lunch that will support a resilient afternoon.

- Top some prewashed, bagged salad with canned beans or tuna, and have whole grain crackers or bread.

- Fill a whole grain pita with turkey and bagged spinach.

- Spread nut butter on a whole wheat tortilla, top with sliced apples and bananas, fold, and eat.

- Eat a couple to a few pieces of string cheese, a piece of fruit, and a small handful of almonds.

- Add hot water to soup in a cup that has protein, vegetables, and grains. (Find natural, low-sodium options.)

- Put cheese on a whole grain tortilla, put it in the microwave for a few seconds, roll, and eat with a piece of fruit or fresh-bagged vegetables.

- Heat a can of refried beans and use as a dip for fresh-bagged vegetables and corn tortilla chips.

Julianna Has a High-Glycemic Snack in the Afternoon

Julianna's lunch was moderately high glycemic. There was not much fiber, the soda was full of sugar, and the only thing that contained protein was the burger. A high-glycemic meal increases insulin secretion, which we know allows the fat, muscle, and liver cells to remove glucose from the bloodstream. Within sixty minutes of a high-glycemic meal, blood glucose levels begin to fall, often to levels below the ideal range. Fatty acids from stored fat are turned off and no longer used as fuel.

The combination of the drop in blood glucose and low concentrations of fatty acids stimulates hunger and subsequently overeating in an attempt to restore glucose levels back to normal.[27] So even though her meal is high in calories (1,780—theoretically enough to last her the whole day), it does not give her sustainable blood glucose over the long term.

It creates a spike and a crash. It makes her seek out more high-glycemic foods to recover from her glucose crash.

She goes cubicle hunting and finds the sugar rush she's looking for: licorice. But if you recall, she's hungry again thirty minutes after she ate it. The high-glycemic nature of the licorice creates another spike and crash, and she's stuck on the glucose rollercoaster. In an attempt to mitigate her hunger and low levels of energy, she has more coffee. Her lunch was high stress, her snack was high stress, and now she's added the stress of caffeine on top.

What to Do: Have a Low-Glycemic Afternoon Snack

Like the midmorning snack between breakfast and lunch, an afternoon snack keeps blood glucose levels from dropping too low between lunch and dinner. The guidelines are the same: aim for 50 to 150 calories of a food (or combination of foods) that is low glycemic, containing a combination of protein, fiber, and healthy fats.

This doesn't have to be a lot of food or take time out of your busy afternoon to prepare. You could grab an apple, have a few chocolate-covered nuts, eat some hummus and whole grain crackers, or have a glass of milk.

Brain Function and Performance in the Afternoon

When we compare the consumption of a high-glycemic meal versus a low-glycemic one, the high-glycemic meal results in worse cognitive performance when it comes to executive function, working memory, and auditory selective attention (that allows us to hear all details).[28]

After Julianna's big lunch, she feels heavy, lethargic, and drowsy. She has a hard time focusing and engaging. She has several important meetings where it's vital she make a good impression. Unfortunately, her performance is mediocre at best, and others mistakenly interpret her lack of energy and focus to mean she doesn't care about what was being said.

Her lack of energy is partly due to her body devoting a lot of re-sources to metabolize the high levels of glucose in her bloodstream from lunch. The pancreas has to crank out large amounts of insulin, and her fat cells have to take up all the extra energy the brain and muscles can't use. Until her glucose levels get closer to their ideal levels, her performance is compromised.

The candy she ate in the afternoon was in response to her body telling her to find a quick source of energy. Unfortunately, the high-glyce-mic licorice gave her a rush of energy (glucose) that was very short lived. Insulin took the excess glucose out of the bloodstream and put much of it into the fat cells, seeing as Julianna was sedentary and her muscle cells didn't require much. The plunge in glucose that occurred left her tired and drinking more caffeine . . . triggering more cortisol. The stress on her body continues to mount.

Julianna Drinks Alcohol

Julianna poured herself several glasses of wine once she got home and started making dinner. It was meant to remove stress, but you can probably guess by now that it didn't have the exact effect she was hoping for.

Honey and many wild fruits can undergo natural fermentation, so the possibility definitely exists that our ancestors were able to tip back a few alcoholic beverages after a long day. This alcohol was less potent than our liquor today because fermentation creates a weaker product than distillation. The amount of alcohol consumed was likely very little, and it mainly occurred on special occasions. The regular use of alcohol is a much later development in our evolution. From a global perspective, we now consume approximately 1.5 gallons (5.6 liters) of alcohol per person each year.[29]

Increased alcohol consumption can be stressful on the body for many reasons: alcohol is toxic to the cells of the liver and can shrink portions of the brain central to memory, planning, problem solving, judgment, and other executive processes. It can damage the pancreas in addition to increasing our risk of high blood pressure, cancer, and cardiovascular disease.

For healthy individuals, moderate drinking seems to have little effect on blood glucose control. But for people with diabetes or reduced glucose or insulin sensitivity, it can cause low blood sugar shortly after drinking and for up to twenty-four hours after. Drinking heavily on an empty stomach can interfere with the liver's ability to release stored glucose into the bloodstream, also resulting in low blood glucose. Low blood glucose is a stress that often leads to cortisol release, overeating, and fat storage.

What to Do: If You Choose to Consume Alcohol, Do So in Moderation

Technically speaking, Julianna did not drink moderately. "Moderate" drinking is defined as no more than one drink per day for women and no more than two per day for men. (This is based on body size.) One drink is equal to a 12-ounce beer, a 5-ounce glass of wine, or 1.5 ounces of distilled spirits (such as vodka, gin, or whiskey). When drinking a distilled spirit, however, be mindful of what you're mixing it with. Juices are high glycemic and sodas are moderate, both of which can cause a spike in blood glucose levels.

There is evidence that light to moderate alcohol consumption can reduce the risk of developing heart disease, but it is not definitive and may not benefit everyone who drinks. Be aware that consuming even moderate amounts of alcohol has been associated with developing several types of cancer in addition to diminished brain function. It can also interfere with the quality of our sleep, and we run the risk of becoming dependent or addicted with regular use.

Julianna Overeats at Dinner

Julianna is stressed—both physically as well as psychologically—

thanks to the glucose spikes and crashes from her high-glycemic lunch and afternoon snack, plus caffeine, plus going too long without eating. Combine that with a tough commute home, and she's in fight-or-flight mode and marinating in cortisol. We all know what happens in response: overeating, fat storage, and the resulting stress it places on the pancreas and body.

She begins the overeating process by drinking wine and munching on cheese and chips before dinner, then continues overeating by downing a full plate of food she knows she's not even hungry for anymore. She tells herself she's "relaxing" after a hard day, but she's only adding to the stress.

What to Do: Eat Frequently Throughout the Day So a Moderately Sized Dinner Is Realistic

It's no wonder Julianna overeats at dinner—even before dinner technically begins. She spent her day on a roller coaster of glucose levels and stress. By now, you're starting to see how every decision we make about eating (or not eating) throughout the day affects the next. You see that if we keep blood glucose levels within the ideal range throughout the span of the day, we diminish the odds we'll stimulate the release of cortisol and overeat at subsequent meals or snacks.

As we discussed, setting ourselves up to be successful for the day starts by eating a T plate breakfast or a snack containing protein right away in the morning. A moderate and steady amount of glucose is released, the brain and muscle cells have adequate energy, and they're not being stressed. Eating frequently throughout the day can also reduce our risk for cardiovascular disease, diabetes, and obesity[30]—all things that either increase stress on the body or are a result of stress. Eating several small snacks and reasonably sized meals keeps us from the high-stress extremes: instead of blood glucose levels looking like mountains and valleys, they look like rolling hills.

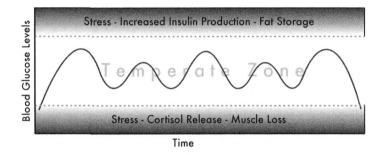

Eating reasonably sized meals and small snacks throughout the day maintains ideal blood glucose levels

WHEN WE EAT MODERATE AMOUNTS
FREQUENTLY THROUGHOUT THE DAY,
WE MINIMIZE STRESS ON THE BODY.

Had Julianna avoided the roller coaster of glucose levels throughout the day, she wouldn't feel the urge to overeat before and during dinner. She would be content to eat a moderately sized T plate meal. She would feel perfectly balanced and fueled for the remainder of the evening.

Sixty-Second Solutions for Dinner

By the time dinner rolls around, you may be in full-on survival mode: rushing home from work, trying to make a meal, getting yourself and/or your children to evening activities, taking care of household duties, and squeezing in more work. It's no surprise many people succumb to the convenience—and temptation—of fast food in these situations. If you're really pressed for time, here are some stress solutions for a fast dinner that will keep you resilient all evening long.

- Put a whole grain English muffin in the toaster; as soon as it's done, top with mozzarella cheese and a couple slices of tomato.

- Scramble two eggs, spoon on salsa and sliced avocado, and have a handful of corn tortilla chips.

- Top a whole wheat tortilla with a handful of packaged salad; cube and add an iPod Classic–sized portion of precooked chicken.

- Open a can of tuna, spoon onto whole grain crackers, and top with sliced cucumber.

- Fill a whole wheat pita with canned tuna and vegetables.

- Microwave frozen vegetables, cut some store-bought rotisserie chicken, and have a whole grain dinner roll.

- Slice French bread; top with cheese and sliced fruit.

- Heat a can of beans, add diced peppers, crush corn tortilla chips on top, and top with salsa.

You may be wondering if it's okay to have a snack in the evening. To determine if one is needed, go back to the suggestion of eating about every three hours to keep blood glucose levels in the ideal range. If dinner was at 6:00 p.m. and you're not going to bed until 11:30 p.m., a small snack between 9:00 and 10:00 p.m. would be warranted. If you were planning to be asleep by 9:30, though, you shouldn't need one. Your snack decision will also depend on how physically active you are in the evening. If you do a lot around the house or work out, you use a lot of glucose and will need to replace it. If you've been sedentary for much of the evening, your requirement for energy will be far less.

Brain Function and Performance in the Evening

Instead, Julianna feels tired and bloated after dinner. She's exhausted after a long day, and eating to the point of a food coma doesn't help. She knows the wine before dinner doesn't help with her lack of energy either—after it brings her down from her day, it leaves her feeling more tired.

As the sole caretaker, it's important for Julianna to feel she's doing her best as a mother—to be emotionally connected to her children, to be a good example, and to let them know they are her most important priority. Unfortunately because of her fatigue, she ends up going through the motions of making sure their homework is done and carrying out the bedtime routine after dinner. She pacifies her distress of not being the mother she wants to be by telling herself tomorrow will be better.

The housework will have to wait as well. She gets frustrated because she spends a good amount of every weekend cleaning, shopping, and doing laundry, but she's just too tired during the week to get it done after work. She knows tomorrow morning she will start the day already behind for not getting any work done on her laptop, but she's so exhausted she has a hard time getting too worked up about it. There's always tomorrow.

Julianna's resilience to stress was seriously compromised the vast majority of the day: She started off in fight-or-flight mode by not eating breakfast, then added to that stress with caffeine and nicotine. Her body went into fat-storage mode and expanded her fight-or-flight fuel allocation station, which added more stress to her body. By not properly fueling her brain and muscle cells, she compromised her cognitive function during the morning and burned precious muscle mass. She then overate while in fat-storage mode, swamped her blood with glucose and fat, and compromised her cognitive function again for the afternoon. She repeated this cycle later in the day, adding alcohol. These eating choices placed a lot of stress on her—in addition to the external stresses of work, family, finances, and everything else she faces!

She wakes up the next day and starts the cycle over again. She does it day after day after day, year after year. Long term, that's a lot of physiological stress on the system. Long term, that's a lot of negative impact on her professional and personal performance. Long term, that's a lot of fat deposited on the body. Long term, that's a lot of muscle mass lost. Each day digs her deeper and deeper into a hole of stress she can't get out of.

It was psychologically stressful for Julianna to go long periods without food, to overeat, and then to feel uncomfortably full. We've all been there. We've gone too long without eating, which makes us short tempered, irritable, impatient, and nasty. In our family, we refer to this state as being "hangry," and it's not pretty. Of course, we know the consequences of going too long without eating are almost always eating too much. We've all been disappointed in ourselves for overeating and for feeling sluggish and tired, not motivated to accomplish much. Imagine continually bouncing between these two emotional states several times each day, while trying to be productive at work and trying to be a caring and compassionate person with your loved ones at home. It's a lot of unnecessary stress and makes life extremely difficult.

If you want to reduce the physiological stress you add to your body and life, and if you want to build your resiliency toward stress, a few simple changes can make a world of difference. To summarize, the big things we can do to minimize stress from a nutrition perspective are:

- Eat a protein-rich breakfast or snack within an hour of waking.

- Eat a low-glycemic snack of 50 to 150 calories midmorning and midafternoon.

- Plate It Out with a T Plate at each meal, consuming only enough to last you about three hours.

- Eat to a level 3 as often as possible at meals.

- Keep caffeine and alcohol to a minimum.

- Cut out nicotine.

Now that we've covered the basics about eating to avoid adding stress to the body, let's take it to the next level. Once we understand the benefits of exercising and eating strategically, some of us may want to undo a few of the effects of our old, stressful habits. That is, some of us may want to reduce body fat.

Let me say this again: this book is not about weight loss or health; it's a way to become more resilient to the stress in our lives. With that being said, if you start employing the resiliency training tools in this book, one of the positive side effects is that you can successfully reduce body fat—if you feel the need to do so—and you can improve your health. Before we discuss how to do that, let's discuss how *not* to.

Dieting Is One of the Most Stressful Things We Can Do

Next time you consider going on a diet, stop and think: *what would a caveman do?* Could you ever imagine Sneaky Pete going completely against his biological drive for survival by purposefully eating less food when it was available?

Having a crazy sweet tooth helped us survive when food was scarce, and having extra body fat was an important life insurance policy. They were both needed for our ancestors to function well and endure their harsh environments. Those who were more driven to eat and those who stored fat had a better chance at survival. And as you know, caveman brain is still very impulsive, not to mention obsessed with seeking comfort and pleasure. It's the part of the brain that screams at us: *Eat that! Drink that! Smoke that!* It wants *what* it wants, *when* it wants it, and it doesn't care much about the future consequences.

....

WE ARE NOT HARDWIRED TO EAT LESS.

....

Dieting couldn't be more opposite to how we're designed to function, which makes it physiologically as well as psychologically stressful. Even worse, dieting is one of the best ways to *gain* weight, not lose it. Research shows that people who diet end up gaining more weight over time than people who never do.[31] Here's the cycle showing why:

- **Dieting releases cortisol.** Research has shown that calorie restriction increases the production of cortisol.[32] This makes sense. Low blood glucose levels from not eating enough or going too long without eating stimulate the release of cortisol. The body thinks no food is available, the HPA axis is activated, and cortisol is released.

- **Cortisol then makes us overeat.** We know cortisol's job is to replace the energy we theoretically spent while fighting and fleeing. When dieting, the only thing we're "fighting" is the urge to eat that chocolate chip cookie, and we usually don't win. The cortisol-induced hunger makes us seek out large amounts of food high in fat and sugar.

- **And cortisol makes us store fat.** Cortisol wants to restock the fight-or-flight fuel allocation station. It takes that food we overeat and converts it into stored fat on the body, primarily around the midsection.

- **Then we lose precious muscle mass.** When the body is in fat-storage mode, it breaks down stored protein from muscle mass and converts it into usable energy. Less muscle mass and more fat make us less sensitive to insulin, the pancreas has to produce more, and body fat levels rise—all events that place additional stress on the body.

- **And it slows our metabolism.** When the body goes into energy-conservation mode, it doesn't just store fat. It also slows metabolic rate in order to conserve precious and limited energy supplies. When we're dieting and we fail to eat when we're hungry, it can suppress resting metabolic rate by up to 20 percent.[33] We not only generate less energy, but we burn less of it as well. Over the long run, this loss of muscle mass and decrease in metabolism can increase body fat—the exact opposite of what we're trying to do on a diet.

One Step Forward, Three Steps Back

The long-term success rate of dieting is 5 percent.[34] That is dismal. All that denial and stress, and it's not going to work for the vast majority of us. What's worse, continually being on and off a diet can create a cycle where the increase in stress actually makes us fatter over the long run. In fact, 66 percent of dieters don't just gain the weight back, but they gain *more* fat, and it's stored preferentially as visceral fat.[35]

Chris is five foot eleven and has gained fifty pounds over the last few years. He currently weighs 225 pounds and would like to lose weight. He decides to go on a very low-calorie diet and eat only two meals per day. These are his stats when he starts the diet:

- Weight: 225 pounds

- Body fat: 27 percent

- Fat mass: 60.7 pounds

- Muscle/lean body mass: 164.3 pounds

He starts his diet, weighs himself on a daily basis, and sees the pounds start to drop off. After six weeks, he's lost twenty-five pounds, but his willpower is completely exhausted, and he can't stay on the diet any longer. He goes back to the way he was eating before he started the diet and gains all the weight back. He thinks he's at square one.

Unfortunately, he's actually *behind* square one. The scale doesn't accurately reflect what really happened while he was on his diet. Because he so drastically reduced his calorie intake and ate only twice a day, his body was in a near-constant state of stress. His body catabolized muscle mass and converted it to glucose, and the continual release of cortisol put his body into fat-storage mode.

Even though he's back to his starting weight, the composition of his body has changed for the worse. He lost 6.8 pounds of valuable muscle mass and instead gained 6.8 pounds of fat mass (most likely around his abdomen). Here are his stats after his diet:

- Weight: 225 pounds

- Body fat: 30 percent

- Fat mass: 67.5 pounds

- Muscle/lean body mass: 157.5 pounds

Several months later, he again becomes frustrated with being over-weight. It happens to be January 1, so he decides his New Year's resolution is to be steadfast about eating less. This time he manages to stay on the diet for twelve weeks and loses all fifty pounds he originally set out to do. It was a struggle, and it seemed as if the weight took forever to come off this time.

He feels good about his success, but can't take the starvation and denial for another minute. He goes back to his old eating patterns. Within a short period of time, he's gained back all fifty pounds. These are his stats after his second diet:

- Weight: 225 pounds

- Body fat: 34 percent

- Fat mass: 76.5 pounds

- Muscle/lean body mass: 148.5 pounds

Chris thinks he's gone back to baseline after each unsuccessful attempt to lose weight. But in reality, he's left himself in worse condition each time he's dieted. Even though he returned to his initial starting weight, his body composition has changed dramatically. Over the course of his two diets, he's lost 15.8 pounds of muscle and added 15.8 pounds of fat, and this has slowed his metabolism.

But that's not all. He's inadvertently set himself up to gain more weight than ever before. He continues his old way of eating, but his body now requires 550 to 790 *fewer calories each day* due to the loss of muscle mass. That's close to an entire meal! He's shocked at how quickly he re-gains the weight each time, but he doesn't realize how much he's altered his metabolic rate.

The increase in body fat and decrease in muscle mass has also made him more resistant to the effects of insulin. As we know, muscle mass helps *increase* sensitivity to insulin, and he has lost a fair amount; fat *decreases* sensitivity, and he has added quite a bit. His pancreas is now working harder each day, and his risk of diabetes and other diseases has increased.

Extreme dieting typically results in "yo-yo weight loss" with a horrible rebound effect each time: losing weight, gaining more back, having a harder time losing weight, gaining more back, having an extremely hard time losing weight, and gaining even more back. The body will go along with a drastic diet a couple times, but eventually it starts fighting back. Evolution favored those who could survive times of famine, which means the body had to develop the capacity to hang on to as much fat as it possibly could. Still to this day, it becomes progressively better at doing it each time it happens. A recent review article found that 30 to 64 percent of diet study participants end up gaining back more weight than they initially lost.[36]

Not that you're a lab rat, but when overweight ones are put on a diet the first time, they lose weight. When they're taken off the diet, they eat more and regain the weight. When put on a diet for the second time, it takes them longer to lose the same amount of weight they did during the first round. When they go off the second diet, they gain weight faster than they did the first time. By the time they hit the third or fourth yo-yo cycle of dieting, the diet stops working completely, even though they're eating fewer calories.[37]

Dieting becomes progressively more stressful each time we do it because we're releasing cortisol, adding more fat to the body, losing more muscle mass, spending more time in fat-storage mode, decreasing insulin sensitivity, and putting our health at risk. It can raise blood pressure and cholesterol, suppress the immune system, and increase the risk of heart attack, stroke, diabetes, and all-cause mortality.[38]

The amount of psychological stress it adds may be even worse. Denying ourselves of eating—and the frustration and anguish that comes along with it—is horrible. We're far more likely to experience negative mood states such as depression, anxiety, decreased self-esteem, nervousness, and irritability when dieting.[39] In addition, restricting a food automatically increases our cravings for it.[40] And when we finally get our hands on it, we end up eating more of it.[41] The hassles of counting calories, weighing out portions, and monitoring food intake also increase perceived stress.[42] Why would we ever want to do this to ourselves? It goes entirely against how our brain and body are designed to function!

Have you ever wondered how sumo wrestlers get so big? For the most part, the Asian body structure is on the smaller, leaner side, so where do the huge sumo guys come from? They train to grow that large by using a very special diet and style of training. If you eat only one or two times per day, you're on the diet. I call it the "Sumo Wrestler Diet," and here's what it looks like:

1. **They skip breakfast.** Skipping breakfast releases cortisol and puts their bodies into fat-storage mode, which is exactly what they want. The more fat mass they can put on their bodies, the greater their advantage over their competitors.
2. **They work out on an empty stomach.** Increasing the need for energy without adequate fuel continues to keep their bodies in fat-storage mode.
3. **They have a large meal after their workout.** Now that they've got their bodies in fat-storage mode, they eat a huge meal along with several glasses of beer or sake to store as much energy into the fat cells as possible. The release of cortisol ensures that a vast majority of it is stored around the midsection.
4. **They take a nap after eating.** They're in a food coma from eating so much, and the less they move around, the fewer calories they expend. (A lot like us sitting at our desk after a big lunch.)

5. **They don't eat again until dinner, and it's another huge meal.** They sit down to gorge on another large meal, again with additional calories from alcohol. Some eat until they become physically ill.

6. **They go to bed.** After eating so much, they're tired again, it's hard to move, so they go back to bed.

Their fat cells love this diet! The wrestlers understand how fat storage works and use it to their "advantage," allowing them to reach weights of five hundred to six hundred pounds.

Unfortunately, the stress of their lifestyle means they have a life expectancy of only fifty to sixty years, more than ten years below the life expectancy of the average Japanese male. Many wrestlers develop diabetes and high blood pressure and are at high risk for heart disease. The excessive amount of alcohol they consume can lead to liver problems, and the daily stress on their joints can cause arthritis.

Is it possible you're occasionally on the Sumo Wrestler Diet? Do you skip breakfast and work hard all morning? When do you eat your largest meal? What do you do right after?

We Have to Eat to Lose Fat

Before joining the Resiliency rEvolution, you may have thought cutting calories was the key to reducing body fat. While we do have to create a calorie deficit, it's also critical to eat those calories in a way that makes the body comfortable with the idea of giving up this precious reservoir of stored energy. Remember, our body is devised to favor storing fat, not getting rid of it.

Being on the Sumo Wrestler Diet is a good example of misunderstanding how the body works: going as long as possible without eating to create a calorie deficit, eating only one or two times per day, and thinking we're doing a good job of eating less. Unfortunately, not eating for extended periods makes blood glucose levels drop, which signals the HPA axis to produce cortisol: the fat-storage hormone. We also lose precious muscle mass that keeps our metabolism going strong and decreases our sensitivity to insulin.

If we alternate between eating moderately sized T plate meals and small low-glycemic snacks about every three hours throughout the day, blood glucose levels stay within the ideal range. Insulin is produced in appropriate amounts, no cortisol is released that would store fat and make us hungry, we don't lose muscle mass, and no excess glucose is stored away in the fat cells.

IN ORDER TO REDUCE BODY FAT, WE'VE GOT TO EAT IN A WAY THAT KEEPS BLOOD GLUCOSE IN THE TEMPERATE ZONE.

In addition to using glucose for energy, the body also relies on fat. When blood glucose levels are within the ideal range, we metabolize a mix of *both* glucose and fat as fuel. The more we can keep blood glucose levels in the temperate zone, the more fat we can use as fuel. However, when glucose levels go above or below the zone, we know that one, if not two, things happen:

1) When blood glucose levels get too low, we secrete cortisol. That puts the body in fat-storage mode, curtailing the use of fat as fuel.

2) When blood glucose levels get too high, large amounts of insulin are produced. It stores much of the extra glucose as fat in the fat cells.

As a hormone, insulin regulates not only glucose but also fat metabolism, controlling how and when it is used or stored. When insulin levels are low, more fat is used as fuel. When insulin levels are high, more fat is being stored away.

LOW INSULIN = FAT BURNING
HIGH INSULIN = FAT STORAGE

No-Stress Eating to Reduce Body Fat

In order to reduce body fat, we have to create a calorie deficit, but it can't be so much that it triggers the stress response. If we eat just a *little bit* less than what the body needs at each meal and snack, we create a deficit, but one that's small enough not be a stressor or make the body think a famine is happening. It will cause blood glucose levels to drop slightly below what the body needs—still within the temperate zone, albeit on the low end. Due to the lower amount of glucose in the system, not much insulin is necessary.

Because we're still in the temperate zone, the body is fine with continuing to use fat as fuel. In fact, when we eat a bit less but still stay within the zone, the body is happy to use fat to shore up the deficit in energy needs—especially when we've consistently been eating about every three hours and the body knows there's always fuel coming in.

I call it no-stress eating, and it's amazingly simple. If we leave a few

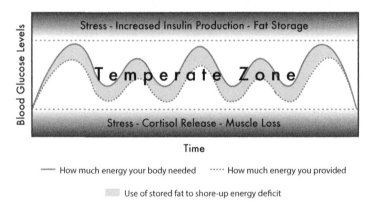

How fat is used as fuel when eating a bit less in the Temperate Zone

bites of food on our plate at meals (or take a bit less to begin with), and if we stop eating at level 3 on the Feast/Famine Scale, we encourage the body to use more fat as fuel. If we eat a smaller amount of food at snacks, closer to fifty calories, we would again encourage the use of fat as fuel.

Bottom line: We're able to lose body fat without having to starve ourselves or add additional stress to our body and mind. We can preserve muscle mass. And we can sustain high levels of cognitive function and performance because we're not hangry or focused on how hungry we are.

When we combine no-stress eating with PowerHouse Hit the Deck (or some other combination of cardiovascular exercise and resistance training), the potential for fat loss is further increased. In a twelve-week study done by researchers at the Pennsylvania State University Department of Kinesiology, volunteers either dieted, dieted and did cardiovascular exercise, or dieted along with cardiovascular exercise and resistance training. At the conclusion of the study, dieting alone resulted in a loss of only 14.6 pounds of fat per participant. When adding cardiovascular exercise to calorie restriction, volunteers lost 15.6 pounds of fat. However, when dieting was combined with cardiovascular exercise and resistance training, fat loss jumped to 21.1 pounds—a 44 percent increase![43]

Feed Your Sneaky Pete Both Essentials and Extras

If we make any changes to how and what we're eating, they have to be sustainable and realistic. Otherwise it creates a lot of stress for nothing and there's no point in doing any of it. As we just discussed, dieting places a large amount of strain on the body and mind, and when we're stressed out, Sneaky Pete takes control.

When he's in command, it can be very difficult to make change. If he thinks we're going to take away things that give him pleasure or do things that put him in danger, he's going to fight us on it. Not eating enough or, worse yet, deciding we'll never eat another piece of chocolate or French fry throws Pete into a state of panic.

There's no getting around the fact that food is designed by nature—and food manufacturers—to be pleasurable so we'll eat it . . . especially when it's full of calorie-rich fat and sugar. It is possible and necessary to "have our cake and eat it too." We can find a balance between eating foods that make us happy because they taste good and eating those that provide the essential nutrients we need for health.

We need to make both our advanced brain and caveman brain content, even though they have different definitions of what "content" means. Advanced brain knows we should choose foods high in the vitamins and nutrients our body needs to be healthy. It thinks about the long-term consequences of today's choices. Caveman brain lives in the now and just wants that dessert—it says we'll eat less or exercise more tomorrow.

When we eat food caveman brain tells us to eat, we can end up feeling guilty, full of regret, ashamed, or "bad." On the other hand, when advanced brain makes rules about what we can or can't eat, we may feel deprived, limited, or frustrated. It can also set up a scarcity mindset, where the conscious effort to *not* eat something actually makes us *want* to eat it all the more. We end up spending a lot of time and energy trying not to think about it. When we try to obey just one of the brains, eventually we have a moment where the other brain manages to take control and make up for "lost time." All this adds more unnecessary stress.

In order to keep both brains happy, think about finding a balance between essentials and extras. Essentials are the foods we know are healthy—they're packed with vitamins, minerals, nutrients, antioxidants, fiber, and essential fatty acids. These would be all the things on your T plate, such as lean proteins, whole grains, and fresh vegetables and fruits. Extras are processed, high-fat, high-sugar, low-nutrient foods, such as sodas, chips, fatty meats, sweets, and desserts. Alcohol can be considered an extra as well.

BALANCE YOUR ESSENTIALS AND EXTRAS.

The key is to find the right balance—it's not an equal division. Most extras are high in sugar and low in fiber, making them high glycemic. The last thing we want to do is spike our blood glucose and place unnecessary stress on the body. For this reason, it's not a good idea to eat an extra as a between-meal snack. It's better to have our extras at mealtimes, where the glucose response will be blunted by the protein, fats, and fiber.

We need to make a little calorie room for the extras in addition to the essentials. Otherwise, we'll consume too much food at meals. This means we've got to eat a bit less of the essentials. But which essentials should we cut back on? Let's give each component a look.

If we refer back to the T Plate, protein is our central side dish and the first thing we should think about when composing a meal. A lean protein is critical for slowing the release of glucose, so it's truly essential, and we can't trade it out. The fruits and vegetables are powerhouses of vitamins, minerals, and other vital nutrients, so these essentials can't be traded either. The only thing left to work with is our whole grains. Whole grains provide fiber and other essential nutrients, so we don't want to get rid of these completely, but we can eat a bit less of them to make room for our extras.

EAT LESS OF YOUR WHOLE GRAINS TO ACCOMMODATE YOUR EXTRAS.

For example, let's say you wanted to have one glass of wine or beer with dinner tonight. (As we discussed, one drink is considered a "moderate" amount.) Instead of having two fistfuls of grains, you would only have one. Or perhaps it's someone's birthday at work, and there's cake to celebrate at lunch. You brought a sandwich, so you remove one slice of bread to account for the cake. Maybe this weekend you're going out to brunch, and you love bacon and pancakes. That high-fat meat would count as your extra, as would the pancake (eating only one fistful). The rest of your breakfast would need to contain an iPod Classic–sized source of lean protein, such as egg whites, in addition to fresh fruit or vegetables.

Try to embrace the philosophy of "some, not all" when it comes to your extras. Allow yourself to have *some* of the extra, but *not all* of the serving. For one thing, serving sizes have continued to grow over the years, and most are more than we need. Just because it comes in a certain size container, just because it came out on a plate, or just because the label says it's a "serving" doesn't mean it's how much we should really eat. Go ahead and have some, but leave a bit behind for later, or share it with someone. I once enrolled the help of a perfect stranger sitting next to me on a flight to eat some of my licorice because it comes in a big bag. It's hard for me not to eat the whole thing. (Seated next to me on a flight: blessing or curse? It's a fine line.)

Also try to remove the emotional labels of "good" and "bad" or "only eat" and "never eat." When is the last time you completely obsessed about eating steamed broccoli, fantasized for days about getting it—and then when you got it, you absolutely couldn't stop eating it and felt really guilty about it later? Probably never. That's how we typically view "forbidden" or "bad" foods. But something like broccoli doesn't take on more meaning or significance than it should. It's simply a food that's always an option to eat, and we don't associate a sense of restriction with it.

When we remove the emotional labels we put on foods, it gets rid of the stigma of a forbidden food and decreases the feeling that it has to be all or none. We can eat our extras every single day and not feel bad about it. We can be resilient, have good health and appropriate levels of body fat—as long as we have extras in a moderate way where we eat some, but not all.

Whenever we label a food as bad, forbidden, or restricted, Sneaky Pete's ears perk up. That's *exactly* the sort of thing he's interested in. He knows it's forbidden because it's seductively high in fat and sugar. He really, really wants it, and he wants all of it.

As a child, I was not allowed to have sugar because my mom said it made me hyper. (She still swears it to this day.) Holy cow, were Sneaky Pete and I ever obsessed about sweets because we weren't supposed to have them. I was allowed only unsweetened cereal for breakfast, so when my mom turned her back, I scooped heaps of sugar onto mine. So much that there would be a half inch of sugar at the bottom of the bowl.

Anytime it was someone's birthday, I couldn't enjoy the party. I

The author and Sneaky Pete getting first dibs—not at her own birthday party, but her brother's.

would hover around the cake in a state of extreme anxiety because I just *had* to get the piece with the most frosting on it. Seriously, I would almost get sick to my stomach with worry that I wouldn't get the piece with the huge frosting flower.

After I grew up and moved out of my parents' house, it took me a long, long time to be able to eat sweets moderately. I still felt as if sweets were something you rarely got, so when you did get them, you'd better get your fill. Eventually I managed to understand that I could eat sweets every single day for the rest of my life, no questions asked. When I got rid of the all-or-none thinking, the desire, guilt, and stress of overeating sweets went away. I get to eat them every single day, so I don't have to binge on them and feel bad about it afterward. I have a moderate amount, enjoy it, and know I can eat it again very soon if I want to.

Eating and Exercise

Many of us exercise to burn excess calories and build muscle mass—in addition to building resiliency to better deal with stress. Exercising on an empty stomach does the opposite. When we exercise without adequate glucose in the bloodstream, our primary fuel source becomes muscle mass. That's right—we lose muscle and hold on to fat. Let's do a quick refresher about why.

Without adequate glucose, the body goes into survival mode, which is fat-storage mode. As we already learned, the body wants to conserve precious energy during times of famine, and fat is a valuable source of stored energy. In order to preserve fat as a critical energy source, the body goes elsewhere to find energy when glucose is not available. The liver begins to break down muscle tissue into amino acids that can be reformulated into glucose (gluconeogenesis), providing fuel to the brain and body.

Being in fat-storage mode also means that when we do finally eat something, it's more likely to be stored as fat so the body is prepared for the next famine. A study conducted by Dan Bernardot, PhD—professor of nutrition and director of the Laboratory for Elite Athlete Performance at Georgia State University—found that female runners and gymnasts who went long periods of time without eating had the highest percentage of body fat. They weren't overweight, but they had more body fat than those who ate at more regular intervals. The longer they went between eating events, the higher their body fat tended to be, especially if they exercised during these periods of calorie deprivation. His research also found that athletes with erratic eating patterns experienced poorer performance and worse concentration than those who ate at regular intervals.

We need to realize that exercise increases the demand for energy. Large, sustained movement requires an increase in calories to provide adequate fuel for the muscles. Without sufficient energy, the body cannot perform at its best—it can only function in a state of stress. This translates to not being able to work out as hard as we want or as long as we want, which means we burn fewer calories and our exercise sessions lose efficiency and effectiveness.

....

IF WE'RE GOING TO FIND THE TIME
TO EXERCISE, IT'S CRITICAL WE FUEL
OUR BODY TO GAIN THE MAXIMUM
BENEFITS FOR THE TIME WE INVEST.

....

A recent study had people exercise once without eating breakfast and then again on another occasion after eating breakfast. Results showed that oxygen consumption and energy (calorie) expenditure was higher after consuming food, and subjects burned more fat as fuel.[44]

The body is amazingly adaptable and will most times do what we ask it to. But it will find workarounds if it doesn't have the right fuel in the right amounts, and these adaptations are often not aligned with our desired outcomes. When we exercise on an empty stomach, it's as if advanced brain creates an action plan based on the rationalization that it's a better way to burn fat, while Sneaky Pete has a different action plan. His plan is to preserve your fat stores. His gets approved, while advanced brain's gets vetoed.

Let's look at how we can properly fuel the body before, during, and after working out.

Before Your Workout: Pre-Fuel

It's ideal to put some glucose in your system anywhere from a few minutes to two hours prior to exercising. Eating beforehand helps maintain blood glucose concentrations during exercise. In addition, it helps you burn a slightly higher rate of fat as fuel.[45] Several studies have shown that eating a low-glycemic meal before exercising burns more fat during exercise than eating one that is high-glycemic in nature.[46, 47] Pre-fueling with a low-glycemic meal before exercise also improves endurance.[48]

EAT A LOW-GLYCEMIC MEAL OR SNACK TO BURN MORE FAT DURING EXERCISE.

The amount of food to eat will depend on how much time you have before your workout. If it's a few minutes before you exercise, have a very light snack. Perhaps half a piece of fruit, a tablespoon or two of nut butter, or a small handful of nuts and dried fruit. Too much food will be hard to stomach once you get moving. If you have more time, have a bigger snack or small T plate meal. You'll want to experiment with which pre-workout foods to eat as well as how much works best for you.

During Your Workout: Stay Fueled

If you're exercising for less than sixty minutes and you've adequately pre-fueled, there should be no need to consume anything other than water. However, endurance exercise of sixty minutes or more may require a glucose replenishment.

Actually, a high-glycemic food or beverage can be a good choice in this instance. It's easily digested and absorbed by the body, making energy rapidly available for the cells. A moderate- or low-glycemic food will work as well.

After Your Workout: Re-Fuel

Pre-fueling ensures glucose levels are within the ideal range to fuel your body adequately during exercise. Because exercise burns glucose and fat, it's important to re-fuel and put energy back into the system to keep blood glucose levels balanced. Try to eat within thirty minutes of completing your exercise session.

A snack composed of protein and carbohydrates or a T plate meal is ideal. It aids the body in recovery in addition to enhancing insulin response.[49] The carbohydrates quickly reestablish blood glucose levels and help replenish glycogen (energy) stores in the muscles and liver. The protein is an essential building block for our muscles.

Most experts recommend eating carbohydrate and protein snacks in a ratio of three to one or four to one after exercise.[50] That means for every gram of protein, you need three or four grams of a carbohydrate. Ideas for easy snacks that contain protein and carbohydrates are any dairy product (milk, cheese, yogurt), a hard-boiled egg and whole grain toast, nut butter and fruit, or a whole grain pita and hummus.

One Step at a Time

As I stated in the chapter introduction, this is a lot of information and a lot of strategies to consider about eating habits. I don't expect you to incorporate everything you've just learned all at once. In fact, you shouldn't. Too much change makes Sneaky Pete wig out. It makes him go on the defensive, and he digs his heels into the comfort of his current behaviors. His resistance overpowers advanced brain, leaving us unsuccessful and extremely frustrated.

This is true not only for changes to our eating habits but for any change we've discussed in this book. The good news is, the final two chapters will help you determine which strategies you should tackle, when, and how. For now, identify one or two strategies you think might be easy for you to begin practicing, then let's learn how to make them stick.

For more information and resources on nutrition for resiliency, go to www.ph-performance.com/plateitout

Success Story

AMY

Amy's Story

As the associate director of a nonprofit caring for people with life-threatening illnesses, Amy manages more than two hundred volunteers, coordinates fundraising efforts, and oversees daily operations at a facility scheduling more than nine thousand client appointments each year. At thirty-three years old, she works each day with patients and their families as they face intense physical and emotional stress.

"Staying focused on fundraising or administrative goals while also maintaining a spirit of compassion and presence for any client who needs a tender connection is challenging," she says. "Keeping the emotions and stress of work at work and not bringing it home is hugely challenging. . . . There's a lot of grief as clients die and relationships end. I feel the temptation to shut off and not connect, but I know that's not how I want to do this job."

Her husband works nights, so her evenings belong to their energetic three-year-old daughter. "When I get home from a long day, it's *all* on me—meals, cleanup, bedtime routine . . . I often feel like I have two full-time jobs."

She struggles to make time for self-care, and me-time often cuts into sleep-time, leaving her exhausted after late nights and early mornings. Her busy schedule and her desire to shed some weight combine to make it easy for her to skip meals during the day and then go out for a single big meal after work, thinking it's the best strategy.

Amy's rEvolution

Amy embraces resiliency training as part of a commitment to self-care—seeking a way to release stress in a healthy way, rather than waiting for it to build to the point of an inescapable and painful meltdown.

Hit the Deck removes the pressure to pick the "right" exercise for workouts; it's easy to simply pull a card and get moving. "Everything you need is in your body—that was a very powerful insight," she says. "You do it for *you* when you need it, on your own timeline." She adds, "My body went from parts—I don't like this part, I don't like that part—to a whole package."

After sixty days of training, Amy is sleeping better and feeling far less vulnerable to the emotional highs and lows at work. She feels better able to connect with her daughter during their evenings together, without feeling overwhelmed or frustrated about her spouse being unavailable to help.

"This process has brought out this strong and powerful me that's always been in there," she says. "I'm me in my body, and I'm my best self."

AMY AFTER SIXTY DAYS
OF RESILIENCY TRAINING

- 20 percent decrease in perceived stress

- 25 percent increase in energy

- 30 percent improvement in quality of sleep

- 30 percent improvement in ability to fall asleep

- Lost 6.7 pounds (2.8 percent) of body fat

- Gained 0.7 pounds of muscle

Chapter 5

CONTROL YOUR ENVIRONMENT

Sean is forty-eight years old, married with three children, and is the vice president of finance at a software and computer systems company. Each weekday morning, he rushes to get ready in the morning, drives to work, takes the elevator up to the third floor, then sits behind his desk in his office. The bulk of his day is made up of conference calls and meetings, often scheduled over lunch. After he gets through as much work as he can, he drives home, sometimes wrestling with whether to stop at the gym on the way. At home he tries to make dinner as often as possible, then spends the evening relaxing with his family. He has a close group of friends who get together for a night out every now and then.

It's a fairly typical life, one many working adults recognize. But a continuous source of stress for Sean is how he feels at the end of each day. Each morning when his alarm goes off, he knows his exercise and nutrition commitments are in his hands. Unfortunately, each evening as he lays his head down on the pillow, he feels frustrated and guilty about not working out and for overeating at lunch and dinner. He makes a promise to himself that tomorrow will be different. He wishes he had more self-discipline and willpower to achieve a healthy, active lifestyle that will allow him to perform to his absolute best and live more in accordance with his values.

Sean assumes he simply needs to be stronger and more committed when it comes to moving more and eating less. He thinks he fails because he is weak and has no willpower, and it frustrates him beyond words. He's successful in so many other areas of his life. Why is taking care of himself so difficult? The constant desire to be more resilient, coupled with his inability to successfully achieve that goal, creates massive amounts of additional stress in his life.

The process of change can create more stress as we try to adapt to new environments or behaviors. When it comes to our health, change usually means doing less of the things we like and more of the things we *don't* like. It can be scary and intimidating. Will we be successful? Our goals may feel out of reach. We think it'll take too long to get there. We don't know where to start. Or we become completely overwhelmed and quit.

In these last two chapters, we'll minimize all these challenges. We'll work with Sneaky Pete as well as your advanced brain to successfully make many of the changes recommended in this book—and likely any other changes you may be trying to make. Change is well within your grasp, and these chapters will set you up to be successful. You'll also learn how to make behavior change that is sustainable over the long term. Being part of the rEvolution means no more committing to a new lifestyle overhaul every Monday morning, only to abandon ship by 6:00 p.m.

In this chapter, we'll specifically focus on how you can use Sneaky Pete and caveman brain to make change. This represents the unconscious elements of change. You'll learn why a lot of the struggles you face are not entirely your fault. You'll learn how to rely less on your advanced brain and "willpower muscles." Chapter six, then, will pick up right on this last point, detailing the most strategic ways to use advanced brain—the conscious aspects. The chapter will ultimately guide you to create an action plan that blends both the unconscious and the conscious aspects—both Sneaky Pete and advanced brain.

That's all to come, but first, let's zero in on how to best use our unconscious brain when making change. When you make so many decisions each day, it's easy for the brain to get exhausted. That often leads you to make easy, expedient choices that thwart your goals. To avoid this, you'll learn how to create microclimates that are *automatically* more conducive to successfully making change in your life. You'll discover how to create optimal defaults that take away the need to make so many small decisions.

This means you'll expend less mental, emotional, and physical energy when integrating these new behaviors into your current habits and routines. You won't have to fight as hard, and you won't be as stressed out about it. You'll have more willpower left for the things that truly matter. A small amount of effort will pay off in large rewards.

The Resiliency rEvolution is not just about Play It Out or eating in a way that balances glucose levels. It's also about finding a way to do these things in a world that's designed to make them difficult, if not unnecessary, to do.

Willpower Is Not so Powerful

Americans name "willpower" and "too much stress" as the top reasons they struggle to meet their health goals. Fewer than one in five people report being successful at making health-related changes, such as exercising more, eating a healthier diet, reducing stress, and losing weight.[1] Many of us desperately want to partake in behaviors that get us closer to our long-term goals, but after a short period of time we get exhausted, quit the plan, and return to our old habits.

What exactly is willpower? We'll be learning a lot about willpower in the next chapter. But in the here and now, one way to define it is "the ability to control impulses." Believe it or not, even Sneaky Pete needed some willpower in order to survive.

Sneaky Pete's survival didn't just rely on his own chances of finding food and avoiding danger. He also needed to be a social creature and get along with his tribe. He needed that whole group of people for survival. They shared resources and took care of each other when they got sick or injured. His odds of making it on his own were slim. The ability to cooperate, fit in with a group, and maintain long-term relationships all required self-control—and willpower.

This means when he was hungry, Sneaky Pete couldn't eat all the food, as tempting as that was. He had to share, and that meant eating less. If he had a conflict with people in the tribe, he couldn't just chuck a rock at their heads. Pissing people off could get him kicked out. He needed a partner to pass on his DNA and help raise his young, but he couldn't mate with just anyone and everyone—as attractive as that caveperson might have been in that bearskin.

As our world has grown more complex, so has our need for additional willpower. Today we have more to resist than urges that would get us kicked out of our "tribes." Now we fight the desire to eat more than we should, to go to the gym instead of watching our favorite show, to not have that cigarette, to not buy that enticing new thing, or to stay focused on work instead of procrastinating online.

Every single decision we make takes precious energy and willpower to accomplish. And each and every day, we make thousands of big and small decisions:

> What time to wake up, whether to hit the snooze button, whether to eat breakfast, what to wear, where to park, whether to say hello to a colleague or pretend to be preoccupied, whether to answer emails first or write that quarterly report, which email to answer first, which to delete, which to put in a folder to be addressed later, where to sit during your 10:00 meeting, whether to eat lunch or work out, where to go for lunch, whether to give

your honest opinion to your boss or sugarcoat it, whom to copy on that email, whether to multitask during a conference call or concentrate, whether to answer the phone or let it go to voicemail, whom to hire, what time to leave work, whether to take your usual route home or take the back roads to avoid traffic, what radio station to listen to, what temperature the car should be, whether to call your mom back now or later, what comfortable clothes to change into, whether to go out for dinner or order in or make something, what to order or make, how much to eat, whether to have dessert, whether to have a beer, whether to watch TV or get more work done, what show to watch, how long to watch, whether to get a snack, what time to go to bed, and whether to brush your teeth or skip it.

That was only thirty-five decisions. Now imagine adding around 2,965 more of them on a daily basis.

Some of these decisions are important, and some are inconsequential. But *all of them* lead to "decision fatigue" and wear out our willpower. We may think only the big decisions take energy, but every choice is an act of willpower, and every act of willpower depletes our willpower reserve.

MAKING DECISIONS WEARS OUT WILLPOWER.

Psychologists have learned that willpower is exactly like a muscle in two ways. One, it gets tired out and exhausted with constant, repeated use. The more we use it, the less power we have. Try doing thousands of squats in a day. Your thigh muscles—like your willpower—are going to burn out. We need to be very strategic about how and when we use willpower when it comes to making behavior change.

Two, willpower can be made stronger with training, like a muscle. It's critical we build this muscle through strategic training over time. We intellectually understand the futility and danger of trying to bench press the heaviest possible weight when first starting a strength-training program. We know the right way is to build our strength over time by beginning with a weight that's just a bit challenging.

Unfortunately, when it comes to making change and using willpower, we immediately try to powerlift when we've only been using tiny hand weights. We try to change several large behaviors all at once, expecting our untrained willpower muscles to be strong enough to stop doing things we've been doing for years or to start doing things we've never done.

A One-Two Punch

When trying to make change, we most often focus on our advanced brain and the *conscious* aspects of behavior modification: using our willpower and self-discipline to either start or stop doing something. In big, general terms, we try to "stop eating so much," "start exercising regularly," "stop drinking coffee," "stop blowing up at a significant other," or "start getting to bed at a reasonable time." But we just learned that relying on willpower alone to make change is a risky proposition because it's not a reliable "muscle" for long-term use.

In the next chapter, we'll learn how to maximize willpower. But there's something critical that needs to be addressed first: what we often fail to recognize is that our environments *unconsciously* impact our rate of success or failure in making lasting change. Sneaky Pete is highly influenced by his external environment, and advanced brain doesn't recognize that fact.

Your advanced brain says you simply have to stop drinking coffee.

But then Sneaky Pete spies about a dozen coffee shops on your way to work, including one with a drive-through right next to your building. The conscious goal crumbles, and advanced brain has no idea why you're suddenly sipping a latte. The only answer it can come up with is that you're weak.

You're not weak. Being in an environment full of temptations means we'll eventually weaken and succumb. No matter how much we want to resist, willpower eventually wears out. But by the same token, when we're in environments where all our options are conducive to a desired behavior, every choice is the right choice. We use very little of our limited supply of willpower.

As you begin to implement some of the strategies you've learned in this book, it's important to acknowledge both the conscious and unconscious aspects of change, both advanced brain and Sneaky Pete. Creating an action plan that focuses only on the conscious aspects and not the unconscious is like creating 50 percent of a business strategy. Devising only half a plan for change—or half a plan for anything—will likely lead to stress, frustration, and failure. By creating action plans that incorporate *both the conscious and unconscious elements of behavior change*, we dramatically increase our odds of success. It's a one-two punch.

Taking Your Cue

Our behaviors are not only shaped by our conscious decisions and goals. They're also influenced by how our brain processes cues about the environments around us: our job, the architecture of our home and office, public policy, city planning, and so on. Our environments subconsciously dictate how and where we move, in addition to how and what we eat—all of which affects our resiliency, performance, and health.

In fact, some scientists have gone so far as to say that "*100% of the increase* in the prevalence of Type 2 diabetes and obesity in the US during the latter half of the 20th century must be attributed to a changing environment interacting with genes, since *0% of the human genome* has changed during this time period."[2] Environment is so influential, research has also shown that when people move to countries where obesity is common, they're more likely to gain weight, while the opposite is also true.[3]

Sean wants to be more active and eat in a way that doesn't add more stress to his body, but the way his office and home climates are set up makes it more challenging. He's living and working in environments that are designed for him to move less and eat more. It's not necessarily one specific element of his environment that's a barrier to his success; it's a combination of many subtle things he's exposed to on a daily basis.

WHAT SEAN DOESN'T KNOW IS, HE'S LIVING AND WORKING IN ENVIRONMENTS THAT ARE STACKED AGAINST HIM.

We don't just eat because of hunger or nutrient needs. We're also eating in response to cues around us, many of which we're completely unaware of. Fast-food companies have known about the unconscious influence of our environments for years and have spent a great deal of money learning about our unconscious behaviors and how to use them to their advantage. They have figured out all the nuances necessary to maximize their bottom line: where we're sitting in the restaurant, who is with us, the décor, what paint colors are used, and even what type of lighting makes us spend and eat more. Restaurants know what size and color of plate, type of drinking glasses and dinnerware, style of music, and even what foods are named in the menu get us to eat more.

For items in the grocery store, marketers know exactly how to package and present foods in a way that lights up our brain's reward pathway and makes us buy them. By using bright colors, appetizing images, ideal product shape, and just the right words on packages, they know Sneaky

Pete can't resist their products. Grocery stores put staples such as dairy, eggs, and meat as far away from the door as possible so we have to walk past thousands of other tempting foods that aren't on our shopping list. Of course, we'll put a few of them in our basket.

Our environments also dictate how much movement we get. Most workplaces have elevators front and center, while you need a map to find the stairwells. Many people live in neighborhoods designed in a way that makes walking to buy groceries or run errands impossible. Stores are located far away from residential areas, and sidewalks are completely missing. Driving is the only way to get just about anywhere. Even people who live close to stores don't think twice about hopping in the car to go a couple blocks. Bike lanes may be nonexistent, as well as bike racks or storage facilities.

Many of our children have been unfortunate victims of some disastrous environments. Many schools have taken physical education out of their curriculums and cut back on recess, ensuring our kids get little to no physical activity each day. School lunches have gone from bad to worse, relying on highly processed, prepackaged foods. A large number of schools have fast-food chains in their cafeterias, giving our children daily access to low-nutrient, high-calorie food. And many after-school activities are funded by the sales of sodas and sugar-sweetened beverages. What these environments have done to their health, weight, stress levels, and cognitive performance is tragic.

The good news is, some environments can also be more conducive to living in a way that's good for resiliency. A great example is the work Dan Buettner has done to identify "Blue Zones"—geographic hot spots of longevity around the world, where people live longer and experience fewer health problems. Research shows a series of common lifestyle behaviors that contribute to longer, healthier lives for people in those communities: being a culture of constant moderate exercise, consuming a plant-based diet, regularly eating legumes, no smoking, making family a top priority, and keeping a high level of social engagement. Buettner says people living in Blue Zones live "rewardingly inconvenient" lives by walking most places they need to go, doing their own yard work, and doing things in the kitchen by hand, such as kneading bread. It's proof that one environment can help us as much as another can hinder us.

Optimal Defaults

Sneaky Pete loves being a sloth, pigging out, and generally getting as much pleasure from unhealthy habits as possible. He lives in the moment and is primarily concerned with "present self." His philosophy is that you only live once, so you better enjoy it while it lasts. Go ahead and eat dessert, watch TV instead of working out, charge that vacation on the credit card, and have that one-night stand.

Advanced brain is focused on "future self" and constantly trying to get Sneaky Pete on board with the program of eating less, moving more, getting to bed on time, saving for retirement, and regretting the morning after. Advanced brain understands why all these habits are good for you. It's all about delaying gratification and sticking to a long-term plan to get a bigger payoff later. (We'll discuss present self versus future self in more detail in the next chapter.)

We know advanced brain has to work hard 24/7 to keep us in line. And we know how quickly and easily willpower is exhausted, especially when our environments seem stacked against us. So it makes sense to prioritize the things in our lives that really need and deserve this precious willpower resource.

We need to save our willpower to support the big changes in our lives, such as the overarching decision to work out regularly or eat more vegetables. If we want to achieve those big goals, we can't burn up our willpower on the little details, such as whether to take the stairs or the elevator, or what snack to eat in the afternoon. We need the little details to require no thought—they should fall into place by default.

OPTIMAL DEFAULTS PRESERVE WILLPOWER.

Some say Albert Einstein had a closet full of the same suits so he didn't have to waste brainpower on such trivialities as deciding what to wear every morning. However debatable that may be, I like the theory. If it's true, it means he created a daily default when it came to getting dressed. He didn't have to stand there every morning and use mental energy to figure out what to put on and whether paisley matched plaid. He opened the door, grabbed one of his only options, didn't think about, and moved on to more pressing matters. He preserved the energy of his advanced brain and willpower.

Creating a default activity, where we don't have to wrestle with a choice, saves willpower. When we create a default activity aligned with a behavior change we're trying to make, it's called an *optimal default*. Optimal defaults almost guarantee our behaviors and choices support our values and goals.

SET YOURSELF UP SO YOU DON'T HAVE TO USE WILLPOWER IN THE FIRST PLACE.

When we have optimal defaults in place, we actually have to go *out of our way* and expend extra effort to do something that doesn't match our goals. Sneaky Pete is all about keeping it easy—he's not about "extra effort." So he falls right in line, totally unaware he's doing what advanced brain wants him to do.

An optimal default means it takes extra effort to *opt out* of a good decision. For example, when looking at organ donor programs, the default makes a large impact. In countries where people have to opt in to donate their organs, the participation rate is a mere 15 percent. In countries where donation is the default, and people must *opt out* if they don't want to participate, 98 percent of people participate.[4] In each case, the individual has full control over the choice. But the optimal default for donation may just save lives.

We see similar results with pension plans. When the default is set for automatic enrollment, and people need to opt out if they don't want to participate, enrollment is close to 100 percent. When the default option is to manually sign up for the plan, only about 50 percent enroll.[5] Again, in both instances, everyone has the same choice: take part or not. But when enrollment is the default setting, you see participation rates that no education program could dream to get.

And that's the key. Now we have both brains on board, even though Sneaky Pete's goals usually differ from advanced brain's. To keep them both on board, we need to create "microclimates" full of optimal defaults where we work and live to keep tricking him into participating in our desired behaviors. I'm not talking about remodeling your home or office. I'm referring to simple changes to your environment that will gradually shift your daily behaviors to match your goals. With microclimates of optimal defaults, you will unconsciously—without realizing what you're doing— become more active and eat the right amounts and types of food.

MICROCLIMATES FULL OF OPTIMAL DEFAULTS MAKE A DESIRED BEHAVIOR AUTOMATIC.

You can set up microclimates for yourself, or they can be set up for you—perhaps without you even realizing it. When our daughter was a child, we would let her choose whatever snacks she wanted out of the pantry. She thought she was quite independent and in control. What she didn't know was that *all* the snacks in the pantry were healthy options. Whatever choice she made would be the right one for her health. It was a microclimate of optimal defaults. (And yes, we chose our own snacks from the same pantry, so it was a microclimate for us too.)

Optimal Defaults as Public Policy

On a much larger scale, optimal defaults have been shown to be extremely effective in a number of public policy scenarios. We talked a bit about trans fat in chapter four. Trans fat, a form of hydrogenated oil, was developed in the late 1800s and soon became a staple in our daily diets. (Remember the large tub of Crisco our mothers had?) Food manufacturers loved the fat because it acted as a preservative and extended shelf life, and consumers loved the taste and texture when it was used for deep frying.

Unfortunately, numerous research studies in the 1990s found a correlation between consuming trans fats, an increase in LDL (bad) cholesterol levels, a decrease in HDL (good) cholesterol levels, and a higher incidence of heart disease. Public education programs were launched to let consumers know they should decrease their intake of trans fats. Health advocacy groups lobbied restaurants to stop using them in their deep fryers.

Then in 2002, the US government released a statement declaring there is no safe level of trans fat consumption. It recommended that people cut them out of their diets or limit consumption. Soon the US government required trans fats be listed on nutrition labels.

Many food manufacturers reformulated their products to remove or reduce the dangerous fats. In 2006, New York became the first US city to pass legislation limiting the use of trans fats in restaurants. As we discussed, the USDA is currently pushing for them to be banned completely while Argentina, Austria, Denmark, Iceland, and Switzerland have already done it.

If the strategy for decreasing the intake of trans fats had stopped at the public education program for us to "simply stop eating them," they would still be around. We'd still be consuming them, even though we'd been told about the dangers. But because the government created an environment conducive to change, making an optimal default of little to no access to trans fats, we're almost all complying with the recommendation.

It's now difficult to find trans fats anywhere. Most consumers haven't noticed a taste difference in the healthier default options. Now every time you walk into a grocery store, you don't have fight Sneaky Pete over whether to buy the forbidden trans fat crackers or the ones without that are much healthier. The optimal default for you, me, and everyone pretty much makes avoiding trans fat a no-brainer.

OPTIMAL DEFAULTS *LITERALLY* MAKE DESIRED BEHAVIOR A NO-BRAINER.

Cigarette smoking has also gone through a very similar process. Over time, it's become more difficult to engage in the unhealthy behavior. You can't smoke in many indoor environments, you can no longer buy cigarettes in vending machines, advertising is limited, and the price continues to increase. More and more, the optimal default is to not smoke.

If optimal defaults can achieve health goals across an entire nation, then they can surely achieve health goals in your own life.

A Deeper Look

Let's go back to Sean and dissect his day step by step at work and at home. On the surface, there's nothing unusual about his average day. However, a deeper look reveals that Sean, like many of us, is living and working in environments with disastrous defaults. Food has become "eatertainment," portion sizes are huge, there's too much access to the wrong foods, too little access to the right foods, and little to no physical exertion required of us. If we look a bit closer at Sean's environments, we can uncover the multitude of forces working against his chances of successfully training to be more resilient. More importantly, we can also find opportunities for him to create microclimates of optimal defaults during his day so he can avoid these obstacles.

As you will see, some of these recommended optimal defaults are more absolute than others. Replacing your rolling office chair absolutely guarantees you'll get up and move more often. But other optimal defaults are not absolute and will become default with practice. For instance, even if you decide the optimal default is to take the stairs instead of the elevator, it doesn't mean the elevator disappears.

The goal is to reduce our decision-making efforts, as you can do by predetermining once and for all you will no longer take the elevator. No more rushing into the building, already late, and listening to both your brains argue over the stairs or the elevator. As you execute the "take the stairs, not the elevator" decision over and over every day, it will quickly become a no-brainer, as if the elevator really did disappear.

Let's see how this works.

What Sean Does

Sean finally manages to rouse himself at 6:45. It's barely enough time to get out of bed, grab some coffee, and get himself and his family ready for the day.

The Issue

Sean hit the snooze button three times, one more than his daily average of two. He's always had trouble getting out of bed in the morning—to the point where he anticipates being too tired to wake up and sets the alarm a half hour before he really needs to. He's gotten to where he hits the snooze button without fully waking up. When he is conscious of pushing the button, he and Sneaky Pete start to time-bargain: if Sean skips breakfast or a workout, he can get some extra sleep.

Sean thinks the nine-minute intervals of extra sleep really help; they feel like "bonus sleep." In truth, they actually do the opposite. We go through several stages and cycles of sleep each night, going progressively deeper into each cycle. These later, deeper cycles that take place close to morning are the ones where quality sleep happens. This deep sleep is where we get the best recovery, both mentally as well as physically. Being roused out of this deep, restorative sleep to have a few minutes of light sleep is a horrible tradeoff.

Staying in bed longer also adds to the urgency and chaos that defines most of his mornings. Even one nine-minute interlude of snoozing can throw off his entire morning—let alone two or three. Getting more quality, uninterrupted sleep may also diminish his need for caffeine in the morning, yet another thing that adds to his stress and cortisol.

Optimal Default

In the evening, set your alarm clock for the absolute, *real* time you need to be up and out of bed in the morning. Don't set it back half an hour just to make room for a couple snoozes. Get as much deep sleep as you can.

Then place the clock across the room—not on a nightstand at arm's reach. When the alarm goes off, you'll have to get out of bed and walk across the room. These few seconds of movement will get your blood and energy flowing, allowing you to wake up enough to remember your commitment to get up on time. If you're more fully awake, and if you're already out of bed, you'll feel more able to get started with your day without wasting time on snoozes.

What Sean Does

He jumps into his car to drive to work. When he arrives, he circles the parking lot several times to find the closest available spot. Just when he's about to snap, he finally nabs the ultimate spot—right by the front door.

The Issue

With the way cities are designed, most of our jobs are located a fair distance from where we live, so we either have to drive or take public transportation to get there. Sneaky Pete, however, stepped out his front door and walked to work. He either worked in the vicinity of his living site or traveled by foot to hunt or gather resources. He didn't have the opportunity to sit behind the wheel of a car, stewing in cortisol as he fought rush hour traffic to find a herd of antelope.

Optimal Default

Many of you don't have any control over your commuting options, but some of you might. Or perhaps you have more control than you realize to make getting to and from work a healthier activity.

Many people aren't even aware they live a bikeable distance to work because we live in an environment where driving is the default for just about everything. If you live close enough to your workplace, you could walk or bike to work even one or two days a week. If you live too far to bike or walk, maybe you could telecommute from home some days, saving yourself the stressful drive and using that time instead to take a morning stroll.

Consider public transportation, if you have the option. Driving to work likely requires you to walk no more than a few steps to and from your car. But public transportation likely involves a decent walk to and from the drop-offs. By making public transportation your default, you gain several opportunities to put your body in motion.

If you already take public transportation, you could make it your optimal default to get off one stop farther away from your usual stop. Want a more absolute optimal default? I know couples who have gone down to one car so they're more likely to bike, walk, or take public transportation.

And even if driving to work is your only option, you still have an opportunity to create an optimal default. Make "your spot" farther away from the entrance so you automatically walk more, both coming and going. Plus, choosing an inconvenient spot means it'll almost always be available. It'll save you time—not to mention the frustrated squirt of cortisol—if you don't circle the lot multiple times, trying to find the "ultimate" parking spot.

What Sean Does

Sean makes the short stroll into the building, then rides the elevator to his office on the third floor. (In fact, he'll go on to use the elevator all day long whenever he needs to get from floor to floor.)

The Issue

We often take elevators up one or two floors, while out-of-the-way stairwells go relatively unused. Most of us take the elevators because we think it's the fastest way to travel. You may be shocked to learn it's not. A study done at a Canadian hospital found that when doctors took the stairs instead of the elevator, it saved them an average of fifteen minutes out of each workday.[6] The stairs are often more efficient because elevators have to stop for people to get on or off, and there's no wait for a lift, especially during peak times.

Optimal Default

Always take the stairs instead of the elevator or escalator. If it's not possible to walk fifty-seven flights up a high-rise building, simply get off the elevator a few floors before your stop and take the stairs the rest of the way.

The great thing about always taking the stairs is that it gives you built-in opportunities to Play It Out by sprinting. It's an optimal default inside an optimal default. (A fast sprint saves even more time too.) Even using the stairs at a leisurely pace is a great way to get much-needed movement—breaking up long periods of sitting and stimulating circulation and energy in the body.

What Sean Does

As he's tending to his many tasks for the morning, Sean rolls his chair around his office space to grab things he needs. Instead of walking over to one of his coworkers sitting not far away, he sends an email to ask an important question. He prints out a report necessary for one of his meetings, but instead of walking over to get it right away, he waits until he's on his way to the meeting to grab it from the printer.

The Issue

Sneaky Pete didn't work out like mad for twenty to thirty minutes, then sit for the rest of the day. We are a species designed to be constantly in motion, doing short bursts of physical activity multiple times throughout the day. Hunting and gathering for the basic necessities of life required a tremendous amount of daily exertion, and this mandatory movement was part of day-to-day life until very recently.

Most of our jobs now require very little physical exertion. The average deskbound American takes only five thousand to six thousand steps per day[7] (about two and a half to three miles), while Sneaky Pete put in around twenty thousand (about ten miles). Even in modern times, we've gone from agricultural and industrial economies necessitating large amounts of physical labor, to those of information and technology. Instead of taxing our muscles, we're working our brain while sitting behind desks for a large part of the day.

Many of us spend close to eight hours sitting in comfortable chairs, rolling them about on wheels instead of simply standing up to retrieve a piece of paper from the filing cabinet. We place plastic mats under our chairs because we don't want to even deal with a little friction from rolling on carpet. The ability to call, text, email, or message someone means we don't have to stand up and walk over to a coworker to communicate. When we do need to walk somewhere, such as to the department printer, we'll hold out until we absolutely must get up.

Optimal Default

You'd be surprised at how much movement you can incorporate into your desk job—and how easily. One, get an office chair that doesn't roll. This means you automatically have to stand up to get things just out of reach. Another option is to use an exercise ball as your chair.

Two, make a rule that if you can see or hear someone, you have to walk over there instead of emailing or texting. Actually, you may be able to gather more information in a shorter amount of time than if you tried to clarify things through multiple emails or texts. (Who doesn't want to cut down on the endless emails, anyway?)

Three, remember that printing something is your cue to take a "movement break" to go get it. Make a special trip—don't leave it sitting there until you have some other trip to make.

What Sean Does

Before lunch, Sean has a long conference call. He makes himself comfortable, then ends up sitting for an hour as the call goes on and on.

The Issue

Sitting is the new smoking. Study after study has warned of the dangers to our health from sitting for extended periods of time. High blood glucose levels, excess fat around the midsection, increased blood pressure, and abnormal cholesterol levels are all consequences of sitting for too long, as is an increased risk of death from cardiovascular disease and cancer.[8]

In contrast, movement increases heart rate, which increases circulation. A higher rate of circulation means more forms of energy, such as glucose and oxygen, are delivered to the brain and body—increasing energy, focus, and productivity.

Because of this, moving regularly throughout the day is a *more* productive way of working, not less. As we know, movement is also the best way to rid our body of the stress hormones that accumulate as the day goes on.

Optimal Default

On the phone = on your feet. Talking = walking. Make being on the phone your cue to stand up. Stand up and pace around your office or workspace while talking. Or take it outside your workspace. I've got clients who walk the skyways in Minnesota during regularly scheduled conference calls, and they get up to sixty minutes of movement while working.

What Sean Does

Next, Sean has a two-hour meeting scheduled over lunch. A buffet is set up in the meeting room. He gets in line, grabs a large plate, and starts scooping food onto it as he moves along. His plate quickly begins to fill—many options look delicious. As he approaches the end of the line, his plate is full, but then he sees an entrée that looks better than anything he's taken so far. He manages to find plate space for it.

The Issue

Imagine how much Sneaky Pete's eyes would bug out over a buffet—such a huge array of deliciously prepared calories to consume! His stomach and brain would be screaming at him to try everything and eat as much as possible.

When we're exposed to a variety of foods instead of a singular option, we're more likely to take and eat a larger amount. Research has shown that if people are given three different flavors of yogurt to choose from, they will eat 23 percent more than if they're offered only one flavor.[9]

Even the *perception* of variety can make us eat more. Brian Wansink and his colleagues from Cornell University's Food and Brand Lab gave people an assortment of 300 M&M candies. Those who were given a bowl with ten different colors ate 43 percent more than those who got a bowl with just seven colors.[10] There was no real variety, beyond different colors of the same exact candy, but color alone was enough to make people reach for more. (Wansink has written a wonderful book, *Mindless Eating: Why We Eat More Than We Think*, that I highly recommend. It's both informative and entertaining.)

Optimal Default

When eating at a buffet, begin with a reconnaissance mission—without a plate—to view all your options. And remember: even at a buffet, you need to Plate It Out. That's still your optimal default. Make a mental note of what you want your protein source to be, what you'll choose for your fruit and/or vegetable, and what grains you'll put on your plate. Also factor in if there's dessert and whether you'll need to leave some essentials off your plate to accommodate for the extras.

After you have everything planned out, next scout out a smaller plate or bowl, if available. (We'll discuss why below.) With your plan in mind and plate in hand, then start adding to your plate, keeping in mind how many fistfuls you need of each item. Beware of large scoops and serving spoons that make a "helping" much bigger than you want it to be.

Don't let Sneaky Pete talk you into taking the very first item you see on a buffet. Researchers have found we're more likely to take the first food we see on a buffet line. They created two different buffet lines for a group of people. Half the group was sent through a line that began with cheesy scrambled eggs, potatoes, bacon, cinnamon rolls, granola, yogurt, and fruit. The other half of the group was sent through a line with the same foods, but in the reverse order. In both lines, more than 75 percent of people dished up the first food they saw, and 66 percent selected the first three foods they saw.

The study also found that people who took the healthier items first ate less overall than those who started with the cheesy eggs. Those who started with cheesy eggs put 31 percent more food on their plate.[11] A broader implication from this study is that if we start by putting healthier foods such as vegetables on our plates at buffets—or any mealtime—we may end up with fewer calories on our plates overall.

What Sean Does

After dishing up at the buffet, Sean realizes he accidentally took too much food, so he makes a mental note not to finish all of it. During the meeting, a highly emotional conflict takes place, and no one is in agreement on how to handle it. Before he knows it, Sean has cleaned his whole plate, and now he's uncomfortably full.

The Issue

We're quite often mindless when we eat. At work and home, we're constantly multitasking while eating: participating in meetings, working on the computer, driving, running through an airport, watching TV, talking on the phone, or going through the mail. We rarely sit down without any distractions to eat a meal, free to tune into how it makes us feel and when we're full.

Distractions not only make us miss our body's satiety cues, but can also create food associations. How many of us *have* to have popcorn when we go to a movie? Do you find yourself snacking in front of the TV or while reading a book? These are examples of food associations, default behaviors we've created by associating two unrelated activities together (such as going to a movie and eating). If we regularly eat while engaging in another activity, that activity very quickly becomes our cue to eat, even though we may not be physically hungry.

Eating while distracted can also result in eating more than we normally would. A recent review of twenty-four studies suggested that when we're focused on a mentally taxing task, our perception of taste decreases and we eat more food.[12] That is, a heavy cognitive load, such as a challenging business meeting, competes with sensory information such as taste or fullness. We find items such as sweet or salty foods less satisfying, and we end up eating more of them in order to satiate our desire for these flavors and tastes.

Optimal Default

Make eating something you do as a singular event, meaning all distractions are removed. This has several implications at work and at home.

Don't schedule work meetings over lunch. If a lunch meeting is necessary, at least schedule it with enough time to eat first, then get down to business second. Or if you must eat during a meeting, be sure to carefully Plate It Out or order a light meal. If you do find yourself eating distractedly, at least there will be less food to begin with.

For regular workday lunches on your own, take a few minutes to leave your desk and eat in a designated eating area. Don't eat with one hand on your sandwich and the other on your mouse or track pad.

Don't use your mealtime to catch up on last night's episode of your favorite show either. In today's connected world, our TV is always with us—on our phones, tablets, and computers. Whether at home or at work, eating in front of a television increases the chance we'll eat high-calorie and low-nutrient foods because of all the advertising. It also increases the chance we'll overeat those foods because we're engrossed in the show and not paying attention to our body's taste and satiety cues. We might only stop when the all the food is gone.

By avoiding any distractions and keeping the focus on food, you'll more likely listen to how much your body is telling you to eat and you'll better enjoy the taste. You won't place unnecessary stress on the body by accidentally overeating, and you'll avoid the subsequent food coma.

What Sean Does

After the lunch meeting, Sean has yet another conference call. While he's sitting and listening, he mindlessly grabs a couple chocolates from the dish always at his desk.

The Issue

Sneaky Pete spied an easy source of fat and sugar on Sean's desk and told him to seize the opportunity. Availability and proximity of food affect how much we'll eat. The less effort it takes, or the more convenient it is, the more we consume. When food is sitting right in front of us, the simple sight of it—not to mention the potential smell—stimulates our caveman brain to want it.

Another one of Wansink's (somewhat diabolical) experiments took place during Administrative Professionals' Week. He and his colleagues placed glass dishesof Hershey's Kisses on admins' desks as gifts. All the dishes had covers, but some of the dishes were clear, and some were opaque. Each night after the admins went home, the researchers counted how many chocolates were eaten and secretly refilled the dishes. They did this for two weeks.

They found if the candy dishes were clear, making the chocolates visible, admins ate 71 percent more often, resulting in seventy-seven additional calories each day.[13] (It may not seem like much, but over a year, that would add up to a weight gain of over five pounds. Thanks, Wansink.)

They did another variation of the study where they placed a dish of chocolate candies either on an admin's desk or two meters away on a filing cabinet. When the candies were on their desks, the admins ate 5.6 more of them each day than when they had to stand up and walk over to get them.[14]

The chocolates on Sean's desk not only tempt him, but their higher glycemic nature also spikes his blood glucose levels. As you know, a spike in glucose is always followed by a crash that stresses his body and negatively affects his afternoon productivity. Because being on the phone distracted him, he wasn't even conscious about taking the first one, let alone the fourth.

(Bonus points if you noticed that during this time, Sean also missed a valuable opportunity for on the phone = on your feet during his conference call.)

Optimal Default

If you want to minimize any unnecessary snacking or eating, keep food out of sight and at a distance. For extras such as chocolates, perhaps don't buy or have them in the first place, but if you do, keep them in a desk drawer or store them down the hall in a communal refrigerator. Out of sight, out of reach, out of mind.

Then again, if it's a challenge to consistently remember to eat every three hours, keep healthy food close and within sight on your desk. Or you could even find yourself a snack buddy, taking turns buying the snacks and reminding each other to eat regularly to maintain blood glucose levels.

What Sean Does

In the late afternoon, Sean facilitates a regular monthly meeting. There are twelve people in attendance besides himself, and they all sit around a conference table. As the meeting progresses, he can tell he's losing people—they're tired, disengaged, multitasking, distracted, and lacking focus. It's been a long, busy day for everyone.

The Issue

When I ask audiences what they do most during the workday, the answer is always "sit in meetings." Many of you rush from one long meeting to the next. Most meetings go over their allotted time on your schedule, which means you and your colleagues are constantly running late. You don't have time to grab your between-meal snacks, have lunch, or even go to the bathroom.

When I probe further, many people tell me these meetings are not very productive and there are too many of them. People in meetings are constantly multitasking, there's often no agenda, and too much time is spent on topics that should be addressed in a follow-up meeting or one on one.

If you tell Sneaky Pete he's got sixty minutes to get something done, he's going to conserve his energy and pace himself. He'll take the full sixty minutes if you give it to him, even though he could have successfully finished in half the time.

So why are meetings automatically scheduled for sixty minutes? I guarantee, if you schedule a meeting for an hour, it will take *at least* that long.

Optimal Default

Break the sixty-minute habit. I've had leaders within companies start scheduling fifty-minute meetings, announcing to everyone in the room exactly what time it will end. They then call for everyone's focus and engagement, asking them to work hard to accomplish everything they need to. To help this goal, they also very clearly communicate the agenda, so people know what to focus on. Many other clients have told me they've even gone down to forty-five-minute meetings. They still do the exact same amount of work that they did in sixty-minute meetings, but in less time.

Not only is this less-than-sixty strategy more productive, it also allows people several minutes to get to their next meeting on time and to get some much-needed mental and physical recovery as they travel from one to the next.

Another optimal default is to ask people to stand up and stretch or move during meetings. It keeps everyone's energy and focus at higher levels. It takes only sixty seconds but makes the meeting more productive in the long run. I regularly build in moments for people to stand up and move around while discussing a concept during my presentations because it's a great strategy to keep people focused and engaged. You can also do meetings without chairs or conduct a walking meeting if you're with one or two other colleagues. (Remember, talking = walking.)

What Companies and Leaders Can Do

Workers represent half the global population and spend about one-third of their lives at work.[15] This means the workplace is the *perfect* setting to make an impact on people's health, resiliency, and performance.

A culture shift toward resiliency does not have to be expensive and complex. In fact, many action steps cost no money whatsoever and are simple to implement. Here are some ideas to consider.

- Conduct walking meetings when there are one to three people in attendance.

- Have standing meetings, get rid of chairs, or designate standing and sitting times.

- Post signs that promote taking the stairs.

- Have Tennis Shoe Tuesday or Sneaker Wednesday, which encourages walking or standing meetings in addition to taking the stairs and getting more movement throughout the day.

- Have healthy food at meetings instead of junk food or sweets.

- Schedule time for both movement and snack breaks during long meetings as well as workouts during multiple-day meetings.

- Have Hit the Deck breaks throughout the day, either as individuals or as a group. Many leaders within organizations go around office areas and lead people through a few cards as a stress break.

- Offer employees standing workstations or create them simply by setting laptops on cardboard boxes. (Ensure they are ergonomically optimal.)

- Purchase or create walking workstations for treadmills. (Check out my PowerHousePerform YouTube channel to see my video on how to create one for less than twenty dollars.)

- Offer smaller portions in the cafeteria.

- Switch from large plates in the cafeteria to smaller ones.

- Swap out large glassware for smaller, taller, skinnier glasses.

- Use smaller silverware.

- Put healthy food options in prominent positions in the cafeteria and put less healthy options in out-of-the-way places.
- Put healthy food and beverage options in vending machines.
- Minimize the amount of caffeinated and alcoholic beverages offered during meetings and events. Offer healthy alternatives.

As a speaker, I conduct anything from one-hour keynote sessions all the way up to full-day training programs to improve employee resiliency, performance, and health. They work well as stand-alone sessions or perfect additions to leadership development programs, annual meetings, and events. For booking information, visit www.ph-performance.com.

What Sean Does

Finally, at the end of the day, Sean gets into his car to head home. On the way, he suddenly remembers he told himself and his family he would stop off at the gym to squeeze in a quick short-burst interval training workout. Unfortunately, he forgot his gym bag and doesn't have any exercise clothes with him. He decides he'll maybe do an exercise video when he gets home instead.

The Issue

Sean has a lot to do in the mornings, with getting himself and his family ready. There are a lot of bags to pack: three lunch bags, three backpacks, two briefcases, and so on . . . Sometimes one little gym bag gets overlooked, especially because he doesn't need to pack it every single day.

And especially because Sneaky Pete is no help whatsoever in this type of situation. He can't fathom why we'd ever want to take time *now* to prepare for something we might do *later*—something he'll likely talk us out of later, at that. Advanced brain may know it's a great idea to pack the gym bag now so we're ready to commit to that workout on the way home. But when we have nothing but coffee for breakfast, and when cortisol levels are shooting through the roof, Sneaky Pete is calling the shots.

So out the door we go without the gym bag.

Optimal Default

Keep a few spare sets of exercise clothes in your car or desk drawer. It ensures you're never lacking the gear to get your workout done. Another option is to pack your gym bag each evening (along with your lunch and snacks for the next day), then put it smack dab in front of the door. Make it so obvious, you'll trip over it in the morning before you leave.

And if you can never seem to remember workout clothes for the gym, don't forget that Hit the Deck doesn't require clothes, gear, or shoes—and saves you a stop at the gym. Make Hit the Deck your optimal default for after-work exercise. So if you realize you somehow stepped right over your bag this morning without seeing it, simply stay and do a couple cards before heading home. Or get home, grab the kids, and enjoy some fun doing cards together.

What Sean Does

When Sean arrives home, everyone is hungry, clamoring, "What's for dinner?" It takes him and his wife a while to finally settle on what to make. But then he realizes they're out of milk and a few crucial ingredients, so he gets back in the car and drives to the grocery store a couple blocks from their house. While making his way to the back of the store where the dairy case is located, he passes by a display of dazzlingly appetizing desserts and grabs one to take home.

The Issue

When you don't plan ahead for meals (keep groceries on hand at home or bring something with you to work), you are forced to become a caveman again. You start searching and hunting for food, happy with the first thing that comes along, even if it's not the healthiest or tastiest! (I've eaten stale, smashed, half-eaten energy bars from the depths of my briefcase in times of desperation. Or have you ever found yourself so hungry you buy one of those nasty sandwiches that sit all day under a heat lamp at a gas station?)

For busy families, a weekly meal plan and shopping list is a must. Sneaky Pete often tells us it takes too much time to make a meal plan and buy the food, saying we'll be fine by winging it each night. But then when dinnertime comes, he's the first one whining when there's no food in the house and no one knows what to make. You end up in the grocery store (if not the fast-food drive-through). The reality is, going to the store several times during the week to "just pick up a few things" means we spend *more total time shopping* than if we would have made one preplanned trip.

Going to the store when we're hungry also increases the chances that Pete puts high-fat, high-sugar foods into the cart—he's starving! Going to the store around the dinner hour also means we're battling all the other people who didn't plan ahead and are hunting and gathering after a long, stressful day at work.

Making matters worse, grocery stores are strategically landscaped to get you to spend as many dollars as possible. The store is laid out in a way that increases the odds we'll buy impulse items as well as the more profitable, highly processed foods. In the produce department, you'll now see things like caramel, whipped cream, and chocolate for dipping, and pastry shells or cakes to top with fruit. The end caps of each aisle feature chips, sugared beverages, cookies, and other junk foods. Both sides of the checkout lane are full of candy, sweets, and sodas. Someone walking into the grocery for one or two items will very likely walk out with a bag or two, typically filled with less than the healthiest choices.

Optimal Default

Pick one day of the week to create a simple meal plan and make a shopping run. Creating a menu for the week decreases the daily stress of answering the question, "What's for dinner?" With a plan, you already know the answer, and you've got the ingredients ready to go.

Stick to the shopping list—as well as to the perimeter of the store. Be aware that the middle of the store contains many of the highly profitable, highly processed foods. The edges are where many of the whole foods are located: fresh fruits and vegetables, dairy products, and meats, in addition to bulk products such as beans and grains. If you do go into the aisles, look both high and low. The products right at eye level are placed there because they're the most profitable for the store. Unfortunately for us, they're also the most highly processed and contain the most sugar, fat, and salt. The less-profitable, less-processed foods are located toward the bottom.

Make sure you've got some food in your stomach before you go. If you go hungry, Sneaky Pete will be in charge no matter how much you're trying to get your advanced brain to override him. He'll be throwing a party in the store with his friends Ben & Jerry, Famous Amos, and Mrs. Fields, while putting up to 44 percent more high-calorie foods in your cart.[16]

And yes, you're right—there's another opportunity for an optimal default in this scenario: Sean lives only a couple blocks from the grocery store. Unlike most people, he can walk to the store when he needs milk and a couple other items.

For some people in some neighborhoods, it actually takes as much time to walk to the store as it does to drive, find a parking space, and make their way into the store. At peak times after work when the lot is packed with people desperate for meal ideas, walking may even be faster—certainly less stressful.

If you happen to be in a neighborhood where the grocery or convenience store is close to your home, make walking the optimal default whenever you need only a few items. As a side benefit, it'll force you to stick to your list, as you can't carry back bags and bags of impulse items. (But the groceries you do carry will add a little resistance training for the trek back home.)

What Sean Does

When dinner's ready, Sean sets the table with large dinner plates, wide drinking glasses, and oversized serving scoops and dinner forks.

The Issue

Which one of these solid black circles is bigger?

The Delboeuf Illusion

Actually, they're both the same size. This illusion is an example of how our brain uses surrounding information to estimate the size of an object. We perceive a difference in the two identical black circles merely because circles of differing diameters surround them.

Now imagine an identical portion of food placed on a large dinner plate and on a small salad plate. Which portion will look bigger—especially to Sneaky Pete? We perceive the same amount of food placed on each plate differently.

This optical illusion affects our portion sizes and the amount of food we eat. As amazing as our brain is, it's incredibly horrible at estimating portion sizes. We're subconsciously influenced by the size and shape of the dinnerware and tools we're eating with.

We're more likely to put more food onto a large plate or into a large bowl than if we were to use a smaller one. We try to "fill" the large plate, and that takes a large amount of food. Putting less food on a large plate looks pathetic. We feel as if we were denying ourselves, and Sneaky Pete doesn't like it.

We will subconsciously—without even realizing what we're doing— eat 22 percent less when using a smaller ten-inch plate than a larger twelve-inch one.[17] But when given larger serving bowls, scoops, plates, and glasses, we'll unknowingly consume more calories. Even *professors of nutrition science* (who should know these things) are not immune to these biases. When several of them were invited to an ice cream social that was actually an experiment, they ate 53 percent more ice cream when using a larger scoop and bowl.[18]

We even have problems when it comes to something so innocuous as judging whether a taller, thinner container holds more than a shorter, wider one. We think the taller, skinnier container is bigger and holds more, even when the volume of both containers is exactly the same. This makes us inadvertently pour 30 percent more into a short, wide glass.[19] Even professional bartenders are fooled and typically pour more alcohol into short, wide glasses than tall, skinny ones. (Now you know what kind of glass to ask for when you go out to a bar. You're welcome.)

Here's another brain bias: Which one of these lines is longer? To most people, the vertical line seems longer than the horizontal one, but they're both exactly the same length.

Our caveman brain will estimate the vertical line as taller because whenever our ancestors came across a potential predator, they perceived the level of danger by its height. When the predator was taller, they perceived it as more of a threat than if it was wider. To this day, we're hardwired to pay more attention to height and to focus more on distance from top to bottom than side to side.

Another good example of this mind trick is the St. Louis Gateway Arch. It's the same distance wide as it is tall (630 feet), but most of us think it's taller than it is wider. Not many people visit the arch and are mesmerized by the width of its base.

Optimal Default

Use these optical tricks to your benefit. When serving food, use smaller dishes and scoops. Eat from smaller salad plates or dessert forks than the larger dinner ones. The average dinner plate has increased in size by close to 30 percent since the 1960s,[20] so seeking out smaller dishes is an easy and important strategy.

In turn, trade your short, wide drinking glasses for tall, skinny ones, and you'll drink less. (Unless it's water, in which case you should be drinking small amounts of it all day long.)

It doesn't seem like much of a strategy to use smaller dinnerware, but unconsciously consuming 22 percent less food each time you eat can make a big difference over the course of a few months, not to mention years. The simple change of dinnerware size means you'll automatically eat less food without going on a diet or consciously restricting yourself.

What Sean Does

As dinner progresses, Sean helps himself to several scoops from each serving bowl sitting in front of him on the table. It smells and looks so good. The family passes the bowls around, and everyone takes another helping.

The Issue

We eat more when dining "family style," by taking food from serving bowls placed on and passed around the table. In contrast, when food was placed in the kitchen instead of left within sight and reach, men ate 29 percent less and women consumed 10 percent less.[21]

Remember the candy dish on Sean's desk? It's the same concept. We eat more because of the increased proximity to our plates and the decreased effort to get another helping. As soon as the idea of taking more food enters our mind, we can execute on it very quickly and easily without a pause to question whether we really need it.

In addition, we're highly sensory creatures. Seeing and smelling foods increases our desire to eat them. Sometimes we say we're full and done eating, but as long as the food is sitting right in front of us, we may consciously or unconsciously decide to have one more bite (a couple of times) or pick at what's left on the plate or in the serving dish.

Optimal Default

Plate It Out first (using the smaller dinnerware, of course), then keep all serving bowls in one place while you eat in another. It depends on your setup: If you eat in the dining room, keep the serving dishes in the kitchen. If you have an eat-in kitchen, keep the serving dishes on the stove or counter rather than on the table.

If you decide you want to stand up, walk over, and get a little more food (more on this below), you'll know it's because you're truly not sated—not because Sneaky Pete is on a "see-food diet" with it right in front of him.

What Sean Does

Sean reminds the children to clean their plates because it's not okay to waste food. He makes sure he cleans his plate too—which has been refilled several times.

The Issue

As mentioned earlier, many of us have been conditioned to clean our plates regardless of whether we're full, to disregard our body, to eat what's in front of us, to not "waste" food, and to not stop eating until the food is gone. We've been conditioned to eat until we can't possibly take another bite, then are rewarded for overeating with more food—a practice commonly known as dessert.

For many of us who were taught to clean our plates, our indication of when to stop eating is when all the food is gone. Based on the fact that most plate and serving sizes are larger than what we may need, we're bound to overeat. Cleaning our plates is an especially dangerous habit when eating out at restaurants with large portions.

In one of Wansink's most famous experiments, participants ate soup out of "bottomless" bowls that slowly and secretly refilled through hidden tubing as they ate. People eating from these bowls ate 76 percent more soup than those who ate out of regular ones. When told about their bottomless bowls, those people estimated they ate *only 4.8 additional calories.*[22]

Perhaps you've heard the statement "French women don't get fat." An interesting study looked into why this adage is quite often the case.

One of the interesting findings was that Parisians reported they usually stopped eating when they no longer felt hungry. In contrast, Chicagoans in the study stopped when they ran out of a beverage, when their plate was empty, or when the television show they were watching was over.[23] We've gotten terrible about listening to the wisdom of our body.

"Cleaning our plate" translates to other food contexts as well. Sometimes we're compelled to finish an entire package or container. In today's food-abundant environment, a "serving size" is typically much more than we really need to eat. Restaurant portions are enormous, fast food wants you to supersize, sodas come in 64-ounce options (that's two quarts, 800 calories, and 219 grams of sugar), and chips and candy come in giant packages. Eating until a "serving size" is all gone could mean a meal of over 1,800 calories or a snack of over 800. Too much!

Adding to the confusion, there is no universal size that all manufacturers use. One brand of ice cream's serving size could be one-third cup, while the next brand's could be a half cup. To be certain of how much food or beverage is in a container or package, read and compare across labels for grams, ounces, or milliliters.

Optimal Default

Simply start with less food—on a smaller plate. One of the sayings at our dinner table is, "You can always have more." But if we start with a full plate of food, the odds of us finishing all of it are high. If you start with the right amount on your plate, you'll still eat the right amount even if the "clean your plate" conditioning kicks in. Cleaning our plates with three handfuls of food is much different than cleaning it with five or six, so starting with less food on our plate is an important strategy.

Remembering to Plate It Out, begin with just three handfuls of food: one classic iPod of protein, one fistful of grain, and one fistful of fruit and/ or vegetable. Eat those three handfuls at a moderate pace, then do the virtual stomach scan. Are you content? Are you at a level 3? Will it last you about three hours?

It might be enough food, and you can stop eating. Or it might not be enough. Perhaps you need one more fistful, and you would choose more fruit and/or vegetable to round out your 25/25/50 T Plate ratio. Maybe you need three-quarters of a fistful. Take it. (That is, walk over to the serving dish and get it.) You can always put more food on your plate, but having too much food on your plate to begin with and not finishing it can be difficult.

When eating packaged foods, read the labels carefully. If a packaged food is an extra—as most are—set aside a moderate amount to eat, regardless of what the serving size says. And plan accordingly for it by eating a little less of your whole grain essentials.

What Sean Does

After dinner, everyone is clamoring for the dessert Sean brought home—even though they're all full and he told them they needed to wait until after he works out. He gives in and lets the rest of the family eat dessert, saying he'll have his after he exercises. Sean tries to remain steadfast, but watching everyone else eat and enjoy the decadent dessert is more than he can stand. His wife tells him it's not a big deal, just go ahead and eat it. He gives in to temptation and has a piece.

The Issue

Our friends, family, and coworkers—also known as our tribes—strongly influence our behaviors. The social aspect of food is an important part of our history. Hunting was a group effort, as was food preparation and consumption. Norms about how we eat in groups are still a central cornerstone of connection with family, friends, and colleagues.

Being around people who eat healthy, exercise more, and engage in fewer negative lifestyle behaviors increases the likelihood we will too. But the opposite is also true: we're more likely to eat less healthy food, be more sedentary, and take part in poor lifestyle choices if our tribes are doing it.

Researchers from the Framingham Heart Study, which tracked more than twelve thousand people over thirty-two years, found that when a friend became obese, a person's future risk of also becoming obese increased by 171 percent.[24] When one person started drinking more, so did other people in the group.[25] They did find evidence of positive behaviors spreading as well, though. If one person gave up smoking, their friends and family were likely to do the same.[26]

It can be very difficult to keep your Sneaky Pete in check while everyone else's Sneaky Petes are running (or sitting) wild and satisfying their base behaviors. Behavior can be contagious. We've all experienced the overt or even covert social pressure to eat or drink more than we had planned or know we should. We may also have been talked out of exercising and going out with friends instead.

Optimal Default

Trying to make Sneaky Pete resist temptation is very difficult. That's why optimal defaults are so important. We're better off putting him into positions where he doesn't have to work as hard to make decisions in line with our goals.

If you find yourself in a similar position as Sean, with family members eating more than you plan to eat, excuse yourself from the table as soon as you're done eating so you're not tempted. Removing yourself from the situation will spare you from not only seeing and smelling that seductive dessert right in front of you (remember proximity and availability), but also from experiencing the hard-to-resist pleasure fireworks that go off just by watching others enjoy it.

Or maybe it's not enough to simply leave the table. Getting your tribes actively on board with your desired behaviors is also very important. Social influence is powerful, and you can definitely use it to your advantage. If you have a specific goal, such as Sean's to eat right and work out afterward, communicate it to your family before dinner and ask for their support in making sure you stick with it. Plus, simply stating your goal out loud makes it more real for you too.

Better yet, why not make yourself the role model of good decisions for your family? Encourage your family to, say, hold off on dessert, saving it for a night when they can plan ahead to eat a little less of the essentials in order to make room for this extra.

Use the power of a support network to boost your own goals. Build an exercise tribe. A workout partner or group is a great way to increase personal accountability. We're less likely to cancel on someone else than we are ourselves, and making an activity social in nature usually makes it more enjoyable.

What Sean Does

After a big meal and dessert on top of that, Sean is now way too full to work out.

The Issue

Sean's situation is familiar to many people. He plans to stop at the gym on his way home from the office, but that doesn't pan out for one reason or another. He then plans to work out sometime in the evening, but that plan goes astray as well.

For some of us, it's very difficult to keep workouts consistent in the evenings. We frequently have to work later than expected, then we're just too tired and exhausted from a stressful day at work. We've got dinner and family obligations demanding our time and attention. Dinner makes us far too stuffed to even think about moving, so we instead slip right into the food coma.

Not to mention, by late in the day we've made thousands of decisions that have depleted our willpower. As we'll discuss more in the next chapter, our willpower muscle gets weaker as the day goes on. This means the odds of us following through with the commitment to exercise after work or dinner are greatly diminished. Sneaky Pete sees the door of opportunity is open a tiny crack—just enough for him to get his foot in. Our resolve is weak, he swoops in, and he delivers the death knell to our workout plans.

Optimal Default

Set up a more realistic or convenient time for exercise. For many people, the best time to exercise is in the morning before work. You'll always have the clothes you need—in fact, you may even want to sleep in pajamas that double as workout gear. You can shower right after, so there's no need to worry about getting all sweaty. Plus, there are typically fewer demands in the morning than as the day progresses, especially if you don't hit the snooze button four times.

Also think about making the 10/10/10 format as your optimal default for workouts. Forget trying to find a big block of time that just doesn't exist in your day. With literally a few minutes here and there, you can accumulate a great workout and give yourself energy-and-bliss boosts throughout your day. Kick off your morning with ten minutes of movement, squeeze in ten more minutes when you need a pick-me-up during work, then declare ten minutes of family fun to get your groove on together in the evening. There's no need for clothes or gear, no need for a shower afterward—no excuses.

What Sean Does

After dinner, Sean gives his friends a call to make plans for their upcoming night out together. They decide to meet up at their favorite bar and grill to catch up over dinner and drinks. They're all trying to watch their weight, so they agree to just split some appetizers.

The Issue

When planning get-togethers with our tribes, the default options very often center around eating and/or drinking. As we just learned, it's possible our tribes' behaviors can put our goals in danger. Researchers have found that we subconsciously model each other's eating styles. If we're typically light eaters on our own, we'll eat more when with a group. If we're heavier eaters, we'll eat less when dining with friends.[27] We will even unconsciously mimic the eating speed of those we're with.[28]

I'm going to date myself a bit here, but when I was growing up, most families didn't go out to restaurants very often. When we did eat out, it meant there was a special occasion. When something is a special occasion and we're in a celebratory mood, we feel we can treat ourselves. We'll eat something decadent—just this once—because it's a rare event. Today, however, eating out is far from a rare event. Some families eat out more often than they eat at home. But unfortunately, we still unconsciously view eating out as a special occasion, even if it's just another Tuesday night.

There are also a greater number of opportunities and options for eating outside the home these days. Our environments are filled with more fast-food and sit-down restaurants than ever before. You can now even find them in hospitals and schools. The restaurant industry wants to make eating their food as convenient and enticing as possible. And if you don't have time to come in and eat, you can order food for your entire family ahead of time, park in a special spot right by the door, and someone will bring it out to your car.

Many of us now eat meals out of the home on a regular basis, but the unconscious "celebration" associations still exist. We may continue to "let go" when eating out, but instead of overdoing it a couple times a year, we're overdoing it several times each week.

Restaurants can be full of landmines and dire obstacles when it comes to our goals to eat light and healthy. A study that analyzed nutrition data on 245 chain restaurants within the United States found that *96 percent* exceed the USDA's recommendations for fat, saturated fat, and sodium per meal.[29] Portions are very large in an attempt to make us feel we're getting the most value for our money, and everything about the restaurant has been designed to get us to spend as much money and eat as much food as possible.

The "lite" entrees are usually listed at the very back of the menu, and for good reason: restaurants want to sell the items with the most markup (the most processed ones), so they feature them up front. By the time we get to the back of the menu, we've drooled over all the high-fat, high-salt, high-sugar options. Sneaky Pete has gotten really excited about those first foods, while the healthy ones sound as appealing as a piece of cardboard.

Sneaky Pete also has a hard time figuring out how much he's eating at a restaurant. We'll typically underestimate the calorie amount in a meal by about 25 percent. The bigger the meal is, actually, the more we'll underestimate it, sometimes by as much as 50 percent.[30]

On a night out with friends, a common temptation—and mistake—is to order an array of appetizers for the group to share. We think they're small, so they've got to be lower in calories—plus, we're sharing. In reality, appetizers have the highest amount of calories, fat, and sodium compared to entrées.[31]

As we learned earlier, we end up eating more when we've got more options to choose from in front of us. (Think about an appetizer sampler: Don't you eat at least one piece of each item?) The fact that a large order of appetizers may come out one at a time and are shared among the group makes it easy to underestimate how much food we've eaten. We never really see how much we're eating, especially if we pick right off the serving platter. The evidence disappears quickly, and we may think we've only had a few bites of each one. Add in the distraction of eating while catching up with good friends—not to mention a couple rounds of beers or cocktails—and we have a recipe for an eating disaster.

Optimal Default

Stop making the bar and grill your go-to for get-togethers. Brainstorm with friends about alternative activities besides eating and/or drinking to spend time together. Ask them to eat on their own, then meet up afterward at someone's house. It *is* possible to socialize without food! Or plan a special get-together to go for a walk, try a new sport or leisure activity, or maybe even volunteer for an organization you care about. Be the leader and encourage your tribe to do something fun *and* healthy.

If you do choose to meet with friends at a restaurant, choose one with healthier or lighter options, and skip the apps. Convince someone to split an entrée with you, or have the staff box half your meal right away for leftovers. Or look up the menu online ahead of time and decide what you'll eat so Sneaky Pete doesn't derail you. (Some menus may even have calorie amounts listed.) Order water or tea, and offer to be the designated driver to save the calories and effect of cocktails.

What Sean Does

When he's off the phone, Sean sees the rest of the family in the living room watching television. He still hasn't worked out, but he finds a spot on the couch and settles in anyway.

The Issue

Watching television has become a less-than-optimal default as an evening activity. I'm not saying we should never watch it, but we need to at least be aware of the ways in which we're consciously and unconsciously affected by it.

The most obvious way is that it makes us couch potatoes. Sneaky Pete loves to kick back and relax, even if advanced brain had plans for a workout or to simply be more physically active. Sitting for large portions of the day at our jobs is damaging to our health, then we often exacerbate the situation by following it with more time sitting in front of a screen (TV or computer). It can be difficult to overcome the inertia of sitting for long periods. Over time, it decreases our energy, making us feel unable to be active even if we wanted to.

Many studies have found that people who watch television are more likely to be obese.[32] It's not just because it's a sedentary activity. It's also because it blasts us like crazy with marketing for unhealthy products. The next time you're watching television—especially in the evening or during a weekend morning cartoon show if you have small children—count how many commercials are for food or beverages. You'll be shocked at how often Sneaky Pete receives the message to eat junk and fast food. It's no wonder many of us find ourselves mindlessly snacking or eating more while watching TV!

Optimal Default

Get rid of your television. I know—that just made Sneaky Pete freak out. But consider it. It's easier to break yourself of the TV habit than you'd ever think.

When my daughter was little, I decided I didn't want her watching TV, and I realized it would be hypocritical for me to do it if she couldn't. I allowed her to watch public television shows for a couple hours on Saturday mornings, but that was it, and I watched only occasionally at night after she went to bed.

With that optimal default in place, our options were to go outside, go for walks, go to a park, play games, make forts, do craft or art projects, and read. It kept us physically active, and we enjoyed our time together. I also found that not having a television helped keep me more connected to my family. (Before, I wanted to talk only during commercial breaks.) It afforded me the opportunity to truly relax, disconnect, and recharge in the evenings.

Currently, our television is at the back of a closet. It's the thirteen-inch one I had in my dorm room in college. We don't have cable. We'll occasionally watch something online, but it's not a regular occurrence.

If you're not ready for such a big step, consider the baby steps along the way: don't eat in front of the TV, turn it on later each night, or turn it off earlier. Turn the radio on if you simply need "background noise." Declare a TV-free night at least once a week. Drop your cable package so there's less to watch in the first place, and so you don't pay an exorbitant amount for something you watch less and less. (And don't forget to apply the TV-free rules to other screens, such as computers, tablets, and phones.)

Replace watching TV with another activity you enjoy but never had the time to do. Work out, plan and cook healthier meals, get to bed earlier—you'll magically find time to do things aligned with your resiliency goals.

If you have a must-see, can't-miss favorite TV show, create an optimal default where you have to exercise while you watch it. You just figured out an easy way to squeeze in a daily workout. (And boy, won't you be motivated to do it!)

Or simply do what I call the "TV Commercial Workout." Pick a different muscle group to work during each round of commercials. During the first commercial break, do some pushups to work your chest muscles. When the commercials are over, sit back down and enjoy your show. When the next round of commercials starts, do some lunges and squats to work your legs. Or you could do a few Hit the Deck cards during each commercial break. During the span of a one-hour show, it's possible to work all your major muscle groups and get in fourteen to twenty-two minutes of exercise.[33] You just figured out an easy way to squeeze in a daily workout!

A New Way Forward

Sean climbs into bed with a heavy heart. He feels guilty about not working out and for overeating at lunch and dinner. He makes a promise to himself that tomorrow will be different. It's the same promise he made the night before and the night before that—each night for a long time now.

What's wrong with Sean? What's wrong with *us*? Have we dEvolved into a society of people who have less self-discipline and willpower when it comes to consistently making good choices about our health? Are we now a population of people who have grown too lazy to get daily exercise? Is our sense of personal responsibility on the decline? Do we lack the capacity to understand public health messaging?

IS SOMETHING WRONG WITH US?

Research indicates the answers to all these questions is no. More people are quitting smoking, getting flu shots, completing college, wearing seatbelts, and using condoms more often when having sex than ever before.[34, 35] Buckling down in a weak economy, many adults are committed to working longer hours and taking on more responsibilities without an increase in compensation or title. All of these examples indicate that awareness of positive behaviors and personal responsibility are still alive and well in our societies.

The problem is that our environments consciously and unconsciously play up to Sneaky Pete's wildest fantasies and make healthy behaviors difficult. Earlier in the book we talked about the dEvolution of food. Well, that's not the only thing that's dEvolved. In many ways, our environments have too.

Big, rich, juicy burgers available everywhere and in minutes? Yes, please! Rooms in houses with nothing but comfortable places to sit and a talking box to entertain me? I never want to leave! Work that involves sitting all day in a climate-controlled room? I'll be there at 8:00 a.m.! Many of our environments have changed for the worse, and it's time we change them for the better.

According to Blue Zones expert Dan Buettner, "Scientific studies suggest that only about 25 percent of how long we live is dictated by genes . . . the other 75 percent is determined by our lifestyles and the everyday choices we make. It follows that if we optimize our lifestyles, we can maximize our life expectancies within our biological limits."[36] I think an important takeaway from this research is that it's not just about living longer lives—it's about living *better* lives.

The point is not to rely on willpower alone, which is rather limited and sometimes powerless when the environment is working against us. The key is to create microclimates at work and home that make change a no-brainer. Our everyday habits then *automatically* create more resiliency, performance, and health in our lives. We suddenly find ourselves moving more, eating less, and reaping the benefits—without thinking about it. We experience fewer negative side effects from stress, we've got better energy, we're more focused and productive, and we're happier.

CONTROLLING THE ENVIRONMENT IS THE ULTIMATE OFFENSIVE MANEUVER AGAINST LIMITED WILLPOWER.

Very few of the things we've talked about will cost you any money (some of them will save you money, actually). They don't require remodeling your home or office. You don't need to ask permission from your boss. They're small, easy modifications that create exponential change. You can now walk into any situation, and instead of you adapting to your environment, you can make the environment adapt to you.

As we mentioned earlier, the next chapter culminates with you creating an action plan for your resiliency training program. In one step of the action plan, you'll design a few optimal defaults for each environment you spend time in—work, home, and on the road—as well as for activities such as eating, exercising, grocery shopping, and dining out. It's the simplest part of the action plan, and it gets Sneaky Pete excited for how easy many of these changes will be.

In fact, I bet you and Sneaky Pete are already quite excited about optimal defaults. Maybe you're so inspired and motivated, you started trying out some no-brainer ideas already. That's a great sign of your readiness, so hold on to that enthusiasm . . . but also don't get too far ahead of yourself. As we discussed, successfully making change involves the unconscious and the conscious. Sneaky Pete is only half of this rEvolution.

The next chapter is all about the conscious side of change. We'll take a closer look at change, willpower, and stress—at the physiological effects they have on each other and on our body and brain. It's the final piece to the Resiliency rEvolution.

For more insights on optimal defaults and ways to control your environment, visit www.ph-performance.com/control

Success Story

TRACEY

Tracey's Story

Before Tracey stepped into a new role as her company's executive director of global business planning, she understood that the many challenges ahead, though exciting, had the potential to raise the stress in her life to dangerous levels. At forty years old, she was making great strides in her career, but her personal life seemed to be in constant chaos.

She had just returned from a leave of absence to treat her bipolar disorder. During the leave, she had also separated from her husband and begun painful negotiations over custody of her two-year-old daughter.

"I knew it was going to be hard, and it was," she says of facing the challenges. "Learning a new role in the company, putting on my game face when I really didn't feel well, mending relationships I had bruised before I stepped back to recover. I had a lot of trouble focusing, and I worried a lot about keeping my job."

Although Tracey felt the leave of absence had improved her mental health, she knew she had to keep herself on track. She was smoking every day and drinking every night, and she had gained about twenty pounds. She remembers, "I needed time and space to figure myself out, and I wasn't feeling good about myself at all."

Her new job had a steep learning curve and required intense, constant communication between departments on high-profile, company-wide initiatives. On evenings and weekends, she struggled to keep up energy and focus during her only shared time with her daughter.

Complicating this stressful period was the fact that her own support system had been badly strained. She recalls, "I lost a lot of people during this time that I thought were my friends, and dealing with that along with mending relationships with my family—it was a really difficult time for me."

Tracey's rEvolution

Tracey learns about PowerHouse through a company program and decides to make resiliency one of her goals. She likes the flexibility of Hit the Deck workouts and soon finds it easy to fit in fifteen minutes in the morning and another fifteen in the evening, even if her schedule is packed. "I especially liked that the exercises were accessible, and if I couldn't do one initially, I could switch out the cards and work up to those I wasn't able to do," she says. With no need for a gym, special equipment, or even good weather, she finds the time commitment very reasonable.

She also makes changes to her nutrition habits, despite some initial reluctance to tackle too much at once. She notes, "The changes were not that hard—they were very realistic, and I never cut out anything I loved. I never felt like there was something that I couldn't have, which is how I like to live."

After sixty days of resiliency training, Tracey feels her day-to-day stress levels have declined, a major relief. After months of restless sleep and insomnia, she is now sleeping soundly on a consistent basis, and she wakes with more energy for work and family.

She has lost over twelve pounds of body fat and replaced it with muscle, and she feels less need to rely on alcohol and nicotine to get through the day. As time passes, she integrates more elements of resiliency training into her daily habits.

With added resiliency, she has replaced feelings of distraction and lack of control with confidence that she can do her work well and still have time for herself and her daughter. "It was perfect for me in that difficult time," she says. "It's easy to follow, the time commitment is not unreasonable, and you see results!"

AFTER SIXTY DAYS
OF RESILIENCY TRAINING

- 25 percent decrease in perceived stress

- 25 percent increase in energy

- 50 percent improvement in quality of sleep

- 10 percent improvement in ability to fall asleep

- Lost 12.7 pounds (5.8 percent) of body fat

Chapter 6

CHANGE

Why Does It Have to Be So Freakin' Hard?

Sunday night you have a come-to-Jesus with yourself. You've *got* to start making your health a priority. Starting tomorrow, you're going to begin eating healthier and working out. No more junk food, no more fast food, no caffeine, and no alcohol. You know it's the right thing to do, and you're even a little bit excited about turning over a new leaf. You go to bed feeling confident and optimistic for morning.

By 4:00 p.m. Monday, you've had coffee, backed out of your plan to work out during your lunch hour, and ate a huge slice of birthday cake during an afternoon meeting. *What just happened?*

Sneaky Pete is what happened. It was too much, too soon.

Human survival has long hinged on getting and conserving energy. For our ancestors, food was scarce, so the more body fat Sneaky Pete had, the better his chance at survival. Sneaky Pete also preferred doing things the easiest way possible and with the most instant gratification. Every day, his goal was to satisfy his immediate urges: eat, reproduce, sleep, do it all over again. It took a lot of energy and physical effort to meet these seemingly simple goals, but he managed.

He wasn't thinking much about the long-term future, whether he'd fit into his bearskin wrap next week, or whether too much meat was raising his cholesterol. In fact, he wasn't thinking much at all. If you recall, caveman brain's job is to react, not to think. Thinking is advanced brain's job.

We are still creatures of these same survival instincts, and we sometimes make irrational decisions through no fault of our own. The problem, as we have discussed, is that our food, environments, and lifestyles have dEvolved while our physiology has not changed. It's a bit ironic that our survival now depends on us resisting many of our primal urges and going against our primitive hardwiring.

In a sense, it's as if Sneaky Pete has been transported forward through time, only to find himself in an environment where he should be doing the *exact opposite* of everything he's ever done. He should walk past those sweets without taking some or all. He should choose food that contains the least amount of calories, fat, and sugar—and even worse, he should leave some of it on his plate. He should plan time to drive to a place (a gym) where people run without going anywhere (on treadmills), and he should pay his hard-earned money for the privilege to do so.

But why would Sneaky Pete *ever* want to purposely eat less when food is right in front of him or waste a bunch of energy at a gym? It makes no physiological sense. He interprets restriction and discomfort as threats. Therefore, these scenarios kick our fight-or-flight response into gear just *thinking* about them. The ensuing stress results in the exact opposite of our health goals. We seek out high-fat, high-sugar foods and eat them in large amounts. Our body goes into fat-storage mode. Our brain switches over to stress mode. And we seek the comfort and security of habit and routine—perhaps the very ones we're trying to change.

We all know we should eat a certain way to be healthy, but many of us aren't. We understand we should get a certain number of fruits and vegetables each day, but we're not. We know fast food and junk food aren't good for us, but we still eat them. We're well aware of the fact we should get regular exercise, but we can't remember the last time we've laced up our sneakers. Most of us now live in obesogenic societies where food is everywhere—especially the high-fat, high-sugar stuff—and our days consist of way too much sitting. We're incredibly vulnerable to food and beverage companies who market to our deep instincts and impulses for survival.

It takes a tremendous amount of willpower and energy to constantly resist urges that have been crucial to our success as a species. This makes us quite susceptible to failing when it comes to making lifestyle changes. We've all made that heartfelt commitment Sunday night only to be flooded with failure and guilt before Monday is even through. The stress of change can often be too much to overcome, but the Resiliency rEvolution shows you how to do it successfully. Remember, Sneaky Pete is here to help us and his intentions are good. We just need to understand how he operates to best use his assets.

In this chapter, we'll focus on the conscious part of change—the other 50 percent of your plan. You'll learn the best way to use advanced brain to make change while also keeping Sneaky Pete on board with the strategy. You'll understand how to get around the limits of self-discipline and willpower, in addition to how to build the strength of your willpower muscle. You will also create your action plan for improved resiliency and devise a strategy to stay on track for making long-lasting change.

Let's begin by looking a little more closely at how and why change typically sends Sneaky Pete—and us—into stress mode.

Change and Sneaky Pete

As soon as our environments change—whether we consciously decide to change them or it happens due to circumstances outside of our control—Sneaky Pete goes on high alert. His number one job is to protect us, so he immediately goes on the offensive to keep us safe. His definition of "safe" includes security, comfort, predictability, and control. He wants to feed us, make us happy, and keep us from feeling vulnerable.

SNEAKY PETE IS NOT A HUGE FAN OF CHANGE.

It's not just external change that Sneaky Pete doesn't like. He even gets twitchy when we try to make internal changes to our behaviors—even if the changes have the potential to benefit us in the long run.

One in four deaths in the United States is due to heart disease,[1] a condition related to lifestyle habits. Simple things such as a healthy diet, regular exercise, and not smoking are some of the best ways to prevent the disease from developing. If left unchecked, heart disease typically leads to a heart attack.

Some people die almost instantly from heart attacks. When people have a heart attack and make it to the hospital, they undergo a traumatic and expensive coronary-artery bypass surgery to save their lives. Experiencing such a significant physical event would motivate anyone to make changes to how they eat and exercise, right? Wrong.

One-fourth of patients hospitalized for heart attacks don't bother to fill their cardiac prescriptions by day seven of their discharge from the hospital.[2] Of those who do fill them, 34 percent stop taking their medication within one month.[3] The seemingly simple task of taking a pill is too much to do. Fast-forward to two years after surgery, and 90 percent of patients have not changed their lifestyle habits.[4] We can experience momentous, traumatic, life-threatening health events, but it doesn't mean we'll automatically change the habits and routines that created the event and increase our chances of a repeat—that may just kill us.

For years, health care professionals have used the fear of death to motivate us to change—telling us we're going to die if we don't quit smoking, go on a diet, or start exercising. What they don't know or realize is, it's not a great motivator. In fact, it can do just the opposite.

The high-stress nature of a life-threatening scenario gets Sneaky Pete's hackles up, and he very quickly goes on the defensive. We may know we need to completely overhaul our lives and change everything about the way we eat, exercise, drink, smoke, sleep, and deal with stress. But ironically, these life-saving changes are too scary to even think about, even when Sneaky Pete knows our life is on the line.

Whether life-saving or simple, change induces stress, and if you re-call, caveman brain *always* overrides advanced brain when we're stressed. We intellectually understand the benefits of changing our negative habits, but to Sneaky Pete, change is a serious red flag. Change means the un-known, discomfort, restriction, denying desires, hard work, and the possi-bility of failure. In short, more stress.

Stress stimulates the fight-or-flight response, and then we're driven by impulse and emotions—we're very reactionary. We lose the ability to think about why we're trying to make change or the long-term positive benefits of the change. We just know we're uncomfortable, and we want to ease our distress as quickly and easily as possible. It's easier and takes less energy to stay the course with our old habits, where there's comfort and security.

Another problem is that change doesn't actually apply to *us in the present moment*—it applies to *a future version of ourselves*. This distinc-tion is just one of the ways in which the "battle of the brains" rages inside us.

The Battle of the Brains, Round One: Present Self vs. Future Self

Making change pits both of our brains against each other. As you know from chapter two, the more primal portion of our brain deals with fight-or-flight, survival, and reproduction. We've been referring to it as Sneaky Pete or caveman brain. We also have what we've called advanced brain, which is a newer portion that evolved over the top of caveman brain. We use it for more advanced cognitive functions like planning into the future, reasoning, decision-making, and keeping track of our goals.

WE CONSTANTLY USE THESE TWO BRAINS IN TANDEM, AND THEY CREATE TWO VERSIONS OF OURSELVES.

Sneaky Pete is the evolutionary default setting for your brain. This means you're "set" to him unless you opt to use your advanced brain. As we briefly discussed in the last chapter, his focus is on the present version of yourself. He is emotional, instinctive, and impulsive. Your comfort, well-being, and security are the top priorities on his list. How are you feeling *right now*? Are you hungry? If so, let's get you fed ASAP. Are you tired? Then let's stay right here on the couch with our feet up or take a nap instead of doing household chores. Did your colleague just say something that made you angry? You should say exactly what you think, in a very loud voice. Did that cocktail make you feel good? Let me pour you another one!

In the distant past, those who followed their immediate impulses were often the ones with higher rates of survival. He who eats first avoids there not being any food left later. He who takes the risk of exploring new territory, hunting large animals, or asking that cavewoman on a date has the potential for higher rewards.

Advanced brain is *not* our default setting, so it takes far more energy and conscious thought to use. As we know, it uses self-control and will-power to resist taking part in behaviors that may provide pleasure in the short-term, but have negative consequences in the long term. It creates a future version of ourselves, whereby controlling impulses today means we will be healthier, smarter, more organized, more successful, more focused, more relaxed, and more loved tomorrow. Weeks and months from now, we will be people who eat healthier, are more excited about exercising, have more time, and consistently take actions that align with our values and long-term goals.

Advanced brain works hard to delay gratification and control Sneaky Pete's impulses. As the more rational part of the brain, it's always trying to motivate us to do the harder thing, such as saying no to more food or alcohol, getting off the couch and exercising, or not participating in office gossip. It's an exhausting job, so advanced brain tires easily.

CAVEMAN BRAIN IS IMPULSIVE AND RELATES TO YOUR PRESENT SELF. ADVANCED BRAIN CONTROLS IMPULSES AND RELATES TO YOUR FUTURE SELF.

Because these two brains often work in opposition, change can be really hard. First off, they can keep passing the buck, trying to make the other one responsible for your failure. Yes, advanced brain is seemingly the more responsible one, but it gets caught up in this pattern too.

Advanced brain honestly believes future self really will have more time, more energy, and more motivation. We get so excited about advanced brain's plan for future self, we say it's okay if present self gets one last hurrah today. We'll create scenarios where we can act crazy in the present moment because we'll make up for it tomorrow. It gives us license to eat this piece of cake now—advanced brain will have us on a diet tomorrow. We can skip the gym today—advanced brain has our workout planned for tomorrow.

Only "tomorrow" is always another day away. When the "future" finally arrives as the new today, future self is nowhere to be found. The only person standing there is present self. Sneaky Pete.

The Battle of the Brains, Round Two: Habit vs. Willpower

It's really not a fair fight when we pit habit against willpower. Willpower has a number of shortcomings when it comes to making change. The good news is, you're about to learn how to even the playing field.

Habit and Routine

Our ancestors had to preserve as much energy as possible because food was often scarce. We've already talked about saving physical energy on the body as fat. But we also developed a way to preserve a tremendous amount of mental energy with habits and routines. As we learned in the last chapter, a good deal of our actions are unconscious defaults.

If you had to decide each and every day whether you should wash your body or your hair first, what side of the bed to sleep on, what route to take to work, or which spot to sit in at home or during a meeting, it would take up ridiculous amounts of valuable energy. In order to save our energy for important or unexpected events, we rely on routines for simple and repetitive decisions of daily life. We do the same thing over and over again without having to invest a lot of conscious thought. Over time it becomes a habit we don't have to think about at all, which preserves a lot of mental energy.

....

CAVEMAN BRAIN IS HABIT.

....

We all have some good habits. We might wake up early every weekday to get a jump on things, listen to the same relaxing radio station on the way to work, create a daily to-do list, keep ourselves on time, ask our kids about their day at the dinner table, and wash our face before bed. For the most part, these good habits don't take a lot of mental energy. In fact, we may find it takes more energy *not* to do them than it does to do them.

The daily repetition of these good habits is a reflection of our values, and they lead to better performance, resiliency, and health.

Unfortunately, though, many of us also have habits that undermine our ability to sustain high levels of performance. We may skip breakfast, leave our workouts up to fate instead of scheduling them, have several glasses of wine with dinner, or tell ourselves we "don't have time" to do things for our health as we watch TV each night. These default negative behaviors add to our stress and diminish our ability to be resilient.

We're completely unconscious about many of our daily decisions, which means we're often not aware of what's driving our actions and their possible consequences. This can make it difficult to execute change. For instance, guess how many food decisions you make on a daily basis. Most people estimate fourteen. The reality is, the average person makes about 227 food decisions every day![5] A great example of how completely unaware we are.

Now extrapolate that figure to the rest of the decisions we make each and every day. As we mentioned in the last chapter, we literally make thousands of choices, many of which have little to no thought process behind them. How can we possibly control or change things we're not even aware of?

Adding to the problem, a lot of distractions in modern society compete for our attention. We constantly juggle a multitude of priorities that continually shift, multitasking to try getting as many things done as possible. We have multiple forms of communication to manage, hundreds of TV channels to watch, several formats of social media to suck us in, and many people whose needs we tend to in our personal and professional lives.

Unfortunately, when we're not paying attention in this distracting world, Sneaky Pete makes most of our choices instead of our advanced brain. We go along with the most expedient way to get things done without thinking of the future consequences.

Willpower

As we learned in the previous chapter, the conscious part of decision-making happens in our advanced brain. It gives careful contemplation of the current situation *and* future consequences, then uses self-control to carry out the best long-term option. It's responsible for the social etiquette needed to get along with our tribes. With willpower on its side, advanced brain works hard to tamp down Sneaky Pete's urges to have every desirable thing that comes along.

ADVANCED BRAIN IS WILLPOWER.

Willpower could also be called "won't-power" because it's the force behind both "I will" and "I won't." You *want* to do something—eat that slice of cake, have another drink, or go smoke a cigarette—but know you shouldn't. Or you *don't want* to do something—work out, choose the vegetables instead of the fries, or call your mother—but know you should. Caveman brain is telling you one thing, while advanced brain is telling you something else. With advanced brain's willpower, you say, "I *will* do this" or "I *won't* do that."

Willpower is very important for making change. We use self-control to reprogram habits and defaults that have been hardwired in our behavior patterns for decades, perhaps. As many of us know from experience, it can be extremely difficult to change our habits. When over a million people were asked about their greatest personal strengths, self-control was not one of them. But when asked about their weakest virtues, self-control was at the top of the list.[6]

Self-control and willpower have been the focus of much research, and here's what we know:

- Willpower is a physiological response.

- Stress is the enemy of willpower.

- Willpower is a limited resource.

- Using willpower depletes resources in the body.

- Willpower is trainable—there's a willpower workout.

Let's learn more about these five very important aspects of willpower and how to best utilize them to make long-lasting change.

Willpower Is a Physiological Response

Just like stress, willpower is not just something that happens in our heads. It has an important physiological aspect. When we make decisions that aren't in accordance with our goals or when we lose control, we often wonder, *What the heck were we thinking?* But a better question may be, *What were we feeling?*

Let's say you're at a client dinner. The meal hasn't started yet, and everyone is milling around talking. Several food servers move about with trays full of appetizers, wine, and beer. As they approach and ask if you'd like some, your brain registers the availability of some pleasing food and beverages.

Dopamine is released, which you'll remember from chapter two is a chemical associated with reward. It heightens Sneaky Pete's sense of desire and brings the attention, motivation, and action centers of the brain to full attention. Now you can't stop thinking about eating a few of those delicious, savory puff pastries and washing them down with a glass of sauvignon blanc. Sneaky Pete tells you to say yes, and to say yes *now* before the server moves on to someone else and they run out.

Your body knows Sneaky Pete usually talks you into these sorts of things. So in response to the mere sight of food, your body prepares for the spike in glucose levels you'll soon get from ingesting it. It preemptively drops blood glucose and releases insulin to keep levels stable while and after you eat. Unbeknownst to you, this drop in blood glucose decreases the strength of your willpower, and you want to eat and drink even more than before.

Still, you try to stay firm. You recently made a commitment to eat and drink less, so you haltingly tell the server, "No, but thank you." That just initiated an internal conflict between caveman brain and advanced brain. And in turn, that stimulated the fight-or-flight response. Everything speeds up: your heart rate, breathing, blood pressure, and other autonomic responses. You feel a mix of anxiety, excitement, and dread. The battle between advanced brain and caveman brain is in full force. Oh god, help . . . you need to save yourself from yourself.

Pause-and-Plan

As soon as your brain registers the fight-and-flight response due to the internal conflict between advanced brain and caveman brain, something called the pause-and-plan response kicks in. In order to resist the urge to indulge, you need to slow things down and use your best judgment. You need to pause, then plan. Your advanced brain needs to gain control.

With pause-and-plan, energy is now directed to the prefrontal cortex of your advanced brain—away from your caveman brain. Heart rate, blood pressure, breathing, and other autonomic functions slow down. This response takes you in the opposite direction of fight-or-flight and buys you some time for rational, thoughtful action.

Pause-and-plan is the antidote to fight-or-flight. It freezes our impulses and allows us to access our long-term goals and future self. It lets advanced brain push back on Sneaky Pete and the fight-or-flight response. Instead of your body tensing up for a physical response, it relaxes you enough that you're not functioning on instinct, autopilot, or habit.

Being able to use pause-and-plan is critical to staying on track with your goals, both personally as well as professionally. It's an important source of willpower. The single best measure of the pause-and-plan ability is heart rate variability (HRV). Remember it from chapter three? It's your resiliency reserve to help you recover from stress more quickly. More notably, it's highly trainable.

THE BEST MEASURE OF PAUSE-AND-PLAN IS HEART RATE VARIABILITY.

Heart Rate Variability

If you recall, HRV represents the beat-to-beat fluctuations in our heart rate. A high variability indicates a healthy, resilient balance between the sympathetic and parasympathetic systems. It means the heart rate is not "stuck" in the sympathetic (fight-or-flight) state. As you also recall, people with high HRV deal with stress more successfully and recover from it more quickly.[7] It improves our physiological resiliency.

Having high HRV also means we have more inner strength, self-control, and persistence, and this makes us more psychologically resilient to stress. It gives us increased capacity to focus our attention, stay calm, and use advanced brain more often than caveman brain. In sum, it gives us more willpower.

HIGH HRV = MORE WILLPOWER

Research has shown that HRV is such a good indicator of willpower, it can predict whether someone is more likely to resist temptation or give in. When recovering alcoholics are exposed to drinks, those whose HRV goes up are more likely to stay sober in the long run. But for those whose HRV drops, their risk of relapse is much higher.[8]

As you learned in chapter three, regular exercise improves HRV.[9, 10] This underscores the importance of physical activity in your life. Not only does it help you deal with stress more effectively by changing the physiology and chemistry of your body, but it also improves your psychological state. Exercise increases the size of your brain—specifically your prefrontal cortex, which is one of the most important portions for willpower and self-control.

As you're about to learn, the more you use willpower to consistently partake in physical exercise, the less of it you need to keep doing it. In addition, the increase in HRV you get from regular exercise increases the amount of willpower you have for *all* areas of your life, not just for your physical activity goals.

Perhaps most importantly, improving your HRV doesn't take you a lot of time. In an analysis of several studies examining the connection between exercise and HRV, it was found that the greatest enhancements to mood and the ability to deal with stress came from five-minute bouts, not hour-long sessions.[11] By following the exercise recommendations in this book, you'll build the muscles in both your body and your brain.

What to Do

- Get regular exercise to improve HRV, which in turn increases your ability to pause and plan.

- Do short bouts of exercise, which are more effective for HRV than longer workouts.

Stress Is the Enemy of Willpower

According to Kelly McGonigal, PhD, a psychologist and willpower researcher who lectures at Stanford, "Nothing drains willpower faster than stress."[12] Many other scientists and experts in the field agree and have found that stress shuts down learning, growth, and change.[13, 14, 15]

Stress is the enemy of willpower because it steals resources from pause-and-plan. During stress and the resulting fight-or-flight response, blood and resources are diverted *away* from the brain and *to* the large muscles of the body, preparing them for action. With no resources going to advanced brain and self-control, caveman brain is free to make decisions based on impulse, instant gratification, and satisfying the desires for comfort and security.

Negative emotions that come from stress—such as anxiety, anger, sadness, and self-doubt—also shift the brain into a reward-seeking state. We want to feel better—and fast. Some of the most immediate ways to feel better are to eat our favorite foods, disconnect from the world by watching TV, have a drink or cigarette, or do some retail therapy.

These things might make us feel better in the short term, but they've got long-term negative consequences. And they may be some of the very habits and activities we're trying to change. Anything we find tempting under normal circumstances becomes *even more* tempting when we're stressed out. Unfortunately, using self-control to try resisting these urges drains even more energy from our willpower reserves. As you can see, stress and lack of willpower can become a downward spiral very quickly.

During times of stress, we're often surrounded by people with whom we have special relationships: coworkers, bosses, clients, significant others, children—our tribes. As tempting as it may be on that impulsive level to lash out, we know we can't yell, swing a fist, or run. Remember that even Sneaky Pete tried his hardest to remain in good graces with his tribe.

Social acceptance is still important for our sense of safety and inclusion today, and advanced brain understands concepts such as kindness and empathy, so we do our best to stifle the urge to fly off the handle during to the fight-or-flight response. Sometimes we succeed, other times we fall short. But every time, trying to control these impulses is further exhausting to our limited resources.

What to Do

Successfully dealing with stress is very important for sustaining and improving willpower, and often all it takes is sixty seconds:

- Play It Out to hit the reset button after each stress event. It's a sixty-second solution with many benefits. As you know, these short bursts of energy mimic the fight-or-flight response, and they are one of the most important things you can do to keep your willpower muscle strong. The resulting bliss molecules help bring the parasympathetic system online, slowing things down so advanced brain can access pause-and-plan.

- Use the nutrition strategies in chapter four to minimize the stress on your body and brain, leaving more energy for willpower. Especially be aware of how eating every three hours—even with just a sixty-second snack—can keep glucose levels balanced.

Willpower Is a Limited Resource

Because advanced brain can become so easily exhausted, it has its limits in the change process. This means we have a limited supply of willpower. Every act to control our emotions, thoughts, or behaviors diminishes this finite—but renewable—internal resource.

When this reservoir of self-control is not replenished, we run on empty, and subsequent tasks that require willpower are greatly impaired. We may be able to exert willpower on one occasion, but we struggle to do it a second time. Think back to the client dinner and that tray of appetizers and wine. You say no the first time, but when the server circles back your way, your odds of saying no again are slim. It's rather ironic that using self-control can lead to losing it!

In addition, exerting willpower in one area of our life depletes it in all other areas. It's the same muscle used for everything and all types of choices. We may have leg muscles for walking and arm muscles for lifting, but we have only one willpower muscle—with one reserve—for nutrition, exercise, sleep, dealing with traffic, handling frustrating work situations, surviving flight delays, and everything else. Overuse it and lose it. Period.

Psychologists studying college students have found that overall self-control decreases drastically during exam periods. Because they spend so much willpower forcing themselves to study, students have less self-control in other areas of their lives: they stop exercising, they smoke more, they drink more alcohol, and they consume 50 percent more junk food.[16]

Chronic dieters are more susceptible to breaking their diets and overeating when exposed to large amounts of tempting foods. The act of eating or not eating is a constant act of self-control, and a whole array of tasty decisions very quickly depletes willpower.[17]

In the same vein, trying to change too many things at once is a surefire way to drain your willpower. (Which is why I keep telling you to work on just one strategy at a time.) Even making seemingly simple daily choices requires self-discipline and willpower. When asked if they think making decisions depletes willpower, most people assume it doesn't, but research paints a completely different picture.[18] When we have to make choice after choice, whether inconsequential or critical, it leads to something called "decision fatigue," where the quality of our choices diminishes after a period of repeated decision making. This helps explain why we're smart, rational people who often make stupid, emotional, or expedient choices.

I recently experienced this firsthand. My wife and I had an appointment with our lawyer to write up our wills. He wanted to ease us into the process of making big decisions, so he started out with the easy questions: is the spelling of your names correct? Is your address correct? Is the person designated as your power of attorney your brother? What is his middle name? Over time, the questions slowly built up to the details of our health care directives, the distribution of assets, and the executor of the wills.

After an hour of this, the questions finally reached the magnitude of decisions such as who would become the guardian of our daughter. To put this in context, you should know I take my role as a mother very seriously—my daughter is one of the most important things in my life. However, at this point I was mentally exhausted with decision fatigue. I didn't have the capacity to care who her guardian should be. I would have given her to the first person who asked or happened to be standing on the street corner. I was done. I didn't have the ability to truly focus and give the energy required to make such an important decision.

When we give caveman brain and advanced brain thousands of decisions each day, it's no wonder we often get exhausted, choose the french fries, tell our kids "Whatever—I don't care," or just put things off for later. Giving in to temptation may seem like the easy "solution," especially to Sneaky Pete, but it doesn't build willpower. Every act depletes resources whether we make the right or wrong decision, and every act brings us that much closer to losing control.

Optimal Defaults Preserve Willpower

Get ready—everything you just read about optimal defaults in the previous chapter is going to sink in even more now. Research has shown that people who successfully act in accordance with their long-term goals don't rely on their willpower—at least not very often. People with high levels of self-control spend less time resisting desires because they arrange their lives in a way that avoids the troublesome scenario in the first place. They create microclimates of optimal defaults. This saves their self-control for emergencies rather than burning it up with a multitude of day-to-day decisions.[19]

In Greek mythology, when Odysseus sailed his ship from Hades, he was warned about the song of the Sirens. These winged monsters were so compelling and powerful, they would make men jump overboard and be killed. In order to save his crew, he put wax in their ears to prevent them from hearing the dangerous melodies. Odysseus was extremely curious and wanted to hear the song of the Sirens himself, but he knew it would tempt him beyond the capacity of his willpower. In order to preserve his willpower and ensure he didn't have to rely on his limited self-control, he ordered his men to tie him to the mast so he would be unable to act on his impulses. When he heard the beguiling tune, he went berserk—begging, screaming, and pleading for his men to untie him—but they were under strict orders to keep him lashed to the mast no matter what he said or tried to do.

Odysseus created an optimal default for himself and his crew. He knew they were heading into a tempting situation, and he formed a strategy ahead of time to ensure success.

As you learned in chapter five, you can create situations that minimize the number of decisions you must face and how much you need to rely on willpower. Those optimal defaults we discussed are crucial to making change because they remove the need for choice or help you automatically make the right one, all of which preserve your willpower.

In particular, organize your life so you don't have to think so much about what to eat or when to exercise. Our weakest moments of self-control come when we're hungry and tired, and we're more likely to opt for fast food, junk food, or takeout, and we're more likely to plop on the couch. Likewise, make difficult choices early in the day when willpower is the strongest. Don't wait for decision fatigue to set in before you tackle something heavy. And don't leave goal-based decisions to chance late in the day. For instance, schedule your workout for the morning, when you'll have the strongest willpower to back it up. Saying you'll exercise on your way home from work or after dinner means you'll have much less willpower to push you.

In fact, optimal defaults don't just preserve willpower—they also allow it a much-needed chance to replenish itself. As we mentioned before, you can't do thousands of squats back to back to back without your legs inevitably turning to mush. You need to take some breaks when working one muscle that much. An optimal default lets you take a break from a decision. The more defaults you build into your microclimates, the more breaks you get. In the meantime, each little break lets your willpower muscle recover. It'll be ready to go when you really do need it.

Not only will you be more successful in making change, you'll have less stress. A recent set of studies found that people with more self-discipline have lower levels of stress. It's not so much that they use their self-control to get through a crisis more successfully, but that they *avoid one in the first place*.[20] They play offense instead of defense by creating optimal defaults. They don't go to restaurants that tempt them to overeat, they don't keep junk food in the house, they bring their lunches to work, they plan their weekly workouts, and they spend time with people in their tribes who share their same values. It's a good cycle to find yourself in, as more willpower leads to less stress, which then leads right back to more willpower.

What to Do

- Trying to change too many things at once exhausts willpower, so set clear priorities on one or two focused, simple strategies.

- Self-control is highest in the beginning of the day, then it deteriorates as the day goes on. Follow through on your change commitments and do important things early in the day when willpower is fresh.

- Use your optimal defaults to preserve willpower and let it recover. If you don't give willpower a chance to recuperate, you can run out of it entirely. Creating microclimates means you conserve much-needed energy for self-control in other areas.

Using Willpower Depletes Resources in the Body

The strength of your willpower is very dependent on the state of your body. Self-control is not just mental power—it's also physiological. Are you hungry? Lack of glucose diminishes your willpower. Are you tired? Your willpower muscle will be tired too.

Recall that glucose is the fuel for all your brain processes, and some mental acts use more of it than others. Our ability to use willpower depends on the availability of glucose in the body. And according to research, few cognitive processes are as expensive as self-control and willpower.[21]

Because the brain cannot store glucose, it's constantly keeping a close eye on supply. When the brain detects a drop in glucose levels, it immediately starts rationing it to the survival portions of the brain. The brain follows the "last in, first out" rule: cognitive abilities that developed later in our evolution are the first to become impaired when resources are limited.

It took us a lot longer to develop the advanced portions of our brain that stop us from acting on every urge. Because caveman brain is an older portion, Sneaky Pete gets first dibs on any available energy. Of course, he's biased to favor instant gratification. We originally evolved to *want* things, not to *not want* things. In times of scarcity, those who favored instant gratification—get it all now—fared better and had an increased chance of survival.

When Sneaky Pete is in charge, advanced brain's supply of energy has been cut off. Once advanced brain's fuel is gone, so is our willpower. Numerous studies confirm that low blood glucose levels and poor glucose utilization are associated with worse self-control of attention, emotions, and behavior.[22]

SELF-CONTROL REQUIRES GLUCOSE. NO GLUCOSE = NO WILLPOWER

Ironically, one of the most commonly resisted desires is the urge to eat.[23] Dieting requires willpower, which means it requires glucose. The problem is that being on a diet means *not* putting glucose in the system. Restricted calorie intake results in low levels of glucose, which reduces the amount of energy available for willpower, which is necessary to restrict calorie intake in the first place. It's the snake eating its own tail—or perhaps not eating it, in this case.

DIETING = NO GLUCOSE AND NO WILLPOWER

To make a diet even more challenging, as we continue to use our limited supply of willpower and as blood glucose levels drop, the body starts craving energy in the most readily available form: sugar. It also wants a sustainable source of energy: fat. We have less willpower to resist Sneaky Pete and our cravings for high-sugar, high-fat foods.

It takes a tremendous amount of energy to recognize, interrupt, and override Sneaky Pete, and being on a diet depletes those energy reserves. This helps explain why dieting is so difficult and why so many of us fail, especially over the long run. It also helps explain why it's a bad idea to be on a diet while trying to make any other changes that require self-control. We've talked about the importance of making one (maybe two) simple, small changes at a time. This recommendation becomes even more important when using limited willpower resources and then exacerbating the situation with a lack of glucose.

We may start each day with loads of resolve to eat less on our diet . . . then we skip breakfast to get a head start on a calorie deficit. Unfortunately, it's also a head start on low glucose levels. It's one of the worst decisions we can make for willpower. As the calorie restriction continues throughout the day, it eventually becomes impossible to resist temptation of all sorts—not just food-related urges. Sneaky Pete talks us into lounging on the couch, having a drink, and who knows what else.

With every decision and act of self-control we make, we use blood glucose. Our levels drop, and they continue to drop with each subsequent task. The ability to discipline ourselves is a bank account that gets depleted quite quickly. Matthew Gailliot, PhD—a social psychologist who has studied how people lose control when they're mentally drained—found that low levels of glucose are associated with worse self-control of attention, emotions, and behavior. In a recent study, he asked participants to control their thoughts, emotions, or behavior, and he measured blood glucose levels before and after the task. After using self-control, participants' blood glucose levels dropped (whereas those in a control group did not). When asked to repeat the tasks of self-control, those whose glucose levels dropped the most on the first task did worse on their second attempt.[24]

Self-regulation of cognitive and emotional tasks uses valuable, limited resources for the entire body, not just the brain. Acts of self-control can deplete *physical* power, stamina, and muscular endurance.[25] It can result in impaired function of the central nervous system. Researchers refer to this as central fatigue. Historically, central fatigue has been connected to mental exhaustion from prolonged physical exercise, such as running for hours. This means using willpower can be just as exhausting as running a marathon!

This lack of glucose and its effect on decision making can also have serious consequences to our professional performance. A team of psychologists analyzed over one thousand decisions judges made over the span of ten months. These judges were ruling on cases for prisoners seeking parole—a serious and complicated decision.

On average, one in three prisoners was granted parole. But there was a striking trend behind who did and didn't receive it, even when cases shared many of the same details. The trend showed that 70 percent of prisoners with cases heard in the morning were granted parole, compared to roughly only 10 percent of those whose cases came up in the afternoon. Over the course of the day, decision fatigue set in with the judges hearing case after case. Less able to wrestle with another barrage of complicated, serious decisions in the afternoon, they almost always defaulted to the safest choice—keeping the prisoners incarcerated.

And within this trend of decision fatigue was a micro trend of central fatigue: right after the judges took their midmorning snack break and just after lunch, the chance of a prisoner getting parole was 65 percent. But when the judges heard case after case, without a chance to eat and get some much-needed recovery and glucose, they granted parole only 20 percent of the time.[26] Each decision used valuable glucose. And with no chance to refuel, over time they had less mental resources available. Again, they defaulted to the least-risky choice: no parole.

Lack of glucose doesn't always mean we'll play it safe, though. Depending on the situation, it can also push us toward more risky behaviors.[27] For Sneaky Pete and his tribe, a food scarcity often required them to be more aggressive in their search for calories. The lack of glucose created a sense of urgency that drove them to engage in riskier activities. When they were hungry, they were more likely to climb higher in a tree and out on a weak limb to get honey. They may have gone after a large animal alone, rather than wait for a fellow hunter to help them out.

To this day, low blood glucose can still make us go out on a limb, metaphorically speaking. It increases short-term thinking and impulsive behavior as resources are being fed to Sneaky Pete and away from advanced brain. When blood glucose levels are low, we're more likely to cheat on a spouse, lie, and engage in several types of criminal behavior.[28]

WHEN BLOOD GLUCOSE LEVELS DROP, THE BRAIN FAVORS SHORT-TERM, IMPULSIVE BEHAVIOR.

On a less dramatic scale, you may not even be aware that you're making hundreds of highly important daily decisions that are not the best to make—all because of a glucose crash from skipping a meal or eating something high glycemic. Do you really use your best judgment when you're hungry? It's possible that your performance has been hindered for the past ____ years (fill in the blank) without you knowing it, simply from not managing your blood glucose levels.

Matthew Gailliot has stated, "The body's variable ability to mobilize glucose may be an important determinant of people's capacity to live up to their ideals, pursue their goals, and realize their virtues."[29] Simply put, maintaining blood glucose levels helps you be the best version of yourself.

The good news is, glucose can restore willpower. When the participants in Gailliot's study were given a sugary drink between the first and second tasks, it replenished their blood glucose levels, and they were better able to exert willpower in their second attempt. The judges who were suffering from decision fatigue were able to restore their focus and self-discipline after putting glucose in their systems.

Blood glucose drops with each act of self-control, but your levels—and your willpower—can be restored by consuming glucose. As you learned in chapter four, consuming low-glycemic food with slow, steady glucose release is best.

Sleep Restores Willpower

Willpower fades not only when our glucose levels are low. When we're sleep deprived, our resolve weakens and we take the path of least resistance. As we discussed in chapter two, lack of sleep impairs our body and brain's ability to effectively utilize glucose. When we're sleep deprived, we don't get the full metabolic benefit of the glucose we put into our system because of the body's diminished ability to use it.

This limits the amount of energy in the body, and what's left goes right to caveman brain because of the "last in, first out" rule. The prefrontal cortex doesn't get sufficient energy, which means there's nothing to supply willpower. Researchers have termed this "mild prefrontal dysfunction." And as we know, when Sneaky Pete gets the vast majority of the resources, we're more likely to overreact to stress and have a much harder time dealing with it.

When we're low on sleep and therefore low on glucose, it leaves us feeling extremely tired all around. The perceived lack of energy cues the body to get more fuel into the system, and we begin to crave high-glycemic foods to give ourselves a boost.

When I've finished an international trip that has left me jet-lagged, it never fails that I start eating in a way that doesn't match my regular routine. I distinctly remember a particular afternoon after returning from work in Dubai. Other work and responsibilities don't stop because you've just arrived from halfway around the world, so I had various meetings to attend. At about 2:00 p.m., I was tired and needed a boost. I knew exactly what I ~~wanted~~ HAD TO HAVE. I stopped off at a convenience store and bought a six-pack of cupcakes and a diet soda for some sugar and caffeine. I put down two cupcakes in quick succession and was about to start on my third when I realized what was happening—and why. At that moment, my top priority was to get to bed as soon as humanly possible. It happens *every* time.

As we know, eating high-glycemic foods begins a spike-and-crash cycle that leaves us exhausted during the crashes. The only thing we want is more high-glycemic food to quickly jack up glucose, but that inadvertently sets us up for another drop. Being sleep deprived adds even more stress to the body in this vicious cycle.

Remember how adding glucose can restore the willpower lost when glucose levels are low? It's the same with sleep. When your "sleep levels" are low, getting some much-needed sleep restores willpower. To avoid the problem of being sleep deprived in the first place, aim to get between seven to nine hours a night. Keep your sleep routine consistent by going to bed and waking up at the same time, even on weekends. It restores our ability to fully process and utilize glucose, the primary fuel for self-control. When advanced brain has all the energy it needs, it can better keep Sneaky Pete in check.

What to Do

- Eat about every three hours to sustain blood glucose levels and willpower. Willpower depends on the last time we ate and the glycemic effects of the food. Consume low-glycemic foods high in lean protein, healthy fats, and fiber.

- If you're trying to eat less, don't "diet" by skipping meals and drastically restricting calorie intake. Instead, spread your total calories throughout the day, and don't go long periods without eating.

- If you know you're about to do something important that requires mental focus and strength, have a low-glycemic snack to fuel your brain for optimal performance.

- Get adequate amounts of sleep each night, and keep your sleep routine.

Willpower Is Trainable: Your Willpower Workout

As you just learned, willpower can easily get fatigued from overuse. But the good news is, it can also be strengthened with the right training. Remember to think of willpower as a muscle: when we use a muscle repeatedly, it gets exhausted. However, when we strategically and continually expose a muscle to *just a bit* more stress than it's used to, and then follow with a period of recovery, it grows and expands its capacity.

WILLPOWER IS EXACTLY LIKE A MUSCLE: THE MORE WE USE IT, THE FASTER IT GETS EXHAUSTED, BUT WE CAN STRENGTHEN IT THROUGH STRATEGIC, REPEATED USE.

As we've said before, you don't strengthen a muscle by finding the heaviest weight you can on the first day and then start trying to crank out the reps. This is akin to trying to strengthen your willpower by overhauling everything in your life all at once. That just makes Sneaky Pete completely freak out, and it shunts all energy to the fight-or-flight response, leaving nothing for pause-and-plan.

You have to start small and train your willpower little by little. It's like searching out a dumbbell that is challenging to lift but not impossible. For example, you use 1 percent milk in your coffee instead of cream. You turn off your email while working on something important. You walk around the block every night after dinner. You put your phone away during meals with family or friends. These little things may seem trivial and inadequate, but they are just enough to stretch the bounds of self-control without completely exhausting it. The "reps" will make your willpower progressively stronger.

Setting and accomplishing little goals releases dopamine. (We've discussed dopamine before, and we'll learn even more about it in a minute.) The rush of accomplishment wires our brain to seek out more and more of the dopamine release. It becomes addictive. These small goals and successes pave the way for progressively larger ones as we gradually make each goal just a little bit more challenging, like tackling that next size dumbbell.

Another great benefit of willpower training is that it's like doing squats and having every muscle in your body reap the benefits too. How cool is that? When you train self-control in one area of your life, it increases in overall strength in other areas as well.[30, 31] Researchers conducted an eight-week willpower training program that focused on participants creating and hitting artificial deadlines. At the conclusion of the study, they found that not only did the participants improve their time-management skills, they also ate healthier, exercised more, smoked less, drank less, and consumed less caffeine—even though these behaviors were not addressed in the program.[32]

The even better news is, willpower training is a cycle that keeps improving itself: the more you strategically train your willpower, the less you'll need for each act of self-control. Remember how we learned that every decision depletes willpower? Well, the stronger your willpower muscle is, the less effort and energy it takes to perform an act, leaving more for the next decision. As time goes by, these small steps gradually improve willpower, and it'll be "strong" enough to make change in the big areas of our lives, such as health, nutrition, exercise, work, finances, and resisting any number of temptations.

Exercise Improves Willpower

Exercise is a self-control wonder drug. If you had only one tool to help enhance your willpower, this is the one you'd want to have. Research has found that participating in a regular exercise routine makes your willpower muscle stronger overall and leaves you less vulnerable to the fatiguing effects of self-control.[33]

Next time you need extra motivation to lace up your sneakers, remember this: using your willpower in one area—such as to meet your regular exercise goals—enhances your willpower in *many* areas. When you focus on using self-discipline to accomplish your exercise goals, the extra willpower you gain spills over into almost every area of your life. It has been found to decrease nicotine, alcohol, and caffeine consumption; increase healthy eating; enhance emotional control; and improve study habits. It's also been shown to increase the regularity of doing chores around the house, improve spending monitoring, and improve follow-through with other commitments.[34]

Who knew using our willpower to say yes to a workout could have so many added benefits? As we also know, exercise improves glucose control,[35] which provides critical fuel for willpower. (And just as a reminder, short bursts of exercise have a more powerful effect than longer workouts. Which is perfect, because it's better to say yes to a couple bursts a couple times a day than to say "maybe" to a long block of time we can't find.)

Not Now, but Later

It often seems as if willpower is yet another all-or-nothing matter. Let's think back to that tray of appetizers hovering under your eyes at the client dinner. Sneaky Pete wants those pastries now. *Now!* But advanced brain says eating the pastries will go against your commitment to eating better—your long-term goal. An internal battle ensues. You begin to feel as though your only options are to either inhale all those pastries right now or never, ever, ever eat another pastry again.

Every time we weigh instant gratification versus our long-term goals, we create stress from an inner conflict between caveman brain and advanced brain. This stress registers as a threat to the system, and it's a fight Sneaky Pete typically wins because he always overrides advanced brain during times of stress. However, if we give Sneaky Pete a few minutes to cool off in these moments, advanced brain can step in and redirect behavior. The key is delayed gratification.

Sneaky Pete gets really excited when he knows a reward is immediate. He starts jumping around like a spastic dog begging for a treat. Give it to me! Now! Now! And this is especially true when he can see it right in front of him. So instead of flat-out saying no to a temptation and putting Sneaky Pete on the offensive, tell him (and yourself) you can eat it, drink it, or do it, *but just not right now.* As soon as you create some distance and buy some time, Sneaky Pete eases up, and advanced brain has a better chance of taking control with pause-and-plan.

Let's say you're sitting in front of a plate of chocolate chip cookies. Mmm . . . just look at their lovely golden-brown color and how full of chocolate chips they are. And the smell! Sweet, vanilla-y, chocolaty goodness. Sneaky Pete has spotted an easy and abundant source of fat and sugar. Your mouth is watering, and your heart is pounding in your chest. The pleasure centers of your brain are going off like a winning jackpot in Vegas. Lights! Noise! The clinking of reward!

But then advanced brain yells out, "Wait! You can eat some of these cookies, but in ten minutes or tonight after dinner." Sneaky Pete pauses. You haven't told him no. He just has to wait. He's willing to go along with the plan. You avoided the head-on conflict between the brains that triggers the fight-or-flight response, and you used less willpower to get Sneaky Pete to calm down than a flat-out no.

In Walter Mischel's famous marshmallow experiments from the late 1960s, children were presented with a single marshmallow. They were told they could eat it right then and there, or they could wait fifteen minutes and get two marshmallows. They were then left alone while researchers observed them. Mischel pitted caveman brain against advanced brain to understand how delayed gratification develops.

It was interesting to see what sorts of strategies the kids would use for self-control. They'd turn away from the marshmallow, cover their eyes, kick the table, sing a song, or even pet or sniff the marshmallow.

Fascinating results from the experiments came many years later as well. The children who were able to use willpower to delay gratification that day went on to have more successful life outcomes. They scored higher on their SATs, pursued more education, had a lower incidence of obesity, had less behavior problems or drug addiction, and were less likely to get divorced. They were better able to cope with stress, more likely to plan ahead and use reason, were more socially competent, and had higher levels of self-esteem.

If there's something you really want to do but know you shouldn't, set a time limit for yourself, then give yourself another activity to do. When the time is up, if you still *really* want it, you can have it. This sounds too easy to work, but you may be surprised at how this small delay allows your advanced brain to wrestle control away from Sneaky Pete. Your other activity may be enough to distract you completely—you may not even remember whatever Sneaky Pete wanted you to do. The tsunami has passed!

Delayed gratification also works for things you *don't* want to do. I typically run twice a week, and depending on the day, it may not be something I'm particularly enthused about doing. As I put on my shoes and head out the door, Sneaky Pete is kicking and screaming about the whole thing. He doesn't want to go. In these instances, I tell myself that if I'm really not into it after a half mile of running, I can turn around and go home. I think I've quit the run once.

It gets me out the door, but it doesn't necessarily mean I've conquered Sneaky Pete. He decides to come with me on the run, complaining the whole time. He tells me several times to stop running because it's too hard—to just walk for a little bit. When this happens, I tell myself that if I really have to walk, I can do it when I reach the next block. When I get to that block, I then ask myself if I *really* need to walk, or if I could make it *just one more* block. If I really need to stop at that point, I can.

I continue to dangle the carrot of walking in front of Sneaky Pete, and a good 95 percent of the time, I can make it all the way home without walking. But if I had flat-out told myself I couldn't stop running until I got home, it would have felt like too much of a challenge. I would have quit the first time Sneaky Pete complained.

Using this time-delay tactic can also prevent the "what the hell" effect. We'll discuss this in more detail later, but the basic idea is that sometimes we tell ourselves no, then we lose all sense of willpower and go off the deep end. Instead of just having one chocolate chip cookie, we say no . . . then end up eating the entire plate. Then because we messed up that moment, we ditch all our efforts for change for the rest of the day—or the rest of the week. We give up and see this as our opportunity to get some much-needed rest from willpower. We pig out, skip our workouts, drink our faces off, and smoke an entire pack of cigarettes, setting ourselves back tremendously.

This is especially common when we're dieting. As we discussed in chapter four, dieting and denying certain foods automatically increases our desire for them, which requires more willpower. Unfortunately, though, when we're dieting, willpower is weak because of low glucose from calorie restriction and because we've exhausted our self-control by denying food all day long. One slip-up, and suddenly we spiral, only to say "What the hell?" when we realize what just happened.

Sometimes a well-planned "not now, but later" delay can prevent the "what the hell" effect and its disastrous consequences. Delayed gratification has short-term and long-term benefits as well. Researchers have found that postponing consumption of a tempting food means you not only avoid eating it (or much of it) in the moment of temptation, but you also eat less of it later. As a long-term strategy, it results in eating less of the food overall.[36]

What to Do

- Set small goals for yourself, knowing they gradually build your willpower muscle to be able to handle larger ones.

- First build willpower in an area of your life that feels easy, and your sense of willpower will strengthen in all aspects of your life.

- Exercise is a wonder drug for willpower, so get your body moving with regular workouts.

- Tell yourself you can give in to a temptation, but just not right now. Set a time limit, keep yourself busy, and allow advanced brain to pause and plan.

Change and the Chemistry of Desire

We just discovered how willpower is the "muscle" of change. If we overuse it, we often fall short of our goals. But if we harness and train it effectively, willpower can bring us closer to resiliency.

Next, we're going to learn about dopamine, the chemical that plays a key role with change. Like the willpower muscle, this chemical can either make or break our goals. The difference is learning how to use it *for* us, not *against* us.

As we discussed in chapter two, dopamine is a neurotransmitter associated with motivation, perseverance, and accomplishing goals. It's often referred to as the reward molecule, but it's a bit more complex and nuanced than that. More specifically, it plays a significant role in signaling feedback about the promise of a reward. In a word, the hunt.

The possibility or promise of a reward is very important in the process of motivation. Nature created an internal reward system that reinforced behaviors necessary for our ancestors' survival. Working hard to hunt, gather, build, raise young, and travel was extremely difficult and used a lot of precious energy. The potential payoff of food, shelter, and family were often far in the future, but just thinking about those rewards released dopamine to keep our ancestors going when they were tired or wanted to quit. The promise of satisfaction or happiness is what kept them working so hard.

It's important to note that dopamine relates to the *promise* of happiness, but not happiness itself. Evolution doesn't really care about our happiness. It's more concerned about the continuation of the species. Dopamine is for taking action, while other chemicals are for happiness. The promise of a reward is what keeps us striving. It's the wanting, the seeking, the desire—which is why it's sometimes also referred to as the "chemical of perseverance and success."

This hit of dopamine can come from the reward itself as well as the anticipation of the reward. When a certain behavior becomes associated with reward, we don't have to wait to actually receive the reward to get a release of dopamine. Once we learn it's coming, the dopamine releases from the anticipation. A good example is Pavlov's dogs: once the bell was associated with the reward of food, the bell itself became a signal of an ensuing award, and they began to drool and get excited whenever they heard it. Dopamine comes from both response and prediction, and it can be inherent or learned.

Dopamine was very helpful for ensuring our ancestors' longevity. But in today's environment, it's one of the shortest paths to extinction. Anything we see with the potential to make us feel good can be mistakenly associated as something critical to our survival. Dopamine makes us think we *need* that burger between two chicken patties instead of buns in the same way Sneaky Pete needed that huge bison steak. The only difference is, Sneaky Pete actually did need that steak in order to survive for at least a few more days, while we need that chicken-burger combo like a kick in the head. Dopamine hijacks our focus and attention. All we can think about is getting the pleasure—and as quickly as possible. We see it, we want it, and we want a *lot* of it.

We live in a world where food and other mind-altering chemicals such as caffeine, nicotine, and alcohol are highly available. Any time we see these items, a flood of dopamine is released in anticipation of getting them. It goes beyond food, though. Every few weeks, there are new fashions, trends, media, and games. We have access to everything on a global, nonstop, twenty-four-hour-a-day level.

Advertising and marketing companies play on our dopamine systems all the time. They understand it's more appropriately the "chemical of desire" rather than the "chemical of perseverance" today. If they can hit it, they can get it—our hard-earned money, that is. They expose us to images with the promise of sex, success, beauty, and happiness. They're all things we can have simply by purchasing their products. The sense of desire takes over, spurs us into action, and we buy it.

From a resiliency perspective, what's worse is that stress and dopamine create a vicious cycle. As the "chemical of desire," dopamine increases our desire for reward even more when we're stressed.

Stress and Dopamine

Neuroscientists have shown that stress puts the brain into a reward-seeking state. In one study, participants experienced stress in a lab setting, and then the researchers observed how that affected the participants' desires for things that made them feel good. The researchers found that smokers craved more cigarettes; binge eaters craved high-fat, high-sugar foods; recovering alcoholics or drug addicts wanted a drink or drugs; and dieters wanted to cheat.[37]

> If you've taken a spoon to a tub of ice cream or found yourself elbow-deep in a bag of chips during a time of stress, that's because junk food is a double whammy. Dopamine puts us in a reward-seeking state when we're stressed, making us hunt for pleasurable food. And that same stress releases cortisol, which also has us seeking high-fat, high-sugar items to replace the energy it presumes we've used fighting or fleeing.

And really making the cycle worse, junk food itself creates additional stress, sending our glucose levels on a roller coaster ride.

Why do we eat, drink, shop, watch TV, surf the web, and play video games when we're stressed out? Because we want to feel better and they hit the brain's reward center. According to the American Psychological Association's "Stress in America" survey, the activities I just listed were rated as the top strategies people use to cope with stress. But they also reported them to be the most ineffective.[38] After the thrilling hunt for food, new clothes, or a secret level on a video game is over, the dopamine is gone. We're back in seeking mode, and the cycle starts over—it never gives us a "stop" signal.

Not even counting food and alcohol, think of all the things we have in society today that release dopamine and create a continual feedback loop of desire:

- **Email.** We're addicted to constantly checking it and opening it. We want to be connected to our tribes and want to feel like valued members, so we get a reward from every message. And there's the thrill of perhaps discovering the reward of a business opportunity we've been hunting for. However, once we open each message, the dopamine is gone—and we're left with 312 emails to answer.

- **Surfing the web.** The Internet is endless, and we get drawn into the anticipation of looking for the next interesting blog, the next funny video, the next great décor or cooking idea, or the best site for pornography. It's a continual search for something that will make us feel good. But as soon as we see something good on the web, we get the reward, and all we want is another one.

- **Facebook, Twitter, and other social media.** We'll post something on our social networks and then be drawn to checking and rechecking how many people liked it or retweeted it. We want validation from our tribes, and social media is a quick and easy way to get it. We also keep checking these networks to get a hit of dopamine from learning the latest piece of gossip or news.

- **Video games.** The promise of reaching the next level or finding the next hidden thing keeps us drawn into games for hours on end. When we talk about dopamine hijacking our attention and focus, this one is a great example: just try and talk to someone who is playing a video game. Online multiplayer games double the dopamine as gamers seek the reward of reaching new levels plus the reward of connecting with tribes.

- **Gambling.** Simply put, lottery tickets, online gambling, and casinos wouldn't exist without dopamine.

- **Work.** The reward of more recognition, another raise, or a new promotion can be very compelling motivation, keeping us working long hours for months or years. When we combine these dangling carrots with email, it creates a very powerful combination where we end up making work a top priority in our lives.

- **Shopping.** Whether online or in a store, the hunt for the perfect new shirt or latest gadget of technology is exciting and alluring. We think the happiness will be long lasting, but it's quite short. And then we're left with the unhappy realization of bills to pay.

We continue to think doing these things will make us happy when we're stressed. But in truth, they end up bringing more stress and misery. Over time, we become sensitized to the effects of dopamine and need more of it to feel better. It's the chemistry behind many types of addictions.

We're also living in a modern world where many achievements and acquisitions aren't a matter of survival. Dopamine kept our ancestors working hard, but the payoff of food, shelter, and a mate resulted in real, lasting happiness. In contrast, a lot of the dopamine hits we get today have no actual reward and instead lead to decreased quality and quantity of life.

It's important to find activities and rewards that truly bring meaning and happiness into our lives. That is, it's important to use dopamine to our advantage when creating meaningful change toward resiliency.

Link Dopamine to Healthy New Habits

Rather than reinforcing empty, unhealthy habits with dopamine, make a conscious decision to reinforce behavior that improves your life and builds a better you. Because dopamine is released when we associate pleasure and reward with a particular behavior, it's possible to use this pathway to our advantage when establishing new rituals and activities in your Resiliency rEvolution. The trick is to make the new habits feel so rewarding, soon even just anticipating them is enough to bring on the dopamine.

Here are a few suggestions about how this can work.

Oh Yeah—That Feels Good: Consciously Associate a Behavior with Feeling Good

When long-term exercisers are asked why they workout, 92 percent say they do it because it makes them feel good.[39] Over time, these people grew to expect and crave the positive feelings endorphins and other neurochemicals provided during and after working out. Intrinsic motivation, such as a positive emotional state, is much more powerful than external motivation, such as fitting into a certain size or losing a particular number of pounds. Sneaky Pete loves to feel good, and nothing feels as good as making your well-being a top priority. It results in a long-lasting positive mood state emotionally, mentally, and chemically.

Immediately after they work out, I encourage many of my clients to write down how they feel physically, emotionally, and mentally, in addition to how it's going to positively affect them over the long run. This simple step creates the association between exercise and feeling good, which reinforces their behavior. Soon, they'll get a hit of dopamine even before they work out.

Connect all your resiliency habits to feeling good. Keep a food log and write down how you feel during and after each time you eat, as well as at the end of the day as you reflect back on your choices. For every night you go to bed on time, think about the benefits you're giving yourself, both to your body and brain, and how it sets you up to be successful the next day. Every time you take a deep breath instead of blowing up at someone or a situation, reflect on how good it feels to treat others in a respectful way and how you've foiled Sneaky Pete. All these things hardwire our brain to seek out these behaviors on a regular basis.

Get High: Frame Your New Behaviors as Opportunities to Raid Your Inner Pharmacy

As we discussed in chapter three, exercise unlocks the pharmacy inside us. It's the best way to get "high." Instead of considering exercise as a punishment or a chore, think about it as a way to get the release of endorphins, endocannabinoids, dopamine, serotonin, brain derived neurotrophic factor, human growth hormone, and other chemicals. You're bathing in bliss molecules!

In addition, exercise uses up the stress hormones and hits the reset button. It also raises your threshold for stress and gives you a natural energy boost and a break from your day. Thinking about exercise as a natural high will get even more dopamine working, pushing you toward it.

In a similar way, see healthy eating as a trip to the inner pharmacy, too. Think about eating natural foods (instead of processed, fast, or junk food) as a way to supply your body with dense nutrients that minimize stress and supply your cells with quality energy to meet the incredibly high demands of your average day.

Break It Down: Divide Your Goal into Several Mini Goals

Imagine your goal is to consistently eat an afternoon snack. When you do, you'll get a nice hit of dopamine, which will reinforce the new behavior. But why settle for just one hit? Why not turn that one goal into many opportunities for dopamine—and many levels of reinforcement along the way?

That's why it's important to break your behavior-change goal into several smaller ones. You not only simplify the steps toward change (which helps Sneaky Pete calm down), but you also get many more releases of dopamine that reinforce your new activity.

For that goal to eat an afternoon snack, say you first set a mini goal to merely remember to pack your snack in the morning. When you remember it (while brushing your teeth, perhaps), you get a nice little hit of dopamine. You then grab the snack from the kitchen and put it in your bag. Bing! There's another squirt of dopamine. Next, you grab your phone and set a reminder to eat your snack at 3:00 p.m. You just got a little bit more dopamine. At 3:00, your phone goes off. Your body shoots out dopamine in anticipation of eating your snack and in reward for the alarm plan being so ingenious. You stop what you're doing and eat, getting one more dose of dopamine before getting back to work. Look at all the dopamine you milked out for just "one" goal.

As this example shows, small successes and wins stimulate the release of dopamine, the fuel for transformation. Over time, this pattern—action followed by internal reward—will wire your brain to *want* to do these behaviors. You won't feel as if you're forcing yourself.

In addition, being successful with little goals toward resiliency increases your confidence to succeed—both overall as well as with the bigger goals. It'll help you see you can build resiliency in spite of a busy schedule, stress, deadlines, and unexpected things popping up.

Winner, Winner: Keep an Internal Scorecard

Train to get dopamine hits from internally validating yourself instead of waiting for external validation that may not come at the right time and place, if at all. When you keep an internal locus of control, where you're the one judging your success, you put yourself in command of your dopamine pathway and can administer the chemical of persistence at will.

No one is going to deliver a present to your door when you eat to a Level 3 at meals this week. Balloons are not going to drop from the ceiling when you finish your workout. In fact, your friends may not notice the physical transformation happening as a result of your consistent training. Your boss might not give you a pat on the back for keeping your cool more often at work. But it doesn't mean your hard work isn't paying off. You're feeling less stress. You're sleeping better at night. You're more focused and productive at work. You're making yourself a priority and following through with your commitments to yourself. Which is quite commendable. (Whoops. I just gave you some external validation. Sorry.)

It's also important to award yourself a "point" and some dopamine for every step you take in the journey of change—not just for every pound lost or clothing size dropped. The rEvolution focuses on small, manageable behaviors you perform every day, often in sixty seconds or less. These action steps make you a stronger leader, a more compassionate significant other, or a more engaged parent. A better version of yourself. It's change you can *feel* from the inside out—change to your physiology, chemistry, cognitive function, energy level, and emotions.

Create a belief that each and every thing you do matters to your resiliency, performance, health, and happiness and gets you one step closer to accomplishing your goals. Recognize when you follow through on a commitment and celebrate your success—even if it's a simple mental "Yes!"

Check It Off: Keep Your Dopamine Pathway Firing with Accomplishments

Ideally, you want dopamine to flow like a river as you work toward your resiliency goals. When we don't release dopamine on a regular basis, we can feel complacent, apathetic, and depressed. That's why it's critical to link little things to a big sense of accomplishment.

Among those long-term exercisers mentioned earlier, 67 percent say working out gives them a big sense of accomplishment.[40] They seek out the sense of triumph and self-reward that comes from making a promise to themselves and following through with the workout, and it keeps them coming back for more.

Working out is just one example, though. The key is to start breaking your whole day into dopamine-worthy accomplishments. This may be too much information... but for me, the act of vacuuming is hands down one of the most rewarding things I do in a week. The instant gratification and satisfaction (i.e., dopamine) I get from transforming something from dirty to clean borders on the obscene.

More importantly, I write a daily to-do list on a piece of paper. Physically drawing a line through each task I accomplish feels ridiculously good in a world where there's always more to do. I plan and log workouts on my calendar, and looking back at all those filled-in spaces gives me a dopamine fix, provides me a huge sense of accomplishment, and reinforces the behavior. Having a to-do list and checking things off, whether large or small, is a great way to get regular doses of dopamine, not to mention a way to keep yourself organized and accountable.

If you're having trouble taking action on your daily to-do list, write down something you've already accomplished, then check it off for some retroactive dopamine. Or add something super easy to accomplish to get you going. As you just learned, you can also simplify an action step or break it into mini goals. (Look at how many accomplishments go into the simple act of eating an afternoon snack.) Find ways to self-administer some dopamine because a sense of progress is critical in keeping us moving forward with our goals.

In fact, let's look next at how to create an action plan that starts you on your way with the Resiliency rEvolution.

Planning Your rEvolution

As I've said throughout the book, the last thing I want to do is add stress to your life. And now you understand what I mean—change can be stressful and unsuccessful if not done strategically. As we've discussed, both the unconscious and the conscious aspects of change need to be addressed. That is, you need both Sneaky Pete and advanced brain on board.

Chapter five focused on the unconscious aspects of change, such as with optimal defaults. Creating optimal defaults is the first piece of your action plan. Now here are six critical steps for planning successful behavior change on a conscious level. These steps are the foundation of your action plan as you embark on the Resiliency rEvolution. (When you're ready to make your action plan, see the template in appendix A.)

Step 1: Ask Yourself, "What's Truly Important Right Now, and in What Ways Do I Feel Ready to Change?"

Many of us may think we're supposed to make certain changes in our lives because everyone else seems to be doing it or it's popular, or because we're feeling pressure from someone else. But forget all that. How would *you* like to take better care of yourself? What would that look like?

Maybe you want to build resiliency with some of the strategies in the book. Or your goals might not have anything to do with what we've directly talked about in this book. Maybe you want to set aside personal time for yourself or quality time with another person. You might designate one hour a week as family time or set up a recurring date night to spend with your significant other.

Your goals may involve your work life as well. Maybe you want to stop multitasking in the presence of other people. You might change the way you run a meeting to make it more effective or to create more of a sense of collaboration.

You be the judge of what *you* want in *your* life. Don't listen to the internal voice that may tell you it's too small of a goal or it's too silly. If it's truly what you want, it's valid and you should go for it.

When I work with clients on this first step of the action plan, they often fall into two categories. Some people have very specific goals. Others aren't sure what they want to do but just know something needs to change in their lives. You likely fall into one category or the other, or maybe you're somewhere in between.

Whichever category you're in, you'll benefit from the "Five Whys," a tool I use with my clients. The purpose is to dig into your goal, pushing past the superficial, external reasoning in order to uncover the meaningful, intrinsic foundation of your desire to change.

For example, let's look at how the Five Whys work for people with very specific goals. When clients tell me they want to lose weight, my first question is, "Why do you want to lose weight?" They look at me as if I were a complete idiot and tell me it's because they want to look better. Then I ask, "Why do you want to look better?" Now their facial expression turns toward confusion. They reply that when they look better, they feel better. Now I ask, "Why do you want to feel better?" No one has asked them this question before, and they certainly haven't asked it of themselves.

Many of them get stuck here, and I really have to push. They finally realize that when they feel better, they act better. "Why do you want to act differently?" They most often share something related to interaction with their loved ones—how they want to be more patient, loving, or engaged. I then ask, "Why does that matter to you?" and the answer is directly tied to their tribe, values, and sense of purpose. Something deeper, more meaningful, and more compelling.

Begin with your initial goal statement, then dig and dig with the Five Whys (or more) until you reach that meaningful level. That's where you'll find your motivation for lifelong change.

Step 2: Identify One Simple, Clear, Practical, and Very Small Action Step

Most people's New Year's resolutions don't work for the long term. Only 8 percent of people who make resolutions are successful.[41] And for the 92 percent who fail, it happens very quickly, typically within the first or second week. It's easy to see why, when most resolutions are sweeping declarations such as "I resolve to lose twenty pounds, stop drinking, and stop smoking."

Changing too much is rarely, if ever, effective, yet it's what many of us continually try. It's an exercise in futility and frustration that often leads to more harm than good, and we have to stop it. *It doesn't work.*

What does work is creating a realistic, long-term plan that starts with one immediate, doable step that sets you up to be successful. By focusing on one singular task, we strategically don't overuse our limited capacity for self-discipline and willpower.

After learning about change and willpower, we know why. Each act of willpower makes us more likely to lose control later, and exerting self-control in one area of our life limits our ability to do so in all others. Resolving to go on a crash diet, quit smoking, and quit drinking all at once is a recipe for failure. It also means we'll probably find ourselves gossiping at work, blowing up at someone, struggling to finish a difficult project, or skipping workouts in the process.

Let's say you want to be more resilient, have steadier levels of energy, and preserve lean body mass for a strong metabolism. You'd like to completely overhaul your diet. You've been eating a lot of fast food because you travel regularly for work, and you often go long periods of time without eating and then eat too much. Great goals—but you can't accomplish that all at once. And you can't go from "zero to sixty." As we've learned, you need to break it down into *one* simple, easy goal at a time.

In order to be strategic with your limited willpower, perhaps you decide to make the commitment to simply eat a lean source of protein at every meal. It's one simple commitment, but it packs a big punch: consuming lean protein at meals means a steady supply of glucose and also better maintenance and growth of muscle tissue. The consistent source of glucose ensures levels don't spike or get too low, which places less stress on your body. And it's fuel for both advanced brain and caveman brain, so you're better able to handle stress. This smaller goal is simple, but it aligns with your larger goals.

Keep It Positive

Keep your action step positive as well. When you identify your goal and write it down, word your statement as something you *will* do instead of something you *can't* or *won't* do. When we frame things negatively or focus on what's missing, it creates a sense of deprivation and denial that Sneaky Pete hates. He immediately starts pushing back.

In addition, behaviors that require thought suppression are more active and prominent in our mind. We've all had this happen: We decide we're no longer going to eat chocolate. (Feel free to substitute something you love here.) No more chocolate, and we're going to be just fine with it. However, we somehow start noticing chocolate everywhere . . . on people's desks, in magazine advertisements, on TV commercials. We catch ourselves daydreaming about eating some and even swear we can smell it at random times throughout the day. By trying to suppress our thoughts about chocolate, we end up focusing on it even more. (And we know how well willpower works in that situation—advanced brain can only fight those obsessive thoughts for so long.)

Keeping it positive removes that entire dilemma. There's no denial, no suppression. For instance, instead of saying, "I'm going to stop eating so much junk food in the afternoons," you could say, "I'm going to eat a delicious piece of fruit for my afternoon snack." (You just got Sneaky Pete's attention—that sounds tasty.) "I'm going to quit watching so much TV at night" could be reframed as, "I'm going to spend an hour each evening doing something I enjoy, such as connecting with family or friends, working on a personal project, or engaging in a leisure-time activity." (Sign him up—Sneaky Pete sure loves leisure time.)

EXAMPLES OF SIMPLE, POSITIVE ACTION STEPS

- Eat lean protein at every meal.
- Exercise for thirty minutes, twenty minutes, or even ten. Every minute counts.
- Accumulate thirty minutes of exercise by the end of the day.

- Sleep at least eight hours every night.

- During each meal, stop when satisfied.

- Twice during the workday, get up and move or stretch.

- Eat every three to four hours.

- Eat a low-glycemic snack midmorning and midafternoon.

- Eat breakfast every day (including protein).

- Do ten minutes of interval training using Hit the Deck.

- Eat three servings of fruit and/or vegetables every day.

- Stretch for ten minutes every Monday, Wednesday, and Friday night before getting into bed.

- Drink one glass of water with every meal.

- Do five minutes of situps Tuesday, Thursday, and Saturday morning right after the alarm goes off. (Set it five minutes early.)

- Do ___ [fill in the blank] minutes of cardiovascular exercise every Monday, Wednesday, and Friday during the lunch hour.

- Order thin crust pizza instead of the thick. Dare: order one with no cheese. (How the vegetables roast without cheese is delicious.)

- Eat white cheese instead of orange.

- Eat whole grain bread instead of white.

- Bring a healthy lunch to work two times per week.

- Drink skim milk instead of 1 or 2 percent.

Step 3: Ask Yourself, "How Confident Am I That I Can Do This Task Consistently?"

The easy part of making change is saying we're going to do it. The hard part is actually *doing* it. We've got to get Sneaky Pete on board with the program. How do we do it? Again, by making the change small, do-able, and nonthreatening so he doesn't even notice it's happening . . . we slip it past him while he's looking the other way. We make the change strategy *so easy a caveman could do it.*

CHANGE: MAKE IT SO EASY A CAVEMAN COULD DO IT.

This step is in some ways a continuation of the previous step. Here's where you test how "simple, clear, practical, and very small" your goal really is. As you identify your singular action step, you need to ask yourself this one critically important question: "On a scale of one to ten, how confident am I that I can successfully follow this goal for the next thirty days?" If you rate your confidence as anything less than a nine or a ten, that means your goal is not simple enough.

As we know, if your goal is too complex, you're very likely to fail. Eventually, you'd need to revise the commitment to make it simpler and easier. Why set yourself up for failure when you can set yourself up for success instead? That's why it's important to test your confidence in your goal before you even begin.

A client I was working with wanted to start exercising regularly. He was under a lot of stress, his fight-or-flight fuel allocation station had grown over the last twelve months, and he wasn't sleeping well. He desperately wanted to feel better and lose weight.

When I asked what his weekly goal for exercise was, he said "every day." I appreciated his excitement to make change, but I knew from years of experience working with people there was no way he could successfully go from not exercising at all to exercising every day, especially with a demanding job and regular travel schedule. Our conversation went something like this:

"Wow," I said. "That would be a lot of exercise. Are you really sure you could exercise *every single day*? You work long hours in the office, at home, and on the road, and that would be really challenging for anyone."

His face fell a little bit. The idea of exercising every day sounded like successful change to him, but he hadn't really stopped to think about the reality of exercising every single day: how much time it would take, where he would do it, what he would do, how he'd have to pack work-out clothes, and so on. Advanced brain had gotten really excited about a future self that would somehow have more time and more commitment than his present self actually had.

"Hmm. Yeah, I suppose every day might be a little tough," he admitted. "Maybe five days a week is more realistic?"

The fact he stated his new commitment as a question rather than a statement was a huge red flag. We were nowhere close to something that would be doable. "On a scale of one to ten, how sure are you that you could find the time to exercise five days per week?" I asked.

Looking up toward the corner of the room, he said, "Well, I think if I was really being realistic, I would rate it a seven."

Using the words "I think" and looking off to the corner instead of looking me in the eye meant he still wasn't close. "Okay. What if you were to exercise three times per week? How confident are you that you could make that happen?"

Looking a little surprised, he said, "Only three times? Probably an eight."

So close, but we're not there yet. "Then how about two times a week for fifteen minutes?"

He laughed. "What? Only two times per week for that short amount of time? Are you kidding me? Of course I can do that—but it sounds too easy."

And that's when I knew I had him. Doing something that sounds laughable is exactly the point. Ease and simplicity make Sneaky Pete happy and content. It's got to be so easy that it sounds *too easy*—so easy a caveman could do it, remember? If our goal is too complex or stretches us too much, caveman brain takes over, and we'll have very little chance at change.

Does your goal make you laugh at how easy it is? Is your confidence at a nine or a ten that you can meet the goal? If yes, great—you're setting yourself on the path to success. If no, then you need to simplify the goal.

The book you hold in your hands is a perfect example of how the right goal—a nine or a ten—can overcome inertia and gets us moving forward toward a larger goal. In the beginning, I tried to sit down to write this book multiple times. But after a few days of working on it, I would quit. There was so much content and so many directions I could go with it, I became *completely* overwhelmed and I shut down. I chose to do nothing instead.

Then I worked with a writing coach, who helped me first come up with an outline—a clear step-by-step plan—for the book. This made me feel a little bit better, but Sneaky Pete was still freaking out. So many chapters! So many words!

My first goal was to write the introduction. In my mind, an introduction isn't technically a chapter, and it only had to be a couple pages for this first draft, so it seemed totally doable. I felt a big sense of accomplishment from getting started, and I was optimistic that more was possible.

I soon identified the right goal: to simply go to my desk and write every day. I didn't set a certain number of pages to accomplish each day because I knew it wasn't realistic for me. I knew there would be days during the process when I wouldn't have time or wasn't as productive. But I was confident I could write *something* every day.

When I sat down to start the first chapter, I didn't think of it as having to write a whole chapter. I just needed to start by writing one page, one paragraph at a time. (Using the delayed gratification trick mentioned earlier, I promised myself I could stop when I needed a break. Sometimes I needed a break after five minutes; sometimes it was after an hour.)

The act of writing consistently, every day, was my goal as well as my measure of success. Did I write today? Awesome. I'm now closer to finishing. Did I not write? Okay, not cool—it's even more important that I write tomorrow. Each day (wait—*most* days) I made progress. As I did, my confidence grew. And so did the book.

Step 4: Put It on Your Calendar

In addition to being very specific about your action step, you need to plan the exact date, time, and place you will perform the new activity. Studies show that being very specific about where, when, and how you'll perform a task helps your brain detect and act on the opportunity, increasing your chances of success by roughly 300 percent.[42] Often times, overcoming challenges has less to do with willpower than it does with planning and scheduling.

Continuing the client story from above, he sat down with his calendar every Sunday morning and looked at his upcoming week to schedule his two fifteen-minute workouts. I often recommend using the weekend as an opportunity for workouts, as it's usually easier than trying to cram exercise into a busy workweek. The client used this strategy, liking the idea of doing one of the workouts on Saturdays and the other on Wednesdays so he could hit the midweek reset button on his stress. Every Wednesday, he would get up twenty-five minutes early, have a quick snack of a banana, then do fifteen minutes of Hit the Deck for both his cardiovascular and resistance training. This routine would also work when he was on the road—he could keep it no matter what.

Saturdays were the other ideal day for him to exercise. He decided to schedule a run at 9:00 a.m., going out for five minutes, then turning around and coming back, for a total of ten minutes. He would then finish the final five minutes of his workout with thirty pushups, thirty crunches, and thirty squats. Everything was spelled out in clear, simple steps.

If your action step is something you do every day, plan it as specifically as you can. If your goal is to, say, eat two servings of fruit and/or vegetables, be clear about which meal or snack you'll "schedule" it for. If your goal is something that happens a certain number of times per week, choose what days it will be, including what time and where it will happen. Set yourself a reminder if you need one.

It's important to be mindful of the limited resource of willpower as you schedule your action. Recall that our self-control is highest in the morning, then it deteriorates as the day goes on. You may want to schedule your most challenging tasks for earlier in the day. It's also important to assess what's getting the bulk of your willpower each day. Do you spend most of it at work or at home? When you're with family or by yourself? How can you prioritize things so you can both preserve and use willpower when you need it most to meet your goal?

Putting an activity on our calendar helps us avoid what's called the Zeigarnik effect, which is when our brain nags us about all the things we haven't done or finished. When we hold things in our short-term memory to do or act on later, we have to continue to rehearse and remember them so we don't forget. (Remember to do laundry, stop at the grocery store, and call mom . . . remember to do laundry, stop at the grocery store, and call mom . . .) All that nagging takes up a lot of our energy.

However, if we make a concrete plan by getting specific about a time, date, and place, the matter will be settled and it will no longer require mental energy. As you can imagine, this saves a lot of willpower.

Step 5: Create Optimal Defaults

Now it's time to incorporate your unconscious efforts toward change. That is, it's time to get Sneaky Pete on board with your commitment without his even realizing it.

Using the ideas from chapter five, create several optimal defaults that will turn your conscious goal into unconscious behavior. Don't let this carefully designed action plan rely on willpower alone. You want this to be a no-brainer, remember? This is where you back up that score of nine or ten from step three. If your optimal defaults are strong, it will take a lot of effort to *not* follow through on your commitment. (It's a win-win: Sneaky Pete likes taking the path of least resistance, and advanced brain likes making decisions in line with your goals.)

Get creative about how you can automatically perform this new behavior at work and home and while traveling. Also think about how to avoid using willpower to follow your action step while eating, exercising, grocery shopping, and dining out. (For quick examples of optimal defaults, see appendix B.)

Consciously identifying what, when, where, how, and especially *why* we want to change can be difficult. And taking conscious action to make that change a reality can be even harder. It requires a lot of energy and focus from advanced brain.

But in some high-stress situations, Sneaky Pete may not be ready to let that happen yet. When in survival mode—especially in extreme situations—Sneaky Pete keeps resources for himself. For some people, each day is truly a matter of survival. Perhaps there's a serious illness, dire financial trouble, or turmoil involving family and relationships. People in survival mode may not be capable of this level of commitment yet. Such a conscious step toward change may not be an option right now, even if they want it to be.

If you are unable to make an official action step due to your current life situation, perhaps you can still begin by following an optimal default or two without committing to a full action plan. Eat a snack. Take those stairs. If it's a no-brainer, do it. You especially could benefit from extra fuel and a chance to reset the stress response.

Of course, you'll see more effective, longer-lasting results when you're ready and able to do an action plan. But a few optimal defaults in the meantime will be small steps with small benefits for much-needed resiliency. It may just be a chance to gather a little momentum, build some confidence, and get ready to start your rEvolution.

Step 6: Write about Your Success

No plan is complete without follow-up. Each time you perform the action step (whether it be twice a week or every day), follow up by logging it in your accountability system (which we're about to get to) and writing a few words about how you feel afterward, both physically and psychologically.

Earlier we discussed how linking dopamine to an activity will help reinforce the behavior. This is why it's important to identify and record your positive feelings about your action. It recruits the emotional caveman brain and gets it on board with the program. We know Sneaky Pete loves feeling good. So write about how your accomplishment, big or small, makes you feel good. This creates a dopamine pathway, leading you and Sneaky Pete to desire the activity.

You may jot down something such as, "I feel really good about eating breakfast. I've given my body a source of energy it needs to function well, and I've balanced my blood glucose levels for the morning. I didn't put additional stress on my body, I made myself a priority, and I'm on the road to taking better care of myself."

As you record your thoughts, it's important to recognize and emphasize behaviors rather than specific outcomes. That is, focus on how the act of performing the task on a regular basis is the reward in and of itself. As we discussed earlier, that's much more motivating than basing your reward on some expected or desired outcome. Writing about making you and your resiliency a priority, about doing the best you can considering the circumstances, and about being consistent will tap into your sense of intrinsic motivation. It connects your emotions to your actions. This drives you to repeat the behavior for the sake of the behavior, rather than attach "success" or "failure" to an external source of measurement.

A client I work with came up with a brilliant way of writing about her action step to eat moderately during the holidays. She wrote, "Tomorrow I'm not going to remember or care that I ate that extra piece of fudge. The comfort of it doesn't stay with me, and there's no long-term value. However, when I make the choice *not* to eat it, I'm proud of myself the next day. The good feeling stays with me."

She focused on the emotion of the action step, not the outcome. She didn't write, "I decided not to eat the fudge." Instead, she went deeper. She celebrated the thought process behind her decision, expressing how that one action aligned with—and reinforced—the goals and values she's building.

Accountability

Sneaky Pete can convince us we're doing just fine with our change goals, but accountability systems don't lie. It's very important we use tracking systems to monitor our follow-through and progress toward our goals.

We use accountability systems in our professional lives to ensure we're following through with commitments. It provides clarity and culpability, and it allows us to perform well. Unfortunately, though, we often leave things to chance when it comes to our personal lives. We just wing it. Sneaky Pete wants to make sure he has an out, so he convinces us we're just fine without any tracking system that may prove otherwise.

As we know, Sneaky Pete focuses on the present moment and what's right in front of us, which means we're easily distracted. Sometimes he's a bit like a bird being sidetracked by something shiny—he's drawn to it, and we end up going down a path we didn't intend.

On top of that, what little attention we can muster goes right to our long to-do list filled with responsibilities that have nothing to do with change or resiliency. And that's not even counting the unforeseen circumstances that command our focus from time to time.

In this constant state of distraction and divided attention, it can be hard to stay consciously focused on change. We remember the *idea* of our goal to change, but we can lose track of the *actions* we're taking—or not taking—to make that change a reality. Yet it always comes as a surprise when we suddenly realize weeks have gone by and we're still at square one (or behind it)—we wonder what happened to this great idea of "change" we once had.

Using a daily accountability system keeps us conscious of the action steps we must take toward change as well as helps keep us focused in a world of distraction. When you create an action plan, you create a contract with yourself. Your accountability system, then, is your way to measure how well you're delivering on your promises. It's your scorecard.

After over twenty years of exercising consistently, I still record every single one of those workout sessions on my calendar. It's my fitness accountability system. First off, it's too easy to think I hit my five workouts for the week when things are busy. When there's a lot going on, things are moving fast, and I'm doing the best I can, I'm certain I'm keeping up on my personal commitments. But then I look at my calendar, and I can see with my own eyes that it just *feels* that way. When there's a glaring white space where a workout is supposed to be, there's no denying I fell short of my commitment to myself. Without visual proof of a skipped workout, I could easily put it out of my mind and choose to ignore it. My calendar keeps me honest.

Second, logging every completed workout is a golden opportunity for dopamine. Remember how we talked about breaking a single goal into mini goals along the way? I get a dose of dopamine when I schedule my workouts for the week, another dose when I get ready with anticipation for the workout, all sorts of doses during the workout itself, another when I finish, and yet another when I log it in my calendar. (And then there's still one more chance for dopamine with the calendar, which I'll get to later.)

Another benefit of an accountability system is that it can help you spot trends in your life and recognize cause-and-effect. I was working with a client who had serious sleep and anxiety issues. He was using sleeping pills and alcohol on a regular basis to fall asleep—a combination he knew was not healthy, but it seemed to be the only solution. Every week I would look at his accountability logs to see if he was following through with his commitments. It didn't take me too long to spot a trend: On the days he exercised, he didn't need to take a sleeping pill. If he didn't exercise, he took one. It was like clockwork. After we discussed the trend, his number of workouts per week increased, he became far more consistent with them, and his intake of sleeping pills dropped dramatically.

It's up to you to determine what sort of accountability system works for you. Some people prefer the primitive system of pen and paper, while others like to use technology. Put your commitments into your calendar, whether paper or digital. Keep a log. Create a spreadsheet. Purchase a tracking device you wear on your body that automatically downloads data to your computer. Download an app that tracks what you eat, how you move, how you sleep, or any other number of indicators. You can join an online community with message boards, and reminders. At the end of every chapter, you may have seen links to www.ph-performance.com, where you can find tools, articles, and videos and you can sign up for regular resources.

Whether with an online tribe or your tribes at work or home, consider using others as an accountability system. Tell your family, friends, and coworkers about your commitment. Post your plans on social media. This gives your tribes an opportunity to support you (we'll discuss this more later), and it can also drive you to be more accountable.

Let's say we make a commitment to do something, but we keep it private—no one knows about it but us. If we don't follow through with it, still no one knows but us. Whew! We just saved face, and we're off the hook. That makes it pretty easy to slough off our commitment.

However, if we make a commitment, tell several people whose opinions we respect, then don't follow through, we'll feel bad. Sharing your goal means creating witnesses to your actions. You can perhaps fool yourself and Sneaky Pete into thinking you're keeping your commitments, but you can't pull the wool over everyone's eyes. If you skip a workout, your family will realize it even if you don't.

And while you don't want to rely on external motivation, there's still something internally motivating about other people following your progress. It raises accountability to a new level—in and outside of yourself. (Again, we'll discuss later how our tribes can provide much-needed support and meaning to our goals.)

Whatever accountability system you choose, another benefit is that it allows you to look back at your progress. That means it's a great tool to propel you forward. My calendar may provide visual proof of missed workouts. But more importantly, it's visual proof of the workout commitments I *did* keep. It feels great to see the hard work I've put in and the progress I've made. Just looking back at my calendar is a great source of dopamine.

Perhaps you have a bad day or two (or five), and you're thinking about throwing in the towel. Just take a look at your accountability log. When you look back at all the time and energy you've invested, in addition to everything you've managed to accomplish so far, there's no way you can quit. It's proof of your success! It shows you've successfully made change—it wasn't always easy, but you did it. And you can do it again.

When to Incorporate a New Action Step

You know by now why it's so important to start with just one simple goal rather than to turn everything in your life upside down at once. Once you see success with that first action step, however, you will be eager and motivated to take on another. But when and how?

Schedule four-week check-ins with yourself and/or your tribe. During this meeting, your first order of business is to determine if you've successfully incorporated the first action step. Has the new behavior become an automatic habit? If the answer is yes, you're ready to commit to a new goal and create a new six-step action plan. If the answer is no, you may need to keep moving forward on your initial goal.

I don't want to give you a hard-and-fast rule for how long you should take to successfully adapt a new behavior. Four weeks isn't a "deadline" but rather a checkpoint to see if a new behavior has become habit, allowing for some ups and downs along the way. Depending on your goal and what has happened to you in the last four weeks, maybe you incorporated your action step fairly quickly. Or maybe you need a little longer. You have to be the judge, and only you know if you're ready to move on.

If you need to give it a little more time, there's nothing wrong with you. We're all on our own journeys, and it's completely unrealistic to expect every one of us to fit into the same time frame. This isn't a race—it's a process. Make this journey uniquely yours. Don't compare yourself to other people or put yourself up against some external standard of who, what, or where you should be.

Move at your own pace, but make sure you check in with yourself on a regular basis to keep yourself moving forward, even if slowly. It's a balance between being mindful of your own pace and keeping yourself accountable. We all need a little fire under our butts to stay motivated.

Overcoming Obstacles

It's important that your action plan includes strategies and backup plans for when things don't go the way you think they will. Because they won't. But if you've got an arsenal of alternative action steps to take, you can easily get yourself back on track. Let's look at how this works.

Trip Your Trigger

One of the biggest challenges to practicing a new behavior is simply remembering to do it. We're all very busy, so not paying attention is one of the main obstacles blocking our progress toward change. As we discussed above, we have only so much brain energy to go around when we're distracted and trying to juggle several things at once (which is the case much of the day). We're more likely to function on reflex, impulse, and old habits to conserve resources.

Changing habits is difficult because by their very nature, habits are things *we don't think about*. A client I was working with had this to say:

It's not so much that the actual changing of behaviors is hard, though it can be. What's harder for me is remaining conscious of the change. I'm trying to change the way I think and the way I act, and to do it in a way that's not just about following a set of rules for the short term, but about changing my reflexes. *The hardest part is remembering to practice a new behavior.*

We had her focus on creating triggers: notes and reminders to help her brain remember that she wants to do something different. She put a sticky note on her desk drawer that said "Snacks in here!" to remind herself (and Sneaky Pete) that food was right there, ready to eat. As simple as that was, it was the perfect trigger, and it kept her from going all afternoon without eating anything. Triggers such as this gave her a chance to practice the new behavior. Soon her new behavior popped on her mental radar without the triggers. Eventually, they turned into new habits, and she was successful.

In addition to putting your new activity on your calendar (per step four of the action plan), you may need to set up a separate system of triggers and reminders for yourself. Set your phone or computer to go off at a certain time, put up sticky notes, set things out in plain view, or enlist a friend's help. I've had clients tell me they find a "snack buddy" at work. Each week, they take turns bringing in healthy snacks and reminding each other to eat at the appropriate time.

Embrace the Gray

Sneaky Pete likes things really simple. Yes or no. I can or I can't. I did or I didn't. Black or white. He gets overwhelmed when there are too many options, so he likes to simplify things in an attempt to conserve energy. Unfortunately, his black-or-white perspective leaves us only two options: success or failure.

This is often our typical way of thinking: we plan a thirty-minute workout for our lunch hour. Then the morning meeting runs long, and now there's only fifteen minutes left to work out. Damn it! Why can't people stay on task? Now we can't work out today. A similar scenario happens twice later that week too, when it takes longer to get home from work one night and when we feel too tired to exercise for our scheduled half hour another night.

In these scenarios, we see only two options: we either do our full workout exactly as planned or we don't do it at all. The plan was to exercise ninety minutes that week—three thirty-minute sessions—but we did zero.

The reality is, we have an *unlimited* number of options. And when it comes to making change and staying on course, we need to tap into them. What if we were to embrace the gray?

Let's try this again: After the meeting, we have only fifteen minutes to work out. So we shrug and tell ourselves a few minutes is better than nothing. We take advantage of that time, do some short-burst interval training with Hit the Deck, and work all our major muscle groups. The night we get home late from work, we decide to still squeeze in ten minutes playing tag with the kids after dinner (they've never seen us run so fast). And we aim for a ten-minute walk the day we feel tired, but end up going for twenty. (Once we get going, it feels pretty good.)

In this second set of scenarios, we see many options—there's always *something* we can do. It may not be the full, exact plan, but at least we do as much as we can. Because of this shift in thinking, we manage to exercise forty-five minutes for the week. It's less than the original plan of ninety, but forty-five is substantially more than zero. It's still progress, it's still change.

Again, there is *always something* you can do. When you find yourself in what seems to be a black-and-white situation, ask yourself, "What is *one thing* I can do that will still move me forward?" You can always modify your original plan or opt for a backup plan (more on this below).

SUCCESS IS DOING *SOMETHING* INSTEAD OF NOTHING, AND THERE IS *ALWAYS* A LITTLE SOMETHING WE CAN DO.

Are you at a social event where you have no say in what is served so you can't Plate It Out? Control your portion size of what they do offer. Stuck in an endless meeting, but your new mantra is "Sitting is the new smoking"? Stand at the back or side of the room and get some blood flowing. At a conference that goes from dawn to dusk with "no time" to exercise? Do twenty pushups and twenty crunches before you get into bed.

Maybe it won't be the big leap forward in progress you had originally planned, but a tiny bit of progress is better than no progress. It's certainly better than saying "What the hell" (more on this below too) and going ten steps backward. These little successes in the face of an obstacle give us a nice shot of dopamine, reinforce our behavior, and help us stay on track.

X = Y

Sneaky Pete is, appropriately, a creature of habit. Once we start paying a little attention to his patterns, we can see him coming from a mile away. That is, sometimes we find ourselves facing the same obstacle time and time again. The good news is, a predictable obstacle can be easily resolved if you plan ahead.

In this situation, it may be helpful to make an "$x = y$" plan: "When I am tempted to do x, I will do y." Planning for an obstacle and precommitting to a default backup action means using less willpower. For example, it may be, "When I'm tempted by alcohol at a client dinner, I'll order a carbonated water." Or it could be something such as, "When I want to have another serving of food, I'll get up from the table and find something to do."

The "x = y" plan is a good backup. Actually, you'll need several back-up plans in place. It's a rare day that goes according to plan, and thinking change will be a cakewalk can leave us unprepared for challenges and setbacks. New stressors and potential derailers pop up all the time: you forgot your workout gear, you were late for your connecting flight and didn't have time to get a snack or meal, or you brought a healthy lunch to work but forgot you're going to a restaurant with a vendor.

I worked with a vegetarian client who wanted to eat enough protein during the day. She normally did a good job when she was at the office, but she regularly had to attend offsite meetings where the "vegetarian option" was just a regular entrée with the meat left out—there was no protein.

In the beginning, she kept hoping she'd luck upon a vegetarian option that would work in these situations, but there almost never was. After discussing what kept showing up on her food logs—a consistent lack of protein when eating at work meetings—we switched her thinking to "assume there will be no source of nonanimal protein." For these work events, she had to have a backup plan. She decided to keep nuts and protein powder in her purse, so that no matter where she was and what the circumstances were, she had protein available. The more we can predict our biggest obstacles or deal breakers, the more we can identify alternative solutions that allow us to adapt and successfully follow through with our desired actions.

And the more we can avoid using willpower to get us through a situation, the better. Backup plans are offensive maneuvers against limited self-control. Participants in an exercise program who wrote down how they would handle obstacles to their workouts were more successful in sticking with a program over the long term.[43] Making only one action plan increases the risk of failure when we hit a bump in the road. We have to have *at least two* backup plans in place, if not more.

As you pre-identify what your obstacles will be (notice I said *will* be, not *might* be), ask yourself the following questions: where and when are they most likely to happen? Is there anything I can do to prevent them from happening in the first place? What specific steps will I take when they happen?

Use Your Tribe

In a world full of obstacles, extend your willpower strength by tapping into the power of your tribes—your family, your friends, or your co-workers. There are several ways to do this.

When you tell others about your commitments, you strategically "outsource" a portion of your self-monitoring duties. It lets you preserve some of your limited willpower energy. You can take a quick willpower break when your coworker immediately reminds you to take the stairs—perhaps even joining you. Or maybe your significant other will choose to make a smaller pot of that mac-and-cheese you can't resist, saving you from the torture of trying to say no to a second portion.

Sharing your goals can also rally your tribe's support in those times when obstacles seem to get the best of you. When they see you stumble, they can reach out to pull you back on your feet. And when they see your perseverance fading, they can cheer you on and provide some much-needed encouragement.

On a deeper level, tapping into the power of your tribes means seeing how your commitment stretches even beyond your own health, resilience, and life. Who else will benefit from you making these changes? And in what meaningful ways?

Many of us have limited motivation to make change when it comes from a place of ego or superficiality. Think about why most people change either the way they're eating or exercising: they want to lose weight or improve their health. Now take a look around North America, for example . . . are those two motivations working for us? They're not. Our self-discipline and willpower get easily exhausted from these external motivations, and we give up.

When we tap into the power of our tribes—what they mean to us and what we want to do for them—we're able to access a cache of motivation and willpower we never knew existed. How will taking care of yourself make you a better leader in your professional and personal lives? How will it affect the energy you use to show your loved ones how much they mean to you? How will your improved resiliency allow you to be a happier, more joyful, relaxed parent? How will creating positive rituals allow you to have more positive exchanges with your significant other? In what ways will you be the best possible version of yourself for your loved ones?

After careful and focused thought about what truly inspires them, many of my clients connect their action plans to someone or something outside of themselves: family, friends, community, or a cause they care about. Many uncover this deeper truth when they answer the Five Whys from step one. They are motivated and excited by how taking care of themselves will allow them to take better care of the people or things they love. And that brings them a sense of happiness, fulfillment, and joy that nothing else can.

Lose Your Tribe

While our tribes often help us avoid obstacles, unfortunately sometimes they can be obstacles themselves. Bad habits can spread like viruses. For instance, remember how we discussed earlier that research has found that if our friends are overweight or obese, our risk of obesity increases by 171 percent?[44]

As social creatures, we're driven to seek the acceptance of our tribes. If our tribe drinks, smokes, and eats fast food on a regular basis, that means it's the social norm of the group. We tend to behave in a similar fashion. Sneaky Pete didn't want to get kicked out of his tribe, and neither do we. The only difference is, Sneaky Pete's tribe didn't have happy hour with several rounds of drinks and a bevy of appetizers every Thursday night.

Depending on the habits and lifestyles of the people around you,

you may need to wean yourself from parts of your tribe. If you can't remove yourself (such as if they're your coworkers or even your own family), you'll need to create optimal defaults specifically designed to avoid getting caught up in their bad habits. Remember Sean from the last chapter? He could make sure he's the first to excuse himself from the table, avoiding any chance of being around when the others bring out the dessert. Maybe his skipping dessert every night will inspire his family to do the same now and then. The good habit could spread like a virus too.

If your usual tribes present more obstacles than support, remember that there are many other tribes out there. If regular exercise, healthy eating, and work-life balance are important to you, then find, join, or create a tribe that agrees. This could mean joining a fitness class or a support group for healthier eating. Maybe it even means getting a magazine subscription.

Being in the company of other people who share your goals and values will decrease your obstacles and increase your odds of success. Belief in what we're doing is essential to success, and it can be fostered in a communal experience, even if that community consists of only two people.

In today's technology-filled world, we have the ability to create and join virtual tribes. Join an online community that offers support, information, and accountability. You may find one where you can connect with other people to learn about their difficulties and how they're able to successfully accomplish a goal similar to yours. Perhaps someone's success inspires you to keep going.

You may want to sign up for the added motivation of a challenge or contest where you perform a certain behavior on a regular basis or hit a designated target by a specific date. Some websites send weekly recipes, workout ideas, or newsletters with information and inspiration relevant to your goal.

Again, at the end of each chapter you may have seen links to www.

ph-performance.com. It's full of helpful tools, articles, and videos for people like you who are ready to join the rEvolution.

How to Deal with Lapses

Behavior change can be challenging—there's no doubt about it. If it were easy, we all would have done it a long time ago and a wide variety of industries wouldn't exist. Expect that you *will* be faced with adversity that leads to lapses from time to time. It's not that I want you to expect to fail, but rather to be realistic about the process of change. It's almost never a straight line from where we are to where we want to be.

Lapses are normal. It's vitally important to read and understand that last sentence: LAPSES ARE NORMAL.

You can create the greatest optimal defaults and the simplest, most specific action plan, but then get knocked off track. It happens to everyone, and there's nothing wrong with you!

When lapses happen, here are a few strategies to pick yourself up and get yourself moving forward again.

The "What the Hell" Effect

One of the biggest threats to our long-term success is the "what the hell" effect: "I just made a mistake, I've completely blown it, so what the hell—I might as well forget the whole thing and go big." As in the example we discussed earlier, it's when one moment of weakness with cookies makes us feel so terrible that we indulge the rest of the day or week.

When we slip up, it often makes us feel frustrated, guilty, and ashamed. We and Sneaky Pete quickly want to escape these negative emotions, so we indulge in behaviors that give us immediate relief and satisfaction—usually the very same ones we're trying to change. Bad choices are followed by more bad choices, and we may set ourselves back weeks in the process. And then after the setback, we beat ourselves up. We tell ourselves we're complete losers and call ourselves every horrible name in the book. We give ourselves a good bout of self-punishment, thinking it will help us shape up and get back on track.

But being hard on ourselves actually makes matters much worse. Studies show that self-criticism increases stress, depletes willpower, and is associated with less motivation and worse self-control.[45] Punishing and putting pressure on ourselves also increases our stress, making it even more challenging to change. We spiral even farther.

Self-forgiveness helps avoid the "what the hell" effect and gets us back on track after a slipup. When we're forgiving and compassionate with ourselves, rather than filled with guilt and shame, there are no negative emotions to escape. We're not driven into the arms of our favorite temptation for relief. Instead, we can pick up the pieces, learn from the situation, and move on. Self-compassion relieves that stress and helps Sneaky Pete back down, allowing us to be more successful with our goals for change.

Carol Dweck—a professor of psychology at Stanford University who studies how our self-concept affects motivation and self-regulation—has found that our mindset determines our success in life. Those with a "fixed" mindset believe that talent alone creates success. They believe effort doesn't matter, that traits such as self-control or intelligence are fixed—either you can do something or you can't. All or nothing. The fixed mindset also focuses on judgment, creating an internal monologue of very harsh self-criticism: "I'm a loser, I suck, and I'm bad because I wasn't successful."

Other people have a "growth" mindset. They believe abilities can be developed through hard work and dedication. They are sensitive to feedback and information, but they focus on how it can help them learn and take action. They think things such as, "Everyone has setbacks. I may not be able to do it well now, but with time and effort, I know I can get there." This view not only creates more success in life, it also improves resiliency.

Change isn't an event—it's a process. Focusing on progress instead of perfection reduces the chances of us even starting down the road of the "what the hell" effect. For example, people who exercise consistently over the long-term aren't as consistent as you think they are. They don't actually work out every single day without fail. From a macroscopic level, they're "consistent" in the long run. But if you look microscopically, their journey is full of setbacks, stops, and starts. They screw up, miss workouts, and lose motivation at times. But they don't let what they did or didn't do yesterday affect what they can do today. If they get off track, they get back on as soon as they can—over and over and over again.

If we had been as hard on ourselves back when we were small children as we are now when we're adults, we never would have learned to do anything. Change, learning, and growth are long processes filled with challenge. We didn't rise up out of our cribs, get down on the floor, and start walking. We first had to realize there was a form of locomotion that required us to be upright. We had to build the strength to pull ourselves up to stand. Then we had to learn how to balance. And we fell down a lot. Eventually we took a single step. And fell down. Then we took a couple steps. And fell down. We "failed" more times than we could count, but we kept at it and eventually learned to walk. If we would have said "what the hell" the first time we tried to pull ourselves up and failed, we'd all still be crawling.

Gradual improvement is the reality of how we function. We expose our body or mind to something new, then give it a chance to recover. During that recovery period, the system grows stronger. It's not realistic to expect to do something once or twice and have it down pat or be an expert. Focus on the process instead of the outcome of "success" or "failure." Sometimes we get so fixated on measuring success in such a specific and limited way, we miss out on the progress and success we're actually making.

There's an infinite number of ways we can measure progress and success in our lives. If you've been reading the success stories between the chapters, you've seen several people make successful changes in their busy, hectic lives. Most of them initially came to me because they just wanted to lose weight.

However, when you ask them about the most exciting benefits of their new routines, they'll tell you they're sleeping so much better and that it feels great to wake up refreshed instead of tired. They'll tell you they have more energy during the day, which makes them more productive and effective at work and makes them more engaged when they get home with their loved ones. They'll talk your ear off about how much stronger they've gotten and how they have muscles they didn't know existed. Their perception is that there's less stress in their lives now, even though nothing about their professional or personal responsibilities have changed. They're more confident in who they are, they feel better about their lives, and they're happier. That's progress, that's success.

There Is No Wagon

If you want to mess with me and make my head explode, tell me you had a plan but then something happened and you "fell off the wagon." Just writing about it gets my blood pressure going, and here's why: show me the wagon. Seriously. Take a picture of it and send it to me. *There is no freakin' wagon.* There is nothing to be "on" or "off." There is only the present moment.

Really, the past and future are figments of our imagination. They're just concepts—advanced brain getting fancy. Don't let what you did or didn't do yesterday or five minutes ago dictate what you will or won't do tomorrow or five minutes from now.

Instead of thinking you "fell off" and blew it, ask yourself this very important question: what is *one* thing I can do *right now* that will get me closer to my goal? Focus on the present moment and what is possible. This immediately helps you regain a sense of control. Pick yourself up and keep moving forward.

Be Realistic

Say your plan is to "make it to the gym two days a week" or to "eat at healthy restaurants when dining out." Then by the second week, you're really struggling, feeling as if you've fallen short of your goal too often to count. After all, something came up on a night you were supposed to go to the gym, so all you could do was make a "game" of burpees, sit-ups, and pushups with your kids in the living room. Or one day, fast food was literally your only option for lunch. You ordered a grilled chicken sandwich with no mayo, didn't finish the whole thing, and had only a few fries—but still. It wasn't a healthy lunch. You're totally lapsing and failing, right?

No. You're actually not lapsing at all. You just need to be more realistic about the spirit and intention behind your goal. You don't always have to take it so literally.

BE REALISTIC—AND FLEXIBLE— ABOUT YOUR ACTION STEP.

We all strive for perfection, especially when it comes to following commitments, but there is no such thing as "perfect." What there is, though, is an ever-changing, fast-paced, high-stress world where anything can and does happen. We *will* run into obstacles we don't foresee and can't avoid. If we're realistic about our goals as well as realistic about balancing all the demands in our lives, our action plan should focus on doing the very best we can on any given day.

So instead of getting hung up on perfection in an imperfect world, be realistic and get creative with the situation. Working out at the "gym" in your living room? Clever! You got the movement you needed, regardless of where it happened. Ordering the healthiest fast food possible and eating a sensible portion? Good call! You handled it quite well. Those are realistic actions for those days, so embrace them as successes, regardless of what your actual goal may have been.

Or sometimes you're realistic about the goal, but not the deadline you arbitrarily set for it. You may feel as though you're lapsing simply because you haven't made your behavior an automatic habit by such-

and-such date.

You check your progress every four weeks, but how long does it really take a habit to form? For some people it takes fourteen days. For others it takes twenty-six. What if it takes you longer? Does that make you a failure? What if you were about to have a huge breakthrough on day thirty-three, but you quit on day thirty-two? Personal change is not a race. It takes time, so give yourself some!

You may want to remove your deadline completely. The word *dead-line* implies a point in time where you'll start or stop doing something. (Not to mention it's stress-inducing and subconsciously negative—*dead* is built right into it!) This is a lifestyle you're creating. It's not a thirty-day project after the conclusion of which you're "done." You're making a commitment to do these behaviors in some way, shape, or form for the rest of your life.

Go Back and Simplify

Change can be a difficult process. We often underestimate how hard it will be. You may have thought your action step was so easy a caveman could do it, but you never know if it's true until you try to make *your* caveman brain do it. There can be a huge difference between what advanced brain thinks is possible and what Sneaky Pete is willing to do. So rather than wallow in failure or quit outright, just create a new action plan with a simpler goal.

It's okay to modify your rituals! Businesses create strategic yearly plans yet rarely stick to the original plan without revising it as the year plays itself out. It's what good businesses do—they take in information and respond accordingly by adapting. As you embark on your plans for change, you need to observe and respond to your environment in a similar fashion and adapt where and when necessary.

It's easy to be overconfident in our ability to resist temptations or to consistently act in a certain way. Sometimes our enthusiasm gets a little carried away, and we find ourselves calling our action plan a nine or ten because we believe in it so much. But then we give it a try . . . it turns out to be more like a six. It consumes and relies on too much willpower, when we've learned that willpower is exhaustible and needs to be preserved as much as possible.

The solution is simple: think about how you can make your action step even simpler. Forget "so easy a caveman could do it." Aim for "so easy and simple, it's stupid to even bother with." If it's too much to do Hit the Deck three days a week, just do some cards during commercials while watching your favorite show once a week. Instead of cutting something out of your diet completely, just cut it in half.

Or perhaps there's a completely different ritual that would work better. Maybe you're not ready to change that part of your life and need to focus on a different area for now. You might have made a commitment around exercise, but maybe it's better to do something related to nutrition or sleep for the time being. Keep that goal simple, set yourself up to succeed, build some dopamine, then try that other goal again.

Reassess Your Optimal Defaults

When mired in a lapse, reflect back on where and when things went haywire. Did something else in the environment exhaust your willpower? Did you have tempting food sitting right in front of you? Did someone talk you into happy hour instead of your workout?

As we learned in the previous chapter, you need to control the effects of your environment as best you can. Ideally, don't put yourself in tempting environments if you can help it. And if you can't help it, assess how you can alter the environment with optimal defaults. So if you're falling short of your commitment, revisit your optimal defaults in step five to see if you can take better control of your surroundings.

Make a new optimal default to sit as far away as possible from the tempting food or in a place where you can't see it. Always share with your friends and coworkers what you're trying to do and why, and ask for their support. Tell them when you work out, so they'll know to skip your happy hour invitation those nights. (Better yet, ask them to join you at the gym instead.) You may be surprised at how much your friends want you to succeed.

When revisiting optimal defaults, don't forget the ones right under your nose. Putting your body into its own "optimal default" state is critical when executing self-control. What state was your body in when you lapsed? Were you hungry? Tired? Of course you're going to be jonesing for some fat and sugar if you haven't eaten since breakfast. And of course Sneaky Pete has no intention of working out when you barely got five hours of sleep last night.

Even the best optimal defaults won't work if your own system is running at less-than-optimal levels. As you know, you've got to ensure you have adequate glucose in your system, or you won't have any willpower. And without enough quality sleep, your body will be in desperate need of energy and will conserve what small amount it has.

Now's the Time

Now that you're at the end of the book, you've got a full toolbox to build a more resilient body and mind. You just need your blueprint to tell you which tools to use at which point in the project. Are you ready? Did you make your action plan? If you haven't yet, this is the time.

Seriously—stop right now and do it. You know your life isn't getting any simpler or easier, and every day you're feeling the effects of your dEvolution. You've taken the time to read the book, now put your knowledge into action with clear, manageable, sixty-second commitments. You'll find the action plan template in appendix A, and you can download as many as you need from www.ph-performance.com.

It's time to officially join the Resiliency rEvolution.

To get additional guidance and direction for successfully making change, go to www.ph-performance.com/change

Success Story

MEGHAN

Meghan's Story

At thirty-five years old, Meghan is vice president and managing director at a digital media company. "It's an always-on industry," she says, explaining her role in overseeing the planning and execution of web, mobile, and application development projects. "I'm pulled in multiple different directions every day."

The constant stream of information from clients and team members demands an intense focus on communication and produces an extremely high volume of email. Meghan feels constant pressure to hit short deadlines and meet customers' high expectations. A driven promoter, she loves her work and quickly became an expert in her field, pursuing side engagements as a blogger, author, and sought-after speaker. She flies nationwide for client meetings and speaking engagements a few times per month.

Meghan's husband is an independent filmmaker, which requires frequent travel and long hours as well as weekend commitments. While they both set aside time for their two children, ages four and two, connections with family and friends are particularly important for Meghan. She makes it a priority to schedule dinners and attend events, both for herself and with the family.

In juggling her commitments to her work, her kids, her spouse, and herself, Meghan sacrifices sleep to get things done. "I've become a night owl, just to get it all in," she admits. In addition to getting very little rest, she struggles to find the energy—much less the time—to exercise. "I'm terrible about remembering to eat," she says, noting that she doesn't plan ahead for healthy meals during the week. "I'm constantly on, whether it's work or family. I'll forget to have lunch, and then I think I should grab a snack and get distracted from that too."

While Meghan knows her life isn't completely out of control, she does know she can't keep up this pace forever.

Meghan's rEvolution

Meghan starts resiliency training by using Hit the Deck because it's easy to bring along on business trips and doesn't require a gym. "I'm just not one of those people who likes to work out," she says, "and the gym can be intimidating when you don't know how to use the machines."

After a few weeks of shutting her office door for five-minute workouts—"nobody even realized what I was doing!" she says—she finds herself fitting in more exercise than ever. The workouts are flexible, and the cards tell her exactly what to do and for how long. It allows her to make the most of her workout time. "No confusing diagrams, no waiting for equipment, no grubby locker room—perfect!" And when she uses the deck at home, her kids think it's a fun game to play with her.

Meghan had thought changing her eating behaviors wouldn't be a big deal. But making some simple changes, she says, "made a huge difference." She explains, "Taking ten extra minutes to make eating a no-brainer later meant that I didn't forget to eat or skip meals for work as often." And again, her kids see what she's doing, and they follow her example.

After sixty days of resiliency training, Meghan notes that she's able to bounce back from stressful situations more quickly. "I'm on much more of an even keel emotionally, even on the craziest days," she says. While nothing has changed at work, she feels less stressed in her high-pressure role and less overwhelmed by challenges that pop up during the course of her day. "I spend less time stressing out and get more done during the day, so I can sleep better at night, so I get up feeling rested. Then I have more energy to get more done the next day—it's a great cycle." As a side benefit, she has also lost a few pounds, exchanging body fat for muscle.

Meghan's success shows how resiliency can make a difference. "I thought what I needed was more hours per day, and that's impossible," she says, laughing. "Now I'm spending less time on the stress that I don't want and getting back more time for what I do want—my family, my career."

MEGHAN AFTER SIXTY DAYS OF RESILIENCY TRAINING

- 10 percent decrease in perceived stress

- 19 percent increase in energy

- 10 percent improvement in quality of sleep

- Lost 5.8 pounds (3.1 percent) of body fat

- Gained 3.8 pounds of muscle

- Lost 3.25 inches

Final Words

Resiliency training is something you do for the rest of your life, and I mean this in two ways: it's something you do on a regular basis, and it's for the benefit of the rest of your days. Your stress will never let up, so neither should you let up your efforts to recover from it more quickly and to handle it successfully. There is no end date to your Resiliency rEvolution.

I often see people successfully achieve a goal, think their obligation is over, and go back to their old ways. The problem is, their old behaviors are what got them into the situation in the first place. What do they think is going to happen after they stop using the tools that made them successful? They'll revert back to the frustration, the unhappiness, and the lack of health and vitality. It makes for more stress in an already stressful life.

Achieving our goals requires time, persistence, planning, and effort. These elements are all critical, but in my opinion the most important is persistence. As a species, we are hardwired for survival. With their tenacity and grit, generations of our ancestors persevered through the most challenging circumstances imaginable. To this day, the primal drive to survive and successfully pass on our DNA fuels our determination to endure and overcome. After our survival needs have been met, we can then strive for a better quality of life for ourselves and our loved ones.

We have made countless adaptations in order to survive, but one thing that's been a constant is Sneaky Pete. None of us could have made it this far without him. He will never stop looking out for us: our safety, comfort, security, and survival. No, his actions aren't always appropriate for our current day and age. But I hope you've come to understand what he's doing, why he's doing it, and how you can work in harmony with him. You really couldn't ask for a better person on your team.

As the pace of work, technology, and communication continues to increase, so will the speed and number of stressors to deal with. They're coming at a rate our ancestors could never have fathomed. Your resilience to the stress in your world and your life will determine how you survive and evolve over the long run.

If you're not part of the rEvolution, you're likely bound for dEvolution. You'll become chronically sleep deprived and barely have enough energy to make it through the day. You won't perform to your best at work or home. You'll struggle with your health. You'll know stress is coming between you and the successful, meaningful life you deserve.

If you start training to become more resilient, you'll evolve to not only survive, but *thrive* despite the demands of your life. You'll live a rich, healthy, long life and be the best possible version of yourself, making a positive impact personally as well as professionally.

This is *your* rEvolution—and Sneaky Pete's got your back. All you have to do is take the first step. And it's only going to take you sixty seconds to get started.

Acknowledgments

Thank you to Dara Beevas and the Wise Ink team. If it weren't for your guidance, enthusiasm, and positivity, I don't know if this project would have happened. You made it all so doable—and dare I say fun. You're the best!

Thank you, Kellie Hultgren, for being my writing coach. In addition to helping me get and stay focused, I loved being accountable to you. You gave me confidence this was possible.

A world of thanks to you, Angie Wiechmann. Words can't express how thankful I am for your editing prowess, and I'm sorry if this book made you stressed! Your polish, insight, eye for detail, and organization resulted in an amazing transformation. I never want to do another project without you.

Thank you, Nupoor Gordon, for the amazing cover design. Your talent made it hard to choose which of your designs was best. It was a gift to work with you.

Thank you, Isabella Evans, for your artistry in making the majority of the illustrations and diagrams in the book. I'm so proud of you.

Thank you, Christina Mahady, for all your incredible design work over the years. Not only do you produce great product, you're always a joy to work with.

To Emily Rodvold: They say people look like their dogs...well, this book looks like me. You swooped in and immediately knew how to translate my energy and personality. Thank you for the fantastic interior design!

Much gratitude goes to Dr. Jim Loehr and Dr. Jack Groppel of the Human Performance Institute. Your love of science, never ending curiosity, drive for growth, professionalism and care have influenced me greatly. It has been a privilege to work with you over the last eleven years and thank you for being incredible mentors.

And to friends, family, and colleagues—thanks for your friendship, love, encouragement, and guidance over the years. I'm insanely grateful to have you all in my life.

Last but never least, thank you, Tiffany Thompson. Your absolute and unrelenting support has allowed me to be and do so much more. Thank you for always believing in me and doing everything in your power to back me up and push me forward.

Appendix A

ACTION PLAN

An action plan is your blueprint to help you use the tools and ideas you learned throughout the book. You'll find this plan is a blend of utilizing both Sneaky Pete and your advanced brain. Use this template to start your personal rEvolution, and to download copies, visit www.ph-performance. com.

Goal Statement

My resiliency training goal is:

_____

Action Steps

Step 1: To ensure you're committing to the right resiliency training goal, ask yourself, "What's truly important to me right now, and in what ways do I feel ready to change? How do I want to take better care of myself?" Then ask yourself the "Five Whys": Ask yourself why your goal is important to you. When you get that answer, ask yourself why that answer matters. Do this at least five times until you have reached an answer connected to your values. (See page 275 for an example.)

Step 2: Identify *one* simple, clear, practical, and very small action step—one immediately doable step—written in positive form. What obstacles do you know you will encounter? What are your backup action steps?

Action step: _____

Backup Action steps: _____

Step 3: Ask yourself, "How confident am I that I can do this task consistently?" Rate it on a scale of one to ten. Keep simplifying it until you rate your confidence a nine or a ten.

Confidence rating: _____

Step 4: Put it on your calendar. Plan the *exact* date, time, and place you will perform the new activity. Keep track of your actions with your accountability system. Schedule a progress check-in four weeks from your start date.

Step 5: Now it's time to focus on Sneaky Pete and your unconscious mind as you create your system of optimal defaults. Come up with a few for each environment as it pertains to your goal. For examples of optimal defaults, see appendix B.

Optimal defaults at home:

Optimal defaults at work:

Optimal defaults for exercise:

Optimal defaults for eating at home:

Optimal defaults while eating out:

Optimal defaults while traveling:

Optimal defaults while food shopping:

Step 6: Write about your success each time you perform the new behavior, at least for the first few weeks. Make the dopamine connection. When you write, answer the questions, "How do I feel physically as well as psychologically after taking my action step? How is this going to benefit me in the long run?" Emphasize the process instead of the outcome.

Four-Week Check-In

Ask yourself, "Has the new behavior become an automatic habit?"

◯ If yes, commit to a new goal and complete a new action plan.

◯ If no, give yourself more time with the behavior and/or consider the tips below.

Things to Remember

◯ Self-forgiveness breaks the "what the hell" effect and gets you back on track. Don't beat yourself up if you slip.

◯ Create triggers that remind you to practice your new activity.

◯ You can always do something, and something is always better than nothing.

◯ Find and use your tribe to support you. Or lose your tribe if they have habits not in alignment with your goals.

◯ There is no wagon.

◯ Be realistic.

◯ Go back and simplify your action steps if you need to.

◯ Reassess your optimal defaults.

Appendix B

Nutrition

○ Put cut-up fruit and/or vegetables on the center shelf of your refrigerator.

○ Keep fresh fruit on the kitchen countertop or table.

○ Don't eat out of a bag or box. Portion out a serving.

○ Eat from smaller plates and bowls.

○ Use smaller silverware.

○ Drink from tall, skinny glasses.

○ Put vegetables on your plate first, especially when taking food from a buffet.

○ Start with a smaller portion than what you think you need. If you need more, you can always take it.

○ Eat with no distractions.

○ Keep serving dishes in the kitchen instead of on the table.

○ Cook less food. Or immediately portion out and store half of what you cook and eat it for lunch the next day.

○ Use food logs to be more conscious of how, when, and what you're eating.

○ Double-cut your pizza into smaller slices. You'll keep reaching for more, and it'll seem as though you're eating a lot.

○ Turn off the TV at mealtime—and any time. You'll have less exposure to junk food ads and more opportunities to enjoy leisure activities.

○ Eat your ice cream from a wine glass.

○ Don't purchase tempting foods. Or at least keep them in inconvenient and out-of-the-way places, such as the basement or the back of a top cupboard. Put them in opaque containers or cover them with aluminum foil.

At the Grocery Store

○ Make a list.

○ Plan your menu for the week.

○ Don't go hungry, or Sneaky Pete will be filling the cart.

○ Stick to the perimeter of the store.

○ Look high and low on the shelves for the less-processed foods.

○ Choose whole foods, which contain only one "ingredient" (beans, fruit, vegetables, lean protein, whole grains).

○ Sign up for something similar to a farm share or community-supported agriculture (CSA), where farm-fresh vegetables and fruits are delivered to you on a weekly basis.

Eating Out

○ Always order the small.

○ Split an entrée or have the server box half of it right away.

○ Ask the server not to bring bread or chips to the table.

○ Volunteer to be the sober driver when out with friends.

○ Go online ahead of time, view the menu, and decide what you'll order before you get there. Don't even open the menu at the table.

○ Look to the light section of the menu first.

○ Sit next to the person who eats the slowest.

○ Eat a small snack before you go.

○ If you're sharing appetizers or small plates of food with others, ask that all items be brought out at once so you can better keep track of how much food you've eaten.

○ Sit at the farthest end of the table, out of reach of the appetizer dishes.

○ First go through the buffet line without a plate to determine what to put on your plate.

○ Take the smallest plate or bowl available at the buffet.

○ Put vegetables and/or fruit on your plate first at the buffet.

○ Sit at a table as far away from the buffet as possible.

Exercise

○ Turn off the TV. You'll move more and skip the junk food and fast-food advertising.

○ If you must watch TV, work out during your favorite show or during commercial breaks.

○ Get rid of your TV remote control.

○ Sleep in your exercise clothes, wake up, and work out.

○ Take your workout gear to work so you don't have to stop at home first.

○ Pack your gym bag the night before.

○ Keep a spare set of workout clothes in your car or office.

○ Get a workout partner.

○ Join a social group centered around exercise (meet-ups, leagues, training groups, etc.).

○ Always take the stairs instead of the elevator or escalator.

○ When using public transportation, get off one to two stops away from your final destination.

○ Walk anyplace you need to go within a few blocks of your home or work.

○ Sit down with your calendar on Sunday nights and schedule your workouts for the upcoming week.

○ Put the alarm clock across the room so you have to get out of bed to turn it off. Don't hit snooze.

○ Keep Hit the Deck on your desk or someplace you can see it.

While Traveling

○ Walk instead of taking the people mover, escalator, or elevator.

○ Walk around or stand while waiting for your flight to board.

○ Walk into the restaurant instead of sitting in the drive-through. (If it's a peak time, going inside may also be faster.)

○ Don't have junk food in the car.

○ Keep a stash of healthy snacks—nuts, nutrition bars, or whole grain crackers—in the car, your briefcase, or purse.

○ Pack workout gear in your suitcase.

○ Stay at a hotel with a gym or pool if possible.

○ See a new city by going for a run or walk. Many hotels have routes with maps you can use.

○ Bring Hit the Deck or an exercise DVD with you.

At Work

○ Wear comfortable shoes on Tennis Shoe Tuesday or Sneaker Wednesday to make standing and walking more conducive.

○ Conduct walking meetings.

○ Conduct standing meetings.

○ On the phone = on your feet.

○ Talking = walking.

○ Park in the "worst" (or best!) spot in the lot.

○ Get an office chair that doesn't roll.

○ Use a standing workstation or create one from a cardboard box.

○ Use or create a walking workstation from a treadmill. Check out my PowerHousePerform YouTube channel to see my video on how to create one for less than twenty dollars.

○ Set your computer with a reminder to get up and move or do a few Hit the Deck cards on a regular basis.

○ Instead of a potentially unhealthy potluck, have a breakfast yogurt bar, a salad bar, or a make-your-own sandwich station (with the healthiest options at the beginning of the line).

○ Keep candies or snacks off your desk or out of sight.

○ Keep healthy food in highly visible places if you're trying to re-member to eat and snack regularly.

○ Set a reminder to break for meals and snacks at the appropriate times.

○ Bring lunch to work.

○ Bring healthy snacks to work.

○ Find a snack buddy. Share the responsibility of bringing healthy snacks and remind each other to eat midmorning and midafternoon.

○ Surround yourself with people who are already modeling some of the behaviors you want.

Endnotes

Introduction

1. Eaton, S. B., Konner M., Shostak, M. (1988) "Stone Agers in the Fast Lane: Chronic Degenerative Diseases in Evolutionary Perspective." *American Journal of Medicine.* 84: 739–49.

2. "Prevalence, Severity, and Unmet Need for Treatment of Mental Disorders in the World Health Organization World Mental Health Surveys." (2004) *Journal of the American Medical Association,* 291 (21): 2581–90.

3. World Health Organization. (2012) "Depression Fact Sheet." http://www. who.int/mediacentre/factsheets/fs369/en/. October. Retrieved 17 Sept. 2013.

4. "Stress in America." (2011) *American Psychological Association.* Vol 42, No.1, print version: 60. January. http://www.apa.org/monitor/2011/01/ stressed-america.aspx. Retrieved 24 July 2013.

Chapter 1: Cavemen Had No Love Handles

1. Mishel, L., Bivens, J., Gould, E., Shierholz, H. (2012) *The State of Working America (12th Ed.)* Cornell University Press. 236–37.

2. Gallup. (2010) "The State of the Global Workplace, a Worldwide Study of Employee Engagement and Wellbeing." 2.

3. McEwen, B. (2002) *The End of Stress as We Know It.* Washington, DC: Joseph Henry Press. 10.

4. McEwen, Bruce. (2011) "Your Brain on Stress." *The Science of Stress: Focus on the Brain, Breaking Bad Habits and Chronic Disease.* Lecture. Yale University. New Haven, CT. June 7.

5. Medina, John. (2008) *Brain Rules.* Seattle, WA: Pear Press. 2.

6. Dalleck, Lance. "Back to the Future: A Paleolithic Exercise Program for the 21 Century." *American Council on Exercise Certified News.* http://www.ace-fitness.org/certifiednewsarticle/2317/back-to-the-future-a-paleolithic-exercise-program. Retrieved 17 February 2012.

7. Robinson, Jo. (2013) *Eating on the Wild Side: The Missing Link to Optimum Health.* New York, NY: Little, Brown and Company. 4–5.

8. Fisk, D. (2001) "American Labor in the 20th Century." *Compensation and Working Conditions,* Fall. 3–8.

9. Blair, S., Nichaman, M. (2002) "The Public Health Problem of Increasing Prevalence Rates of Obesity and What Should Be Done About It." *Mayo Clinic Proceedings*. 77 (2): 109–13.

10. Booth, F. W., Chakravarthy, M. V., Gordon, S. E., Spangenburg, E. E. (2002) "Waging War on Physical Inactivity: Using Modern Molecular Ammunition Against an Ancient Enemy." *Journal of Applied Physiology*, 93, 3–30.

11. Ibid.

12. Eaton, S., Konner, M., Shostak, M. (1988) "Stone Agers in the Fast Lane: Chronic Degenerative Diseases in Evolutionary Perspective." *The American Journal of Medicine*, 84: 739–49.

Chapter 2: The Chemistry of Stress

1. Sapolsky, R., Romero, M., Munck, A. (2000) "How Do Glucocorticoids Influence Stress Responses? Integrating Permissive, Suppressive, Stimulatory, and Preparative Actions." *Endocrine Reviews*. 21 (1): 55–89.

2. Ibid.

3. "Brain Energy Metabolism." *Brain Energy Metabolism*. N.p., n.d. http://www.acnp.org/g4/gn401000064/ch064.html. Retrieved 14 Aug. 2013.

4. "Why High Blood Sugar Is Bad." Mayoclinic.com. http://www.mayoclinic.com/health/high-blood-sugar/MY01701. Retrieved 12 Sept. 2013.

5. Umpleby, A., Russell-Jones, D. (1996) "The Hormonal Control of Protein Metabolism." *Baillière's Clinical Endocrinology and Metabolism*. 10 (4): 551–70.

6. Nistala, R., Stump, C. (2006) "Skeletal Muscle Insulin Resistance Is Fundamental to the Cardiometabolic Syndrome." Review paper. *The Journal of Cardiometabolic Syndrome*. 47–52.

7. Sapolsky, R., Romero, M., Munck, A. (2000) "How Do Glucocorticoids Influence Stress Responses? Integrating Permissive, Suppressive, Stimulatory, and Preparative Actions." *Endocrine Reviews*. 21 (1): 55–89.

8. McEwen, B., Winfield, J. (2002) "The Concept of Allostatis in Biology and Biomedicine." *Hormones and Behavior*. 43. 2–15.

9. Sapolsky, R., Romero, M., Munck, A. (2000) "How Do Glucocorticoids Influence Stress Responses? Integrating Permissive, Suppressive, Stimulatory, and Preparative Actions." *Endocrine Reviews*. 21 (1): 55–89.

10. Sapolsky, R. M. (2004) *Why Zebras Don't Get Ulcers*. New York: Henry Holt and Company. 71.

11. Adam, T., Epel, A. (2007) "Stress, Eating and the Reward System." *Physiology and Behavior*. 91: 449–58.

12. Richards, Dave. (2013) *Human Physiology*. Oxford University Press. 289.

13. Carruth, L. L., Jones, R. E., Norris, D. O. (2002) "Cortisol and Pacific Salmon: A New Look at the Role of Stress Hormones in Olfaction and Home-Stream Migration." *Integrative and Comparative Biology*. 42: 574–81.

14. Farrell, AP. (2002) "Coronary Arteriosclerosis in Salmon: Growing Old or Growing Fast?" *Comparative Biochemistry and Physiology Part A: Molecular & Integrative Physiology*. 132 (4): 723–35.

15. Cockburn, A., Lee, A. (1988) "Marsupial Femmes Fatales." *Natural History*. 97: 40–47.

16. Sapolsky, R., Romero, M., Munck, A. (2000) "How Do Glucocorticoids Influence Stress Responses? Integrating Permissive, Suppressive, Stimulatory, and Preparative Actions." *Endocrine Reviews*. 21 (1): 55–89.

17. Kyrou, I., Tsigos, C. (2007) "Stress Mechanisms and Metabolic Complications." *Hormone and Metabolic Research*. 39: 430–38.

18. Sapolsky, R. M. (2004) *Why Zebras Don't Get Ulcers*. New York: Henry Holt and Company. 238.

19. Epstein, L. (2008) *Improving Sleep: A Guide to a Good Night's Rest*. Cambridge, Massachusetts: Harvard University Medical School. 8. www.health.harvard.edu.

20. Lacerda, L., Kowarski, A., Migeon, C. (1973) "Integrated Concentration and Diurnal Variation of Plasma Cortisol." *The Journal of Clinical Endocrinology & Metabolism*. 36 (2): 227–38.

21. McKay L., Cidlowski, J. (2003) "Pharmacokinetics of Corticosteroids." *Holland-Frei Cancer Medicine*. (6th Ed.)

22. McEwen, B. (2002) *The End of Stress as We Know It*. Washington, DC: Joseph Henry Press. 142.

23. Sapolsky, R. M. (2004) *Why Zebras Don't Get Ulcers*. New York: Henry Holt and Company. 236.

24. Vgontzas, A. N., Bixler, E. O., Lin, H., Prolo, P., Mastorakos, G., Vela-Bueno, A., et al. (2001) "Chronic Insomnia Is Associated with Nyctohermeral Activation of the Hypothalamic-Pituitary-Adrenal Axis: Clinical Implications." *The Journal of Clinical Endocrinology & Metabolism*, 86 (8): 3787–94.

25. Sapolsky, R. M. (2004) *Why Zebras Don't Get Ulcers*. New York: Henry Holt and Company. 236.

26. Medina, J. (2008) *Brain Rules*. Seattle, WA: Pear Press. 165.

27. McEwen, B. (2002) *The End of Stress as We Know It*. Washington, DC: Joseph Henry Press. 84.

28. Patel, S., Malhotra, A., White, D., Gottlieb, D., Hu, F. (2006) "Association Between Reduced Sleep and Weight Gain in Women." *American Journal of Epidemiology*. 164 (10): 947–54.

29. "Unexpected: Surprising Findings From the Last 40 Years." (2011) *Nutrition Action Healthletter*. January/February. 3–8.

30. Magee, C., Huang, X., Iverson, D., Caputi, P. (2010) "Examining the Pathways Linking Chronic Sleep Restriction to Obesity." *Journal of Obesity*. Article ID 821710.

31. Epstein, L. (2008) *Improving Sleep: A Guide to a Good Night'sRest*. Cambridge, Massachusetts: Harvard University Medical School. 4. http://www.health.harvard.edu.

32. Ibid. 12.

33. McEwen, B. (2002) *The End of Stress as We Know It*. Washington, DC: Joseph Henry Press. 140–141.

34. "Cushing's Syndrome." MedicineNet.com. http://www.medicinenet.com/cushings_syndrome/article.htm. Retrieved 29 Aug. 2013.

35. McEwen, B., Winfield, J. (2002) "The Concept of Allostatis in Biology and Biomedicine." *Hormones and Behavior*. 43. 2–15.

36. Epel, E., et al. (2000) "Stress and Body Shape: Stress-Induced Cortisol Secretion Is Consistently Greater Among Women with Central Fat." *Psychosomatic Medicine*. 62 (5): 623–32.

37. Kyrou, I., Tsigos, C. (2007) "Stress Mechanisms and Metabolic Complications." *Hormone and Metabolic Research*. 39: 430–38.

38. Despres, J. (2001) "Health Consequences of Visceral Obesity." *Annals of Medicine*. 33: 534–41.

39. Björntörp, P. (1991) "Visceral Fat Accumulation: The Missing Link Between Psychosocial Factors and Cardiovascular Disease?" *Journal of Internal Medicine*, 230: 195–201.

40. Zhang, C., Rexrode, K., van Dam R., Li, T., Hu, F. (2008) "Abdominal Obesity and the Risk of All-Cause, Cardiovascular, and Cancer Mortality: Sixteen Years of Follow-up in US Women." *Circulation*. 117: 1658–67.

41. Lapidus, L., Bengtsson, C., Larsson, B., Pennert, K., Rybo, E., Sjostrom, L. (1984) "Distribution of Adipose Tissue and Risk of Cardiovascular Disease

and Death: A 12 Year Follow Up of Participants in the Population Study of Women in Gothenburg, Sweden." *British Medical Journal (Clinical Research Edition)* 10: 289 (6454): 1257–61.

42. "Classification of Overweight and Obesity by BMI, Waist Circumference, and Associated Disease Risks." *Losing Weight, Body Mass Index*. N.p., n.d. 7 June 2014.

43. Lupien, S., Maheu, F., Tu, M., Fiocco, A., Schramek, T. (2007) "The Effects of Stress and Stress Hormones on Human Cognition: Implications for the Field of Brain and Cognition." *Brain and Cognition*. 65: 209–73.

44. McEwen, B. (2007) "Physiology and Neurobiology of Stress and Adaptation: Central Role of the Brain." *Physiol Rv*. 87. 873–904.

45. Ansell, E., Rando, K., Tuit, K., Guarnaccia, J., Sinha, R. (2012) "Cumulative Adversity and Smaller Grey Matter Volume in Medial Prefrontal, Anterior Cingulate, and Insula Regions." *Biological Psychiatry*. 72 (1): 57–64.

46. Pittenger, C., Duman, R. (2008) "Stress, Depression, and Neuroplasticity: A Convergence of Mechanisms." *Neuropsychopharmacology Reviews*. 33: 88–109.

Chapter 3: Play It Out

1. Goldfarb, H., Hatfield, B., Armstrong, D., Potts, J. (1990) "Plasma Beta-Endorphin Concentration: Response to Intensity and Duration of Exercise." *Medicine and Science in Sports and Exercise*. 22 (2): 241–44.

2. Goldfarb, H., Hatfield, B., Potts, J., Armstrong, D. (1991) "Beta-Endorphin Time Course Response to Intensity of Exercise: Effect of Training Status." *International Journal of Sports Medicine*. 12 (3): 264–68.

3. deVries, W., Bernards, N., deRooij, M., Koppeschaar, H. (2000) "Dynamic Exercise Discloses Different Time-Related Responses in Stress Hormones." *Psychosomatic Medicine*. 62 (6): 866–72.

4. Schwarz, L., Kindermann, W. (1989) "ß-endorphin, Catecholamines, and Cortisol During Exhaustive Endurance Exercise." *International Journal of Sports Medicine*. 10: 324–28.

5. Brooks, S., et al. (1988) "The Responses of the Catecholamines and ß-Endorphin to Brief Maximal Exercise in Man." *European Journal of Applied Physiology*. 57: 230–34.

6. Meyer, T., Schwarz, L., Kindermann, W. *Contemporary Endocrinology: Sports Endocrinology*. Totowa, NJ: Humana Press, Inc., 31–42.

7. Viru, A., Viru, M. (2003) "Hormones in Short-Term Exercises: Anaerobic Events." *Strength Conditioning Journal*. 25 (4): 31–37.

8. Schwarz, L., Kindermann, W. (1990) "ß-Endorphin, Adrenocorticotropic Hormone, Cortisol and Catecholamines During Aerobic and Anaerobic Exercise." *European Journal of Applied Physiology and Occupational Physiology*. 61 (3–4): 165–71.

9. Schwarz, L., Kindermann, W. (1992) "Changes in Beta-Endorphin Levels in Response to Aerobic and Anaerobic Exercise." *Sports Medicine*. 13 (1): 25–36.

10. Mayo Clinic. (2009) "Depression and Anxiety: Exercise Eases Symptoms." Retrieved 23 May 2009. http://www.mayoclinic.com/health/depression-and-exercise/MH00043

11. Cota, D. (2008) "The Role of the Endocannabinoid System in the Regulation of Hypothalamic-Pituitary-Adrenal Axis Activity." *Journal of Neuroendocrinology*. 20 (s1): 35–38.

12. Bergland, C. (2007) *The Athlete's Way*. New York: St. Martin's Press. 105.

13. Chaouloff, F. (2008) "Physical Exercise and Brain Monoamines: A Review." *Acta Physiologica Scandinavica*. 137, 1–13.

14. Ratey, John. (2008) *Spark*. New York: Little, Brown and Company. 256.

15. Ibid. 257.

16. Medina, John. (2008) *Brain Rules*. Seattle, Washington. Pear Press.

17. Voss, M. W., et al. (2011) "Exercise, Brain, and Cognition Across the Lifespan." *Journal of Applied Physiology*. April 28.

18. "Can Exercise Make Us Smarter?" *Harvard Health Beat Newsletter*. Issue #3. April 2011.

19. Fox, K. (1999) "The Influence of Physical Activity on Mental Well-Being." *Public Health Nutrition, 2* (3a), 411–18.

20. Ströhle, A. (2009) "Physical Activity, Exercise, Depression and Anxiety Disorders." *Journal of Neural Transmission*. 116: 777–84.

21. Scully, D. et al. (1998) "Physical Exercise and Psychological Well-Being: A Critical Review." *British Journal of Sports Medicine*. 32: 111–20.

22. Hassmen, P., Koivula, N., Uutela, A. (2000) "Physical Exercise and Psychological Well-being: A Population Study in Finland." *Preventative Medicine*. 30 (1): 17–25.

23. Traustadottir, T., Bosch, P., Matt, K. (2005) "The HPA Axis Response to Stress

in Women: Effects of Aging and Fitness." *Psychoneuroendocrinology*. 30: 392–402.

24. Rimmele, U., Seiler, R., Marti, B., Wirtz, P., Ehlert, U., Heinrichs, M. (2009) "The Level of Physical Activity Affects Adrenal and Cardiovascular Reactivity to Psychosocial Stress." *Psychoneuroendocrinology*. 34 (2): 190–98.

25. Thayer, J. F., et al. (2011) "A Meta-Analysis of Heart Rate Variability and Neuroimaging Studies: Implications for Heart Rate Variability as a Marker of Stress and Health." *Neuroscience and Biobehavioral Reviews*, 36 (2), 747–56.

26. Souza, G. G. L., et al. (2007) "Resilience and Vagal Tone Predict Cardiac Recovery From Acute Social Stress." *Stress*, 10 (4), 368–74.

27. Rennie, K., et al. (2003) "Effects of Moderate and Vigorous Physical Activity on Heart Rate Variability in a British Study of Civil Servants." *American Journal of Epidemiology*. 158(2): 135–43.

28. DeMeersman, RE. (1993) "Heart Rate Variability and Aerobic Fitness." *American Heart Journal*. 125 (3): 726–31.

29. Mandigout, S. et al. (2002) "Physical Training Increases Heart Rate Variability in Healthy Prepubertal Children." *European Journal of Clinical Investigation*. 32 (7): 479–87.

30. Pichot, V. et al. (2005) "Interval Training in Elderly Men Increases Both Heart Rate Variability and Baroreflex Activity." *Clinical Autonomic Research*. 15 (2): 107–15.

31. Munk, P., Butt, N., Larsen, A. (2010) "High-Intensity Interval Training Improves Heart Rate Variability in Patients Following Percutaneous Coronary Intervention for Angina Pectoris." *International Journal of Cardiology*. 145 (2): 312–14.

32. Camillo, C. et al. (2011) "Improvement of Heart Rate Variability After Exercise Training and It's Predictors in COPD." *Respiratory Medicine*. 105 (7): 1054–62.

33. Trapp, E., Chisholm, D., Freund, J., Boutcher, S. (2008) "The Effects of High-Intensity Intermittent Exercise Training on Fat Loss and Fasting Insulin Levels of Young Women." *International Journal of Obesity*. 32 (4): 684–91.

34. Koivisto, V. et al. (1979) "Insulin Binding to Monocytes in Trained Athletes: Changes in the Resting State and After Exercise." *Journal of Clinical Investigation*. 64: 1011–15.

35. Rosenthal, M. et al. (1983) "Demonstration of a Relationship Between Level of Physical Training and Insulin-Stimulated Glucose Utilization in Normal Humans." *Diabetes*. 32: 408–11.

36. Gibala, M. (2007) "High-intensity Interval Training: A Time-efficient Strategy for Health Promotion?" *Current Sports Medicine Reports*. 6: 211–13.

37. Lamport, D., Lawton, C., Mansfield, M., Dye, L. (2009) "Impairments in Glucose Tolerance Can Have Negative Impact on Cognitive Function: A Systematic Research Review." *Neuroscience and Biobehavioral Reviews*. 33 (3): 394–413.

38. Nilsson, A., Radeborg, K., Björck, I. (2009) "Effects of Differences in Postprandial Glycaemia on Cognitive Functions in Healthy Middle-Aged Subjects." *European Journal of Clinical Nutrition*. 63: 113–20.

39. Steyn, N. et al. (2004) "Diet, Nutrition and the Prevention of Type 2 Diabetes." *Public Health and Nutrition*. 7 (1A): 147–65.

40. Little, J., et al. (2011) "Low-Volume High-Intensity Interval Training Reduces Hyperglycemia and Increases Muscle Mitochondrial Capacity in Patients with Type 2 Diabetes." *Journal of Applied Physiology*. 111: 1554–60.

41. Helgerud, J., et al. (2007) "Aerobic High-Intensity Intervals Improve VO-2max More Than Moderate Training." *Medicine and Science in Sports and Exercise*. 39 (4), 665–71.

42. Wisløff, U., Ellingsen, Ø., & Kemi, O. J. (2009) "High-Intensity Interval Training to Maximize Cardiac Benefits of Exercise Training?" *Exercise Sport Science Review*. 37 (3), 139–46.

43. Schwager, Tina. (2009) "Short-Burst Training." *IDEA Fitness Journal*. September. 27–29.

44. Daussin, F. N., et al. (2008) "Effect of Interval Versus Continuous Training on Cardiorespiratory and Mitochondrial Functions: Relationship to Aerobic Performance Improvements in Sedentary Subjects." *American Journal of Physiology: Regulatory, Integrative and Comparative Physiology*. 295: R264–72.

45. Burgomaster, K. et al. (2008) "Similar Metabolic Adaptations during Exercise After Low Volume Sprint Interval and Traditional Endurance Training in Humans." *Journal of Physiology*. 586: 151–60.

46. Gibala, M. et al. (2006) "Short-Term Sprint Interval Versus Traditional Endurance Training: Similar Adaptations in Human Skeletal Muscle and Exercise Performance." *Journal of Physiology*. 575 (3): 901–11.

47. Buchan, D. et al. (2011) "The Effects of Time and Intensity of Exercise on Novel and Established Markers of CVD in Adolescent Youth." *American Journal of Human Biology*. 23 (4): 517–26.

48. Perry, C. G., et al. (2008) "High-Intensity Aerobic Interval Training Increas-

es Fat and Carbohydrate Metabolic Capacities in Human Skeletal Muscle." *Applied Physiology, Nutrition, and Metabolism.* 33 (6), 1112–23.

49. Talanian, J. L., et al. (2007) "Two Weeks of High-Intensity Aerobic Interval Training Increases the Capacity for Fat Oxidation During Exercise in Women." *Journal of Applied Physiology.* 102 (4), 1439–47.

50. Macpherson, R., Hazell, T., Olver, T., Paterson, D., Lemon, P. (2011) "Run Sprint Interval Training Improves Aerobic Performance but Not Maximal Cardiac Output." *Medicine and Science in Sports and Exercise.* 43 (1): 115–22.

51. Trapp, E., Chisholm, D., Freund, J., Boutcher, S. (2008) "The Effects of High-Intensity Intermittent Exercise Training on Fat Loss and Fasting Insulin Levels of Young Women." *International Journal of Obesity.* 32 (4): 684–91.

52. Tremblay, A, Simoneau, JA, Bouchard, C. (1993) "Impact of Exercise Intensity on Body Fatness and Skeletal Muscle Metabolism." *Metabolism.* 43 (7): 814–18.

53. Gibala, M. (2007) "High-intensity Interval Training: A Time-efficient Strategy for Health Promotion?" *Current Sports Medicine Reports.* 6: 211–13.

54. Talanian, J. et al. (2007) "Two Weeks of High-intensity Aerobic Interval Training Increases the Capacity for Fat Oxidation During Exercise in Women." *Journal of Applied Physiology.* 102: 1439–47.

55. Gibala, M. (2007) "High-intensity Interval Training: A Time-efficient Strategy for Health Promotion?" *Current Sports Medicine Reports.* 6: 211–13.

56. Burgomaster, K., Hughes, S., Heigenhauser, G., Bradwell, S., Gibala, J. (2005) "Six Sessions of Sprint Interval Training Increases Muscle Oxidative Potential and Cycle Endurance Capacity in Humans." *Journal of Applied Physiology.* 98(6): 1985–90.

57. Gibala, M. (2009) "Molecular Responses to High-Intensity Interval Exercise." *Applied Physiology, Nutrition, and Metabolism.* 34 (3), 428–32.

58. Daussin, F. N., et al. (2008) "Effect of Interval Versus Continuous Training on Cardiorespiratory and Mitochondrial Functions: Relationship to Aerobic Performance Improvements in Sedentary Subjects." *American Journal of Physiology: Regulatory, Integrative and Comparative Physiology.* 295, R264–72.

59. Vella, C., Kravitz, L. "Exercise After-Burn: Research Update." The University of New Mexico. http://www.unm.edu/~lkravitz/Article%20folder/epocarticle. html. Retrieved 18 Sept. 2013.

60. Withers, R, et al. (1993) "Oxygen Deficits Incurred During 45, 60, 75 and 90-s

Maximal Cycling on an Air-Braked Ergometer." *European Journal of Applied Physiology*. 67 (2): 185–91.

61. Kravitz, Len. (2006) "Controversies in Metabolism." *IDEA Fitness Journal*, Volume 3, Number 1.

62. Talbott, S. (2007) *The Cortisol Connection*. Hunter House, Inc. 76.

63. Ibid.

64. Srikanthan P., Karlamangla, A. (2011) "Relative Muscle Mass Is Inversely Associated with Insulin Resistance and Prediabetes." Findings from the Third National Health and Nutrition Examination Survey. *Journal of Clinical Endocrinology*. 96 (9): 2898–903.

65. Smutok, M. A., Reece, C., & Kokkinos, P. F. (1993) "Aerobic vs. Strength Training for Risk Factor Intervention in Middle-Aged Men at High Risk for Coronary Heart Disease." *Metabolism*. 42, 177–84.

66. Hurley, B. F., Hagberg, J. M., & Goldberg, A. P. (1988) "Resistive Training Can Reduce Coronary Risk Factors Without Altering VO2max or Percent Body Fat." *Medicine and Science in Sports and Exercise*. 20, 150–54.

67. Sigal, J., Kenny, G., Boule, N., et al. (2007) "Effects of Aerobic Training, Resistance Training, or Both on Glycemic Control in Type 2 Diabetes: a Randomized Trial." *Annals of Internal Medicine*. 147 (6): 357–69.

68. O'Connor, P., Herring, M., Caravalho, A. (2010) "Mental Health Benefits of Strength Training in Adults." *American Journal of Lifestyle Medicine*. 4 (5), 377–96.

69. Ibid.

70. Ibid.

71. Ramirez, A., Kravitz, L. (2012) "Resistance Training Improves Mental Health." *IDEA Fitness Journal*. Volume 9, Number 1. January.

72. Eaton, B., Konner, M., Shostak, M. (1988) "Stone Agers in the Fast Lane: Chronic Degenerative Diseases in Evolutionary Perspective." *The American Journal of Medicine*. 84: 739–49.

73. Quelch, Fraser. "The Science and Application of Metabolic Training." IDEA Health and Fitness Association Continuing Education Course.

74. Murphy, M., Hardman, A. (1998) "Training Effects of Short and Long Bouts of Brisk Walking in Sedentary Women." *Medicine and Science in Sports and Exercise*. 152–57.

75. Bhammar, D., Angadi, S., Gaesser, G. (2012) "Effects of Fractionized and Continuous Exercise on 24-h Ambulatory Blood Pressure." *Medicine and*

Science in Sports and Exercise. 44 (12): 2270–76.

76. Francois, M., et al. (2014) "'Exercise Snacks' Before Meals: A Novel Strategy to Improve Glycaemic Control in Individuals with Insulin Resistance." *Diabetologia,* 57 (7): 1437–45.

77. "Super-short Exercise Bouts (at the Right Intensity) Offer Big Weight-loss Benefits." *American Council on Exercise Pro Source.* http://www.acefitness.org/prosourcearticle/3512/super-short-exercise-bouts-at-the-right?utm_source=ProSource&utm_medium=email&utm_term=September%2B2013&utm_campaign=ProSource. Retrieved 19 Sept. 2013.

78. "Short Bouts of Exercise Reduce Fat in the Bloodstream After Meals." (2004.) American College of Sports Medicine. News Release. August 5. Retrieved 23 May 2009. http://www.acsm.org/AM/Template.cfm?Section=Search&template=/CM/HTMLDisplay.cfm&ContentID=4221

79. Ibid.

80. Ibid.

81. Shaw, Johnathan. (May–June 2011) "Fathoming Metabolism. The Study of Metabolites Does an End Run Around Genomics to Provide Telling Clues to Your Future Health." *Harvard Magazine.* http://harvardmagazine.com/2011/05/fathoming-metabolism?page=0,0. Retrieved 19 Sept. 2013.

82. Barton, J., Pretty, J. (2010) "What is the Best Dose of Nature and Green Exercise for Improving Mental Health? A Multi-Study Analysis." *Environmental Science & Technology.* 44: 3947–55.

83. Nieman, D. (1997) "Risk of Upper Respiratory Tract Infection in Athletes: An Epidemiologic and Immunologic Perspective." *Journal of Athletic Training,* 32 (4), 344–49.

84. Smith, T., Kennedy, S., Fleshner, M. (2004) "Influence of Age and Physical Activity on the Primary in Vivo Antibody and T Cell-Mediated Responses in Men." *Journal of Applied Physiology.* 97, 491–98.

85. Silveira, M., Rodrigues, M., Krause, M., et al. (2007) "Acute Exercise Stimulates Macrophage Function: Possible Role of NF-KappaB Pathways." *Cell Biochemistry and Function.* 25 (1), 63–73.

Chapter 4: Plate It Out

1. Liebman, Bonnie. (2014) "Tip of the Iceberg: Most People with Prediabetes Don't Know It." *Nutrition Action Healthletter.* July/August. 1–7.

2. Shetty, P. (2012) "Public Health: India's Diabetes Time Bomb." *Nature.* 485:

S14–S16.

3. "Diabetes in India." Diabetes.co.uk. http://www.diabetes.co.uk/global-diabetes/diabetes-in-india.html. Retrieved 20 Feb. 2014.

4. Cukierman, T., Gerstein, H., Williamson, J. (2005) "Cognitive Decline and Dementia in Diabetes—Systematic Overview of Prospective Observational Studies." *Diabetologia*. 48: 2460–69.

5. "The Cost of Diabetes: American Diabetes Association." *American Diabetes Association*. N.p., n.d. Retrieved 3 Mar. 2014. http://www.diabetes.org/advocacy/news-events/cost-of-diabetes.html.

6. Bowen, R. "Physiologic Effects of Insulin." http://www.vivo.colostate.edu/hbooks/pathphys/endocrine/pancreas/insulin_phys.html. Retrieved 12 Dec. 2014.

7. Leidy, H. et al. (2013) "Beneficial Effects of a Higher-Protein Breakfast on the Appetitive, Hormonal and Neural Signals Controlling Energy Intake Regulation in Overweight/Obese, 'Breakfast Skipping', Late-Adolescent Girls." *American Journal of Clinical Nutrition*. 97 (4): 677–88.

8. Benton, D. et al. (2003) "The Delivery Rate of Dietary Carbohydrates Affects Cognitive Performance in Both Rats and Humans." *Psychopharmacology*. 166 (1): 86–90.

9. Lovallo, W. et al. (2005) "Caffeine Stimulation of Cortisol Secretion Across Waking Hours in Relation to Caffeine Intake Levels." *Phychosomatic Medicine*. 67 (5): 734–39.

10. Lovallo, W. et al. (2006) "Cortisol Responses to Mental Stress, Exercise, and Meals Following Caffeine Intake in Men and Women." *Pharmacology Biochemistry and Behavior*. 83 (3): 441–47.

11. Badrick, E., Kirschbaum, C., Kumari, M. (2007) "The Relationship Between Smoking Status and Cortisol Secretion." *Journal of Clinical Endocrinology & Metabolism*. 92 (3): 819.

12. Convit, A., Wolf, O., Tarshish, C., deLeon, M. (2003) "Reduced Glucose Tolerance is Associated with Poor Memory Performance and Hipppocampal Atrophy Among Normal Elderly." *Proceedings of the National Academy of Sciences of the United States of America*. 100: 2019–22.

13. Benton, D., Nabb, S. (2003) "Carbohydrate, Memory, and Mood." *Nutrition Reviews*. (61) 5: S61–S67.

14. Ingwersen, J., Defeyter, M., Kennedy, D., Wesnes, K., Scholey, A. (2007) "A Low Glycaemic Index Breakfast Cereal Preferentially Prevents Children's Cognitive Performance from Declining Throughout the Morning." *Appetite*.

49 (1): 240–44.

15. Tataranni, P., et al. (1999) "Neruoanatomical Correlates of Hunger and Satiation in Humans Using Positron Emission Tomography." *Proceedings of the National Academy of Sciences of the United States of America.* 96 (8): 4569–74.

16. Brownlee, M. (2001) "Biochemistry and Molecular Biology of Diabetes Complications." *Nature.* 414: 813–20.

17. McMillan-Price, J., Miller-Brand, J. (2006) "Review: Low-Glycaemic Index Diets and Body Weight Regulation." *International Journal of Obesity.* 30: S40–S46.

18. Bornet, F., Jardy-Gennetier, A. E., Jacquet, N., Stowell, J. (2007) "Glycaemic Response to Foods: Impact on Satiety and Long-Term Weight Regulation." *Appetite.* 49 (3): 535–53.

19. McMillan-Price, J., Miller-Brand, J. (2006) "Review: Low-Glycaemic Index Diets and Body Weight Regulation." *International Journal of Obesity.* 30: S40–S46.

20. Ludwig, D. (2000) "Dietary Glycemic Index and Obesity." *Journal of Nutrition.* 130: 280S–283S.

21. Ludwig, D. et al. (1999) "High Glycemic Index Foods, Overeating, and Obesity." *Pediatrics.* 103 (3): e26.

22. McMillan-Price, J., Miller-Brand, J. (2006) "Review: Low-Glycaemic Index Diets and Body Weight Regulation." *International Journal of Obesity.* 30: S40–S46.

23. "Burger King USA Nutritionals: Core, Regional and Limited Time Offerings November 2012." BurgerKing.com. http://www.bk.com/cms/en/us/cms_out/digital_assets/files/pages/MenuNutritionInformation_November2012.pdf. Retrieved 2 Nov. 2014.

24. Calder, P. (2001) "Polyunsaturated Fatty Acids, Inflammation, and Immunity." *Lipids.* 36 (9): 1007–24.

25. Mozaffarian, D. et al. (2004) "Dietary Intake of Trans Fatty Acids and Systemic Inflammation in Women." *American Journal of Clinical Nutrition.* 79 (4): 606–12.

26. Matthews, J. (2009) "Are There Health Risks Concerning Too Much Protein?" *ACE Fit Share.* American Council on Exercise. http://www.acefitness.org/acefit/healthy-living-article/60/122/are-there-health-risks-concerning-eating-too/. Retrieved 31 Oct. 2013.

27. Ludwig, D. (2007) "Clinical Update: The Low-Glycaemic-Index Diet." *The*

Lancet. 369 (9565): 890–92.

28. Papanikolaou, Y. et al. (2006) "Better Cognitive Performance Following a Low-Glycaemic-Index Compared with a High-Glycaemic-Index Carbohydrate Meal in Adults with Type 2 Diabetes." *Diabetologia.* 49 (5): 855–62.

29. World Health Organization. "Global Status Report on Alcohol and Health 2011." http://www.who.int/substance_abuse/publications/global_alcohol_report/en/index.html. Retrieved 30 Oct 2013.

30. Timlin, M., Pereira, M. (2007) "Breakfast Frequency and Quality in the Etiology of Adult Obesity and Chronic Diseases." *Nutrition Reviews.* Special Article. 65 (6): 268–81.

31. Mann, T., et al. (2007) "Medicare's Search for Effective Obesity Treatments: Diets are Not the Answer." *American Psychologist.* 62 (3): 220–33.

32. Tomiyama, J., et al. (2010) "Low Calorie Dieting Increases Cortisol." *Psychosomatic Medicine.* 72: 357–64.

33. Hill, A. J. (2004) "Does Dieting Make You Fat?" *British Journal of Nutrition.* 92 (Suppl. 1), S15–S18.

34. Hafekost, K., et al. (2013) "Tackling Overweight and Obesity: Does the Public Health Message Match the Science?" *BMC Medicine,* 11, 41.

35. Benasik, J., et al. (2013) "Low-Calorie Diet Induced Weight Loss May Alter Regulatory Hormones and Contribute to Rebound Visceral Adiposity in Obese Persons with a Family History of Type-2 Diabetes." *Journal of the American Association of Nurse Practitioners.* 25 (8): 440–48.

36. Mann, T. et al. (2007) "The Search for Effective Obesity Treatments: Should Medicare Fund Diets?" *American Psychologist.* 62: 220–33.

37. Baumeister, R., Tierney, J. (2011) *Willpower.* New York: Penguin Group.

38. Mann, T. et al. (2007) "The Search for Effective Obesity Treatments: Should Medicare Fund Diets?" *American Psychologist.* 62: 220–33.

39. French, S., Jeffery, R. (1994) "Consequences of Dieting to Lose Weight: Effects on Physical and Mental Health." *Health Psychology.* 13: 195–212.

40. Hill, A. (2007) "The Psychology of Food Craving." *Proceedings of the Nutrition Society.* 66: 277–85.

41. Polivy, J., Coleman, J., Herman, C. (2005) "The Effect of Deprivation on Food Cravings and Eating Behavior in Restrained and Unrestrained Eaters." *International Journal of Eating Disorders.* 38 (4): 301–09.

42. Tomiyama, J., et al. (2010) "Low Calorie Dieting Increases Cortisol." *Psychosomatic Medicine.* 72: 357–64.

43. Kraemer, W., et al. (1999) "Influence of Exercise Training on Physiological and Performance Changes with Weight Loss in Men." *Medicine & Science in Sports & Exercise.* 31 (9): 1320–29.

44. Paoli, A. et al. (2011) "Exercising Fasting or Fed to Enhance Fat Loss? Influence of Food Intake on Respiratory Ratio and Excess Postexercise Oxygen Consumption After a Bout of Endurance Training." *International Journal of Sport Nutrition and Exercise Metabolism.* 21 (1): 48–54.

45. Bernard, P., Imbeault, P., Doucet, E. (2005) "Maximizing Acute Fat Utilization: Effects of Exercise, Food, and Individual Characteristics." *Canadian Journal of Applied Physiology.* 30 (4): 475–99.

46. Stevenson, E., et al. (2006) "Influence of High-Carbohydrate Mixed Meals with Different Glycemic Indexes on Substrate Utilization During Subsequent Exercise in Women." *American Journal of Clinical Nutrition.* 84: 354–60.

47. Wu, C., et al. (2003) "The Influence of High-Carbohydrate Meals with Different Glycaemic Indices on Substrate Utilization During Subsequent Exercise." *British Journal of Nutrition.* 6: 1049–56.

48. DeMarco, H., et al. (1999) "Pre-Exercise Carbohydrate Meals: Application of Glycemic Index." *Medicine & Science in Sports & Exercise.* 31 (1): 164–70.

49. Kundrat, S. (April 2000) "Refueling After Exercise." *IDEA Health and Fitness Source.*

50. Ibid.

Chapter 5: Control Your Environment

1. American Psychological Association. (2010) "Americans Report Willpower and Stress as Key Obstacles in Meeting Health-Related Resolutions." Press release. http://www.apa.org/news/press/releases/2010/03/lifestyle-changes.aspx.

2. Booth, F., Gordon, S., Carlson, C., Hamilton, M. (2000) "Waging War on Modern Chronic Diseases: Primary Prevention Through Exercise Biology." *Journal of Applied Physiology.* 88: 774–87.

3. Brownell, K., et al. (2010) "Personal Responsibility and Obesity: A Constructive Approach to a Controversial Issue." *Health Affairs.* 29 (3): 379–87.

4. Johnson, E., Goldstein, D. (2003) "Medicine: Do Defaults Save Lives?" *Science.* 302 (5649): 1338–39.

5. Choi, James J., David Laibson, Brigitte C. Madrian, and Andrew Metrick. (2002) "Defined Contribution Pensions: Plan Rules, Participant Decisions,

and the Path of Least Resistance." James Poterba (Ed.) *Tax Policy and the Economy*. 16, 67–114.

6. Shah, S., O'Byrne, M., Wilson, M., Wilson, T. (2011) "Elevators or Stairs?" *Canadian Medical Association Journal*. 183 (18): E1353–E1355.

7. Levine, James, Yeager, Selene. (2009) *Move a Little, Lose a Lot*. Crown Publishers.

8. Levine, James. (2013) "Sitting Risks: How Harmful Is Too Much Sitting?" *Mayo Clinic*. http://www.mayoclinic.com/health/sitting/AN02082. Retrieved 10 Dec. 2013.

9. Rolls, B. et al. (1981) "Variety in a Meal Enhances Food Intake in Men." *Physiology & Behavior*. 26: 215–221.

10. Kahn, B., Wansink, B. (2004) "The Influence of Assortment Structure on Perceived Variety and Consumption Quantities." *Journal of Consumer Research*. 30: 455–69.

11. Wansink B., Hanks, A. (2013) "Slim by Design: Serving Healthy Foods First in Buffet Lines Improves Overall Meal Selection." *PLOS ONE* 8 (10): e77055. doi:10.1371/journal.pone.0077055

12. Robinson, E., et al. (2013) "Eating Attentively: A Systematic Review and Meta-Analysis of the Effect of Food Intake Memory and Awareness on Eating." 97 (4):728–42.

13. Wansink, B. (2006) *Mindless Eating*. Bantam Books.

14. Wansink, B. (2004) "Environmental Factors That Increase the Food Intake and Consumption Volume of Unknowing Consumers." *Annual Review of Nutrition*. 24: 455–79.

15. Dunstan, D., Howard, B., Healy, G., Owen, N. (2012) "Too Much Sitting—A Health Hazard." *Diabetes Research and Clinical Practice*. 97 (3): 368–76.

16. Tal, A., Wansink, B. (2013) "Fattening Fasting: Hungry Grocery Shoppers Buy More Calories, Not More Food." *JAMA Internal Medicine*. 173 (12): 1146–48.

17. Harvard Medical School. (2011) "Controlling What—and How Much—We Eat." *Healthbeat Newsletter*. 8 Nov.

18. "Fooled By Food." (2013) *Nutrition Action Healthletter*. April.

19. Wansink, B. (2006) *Mindless Eating*. Bantam Books.

20. Ibid.

21. Payne, C., Smith, L., Lee, J., Wansink, B. "Serve It Here; Eat It There: Serving Off the Stove Results in Less Food Intake Than Serving Off the Table." http://

foodpsychology.cornell.edu/images/posters/serveofftable.pdf. Retrieved 17 Dec. 2013.

22. Wansink, B. (2004) "Environmental Factors That Increase the Food Intake and Consumption Volume of Unknowing Consumers." *Annual Review of Nutrition.* 24: 455–79.

23. Wansink, B. (2006) *Mindless Eating.* Bantam Books.

24. Christakis, N., Fowler, J. (2007) "The Spread of Obesity in a Large Social Network Over 32 Years." *New England Journal of Medicine.* 357: 370–79.

25. Rosenquist, J., et al. (2010) "The Spread of Alcohol Consumption Behavior in a Large Social Network." *Annals of Internal Medicine.* 152 (7): 426–33.

26. Christakis, N., Fowler, J. (2008) "The Collective Dynamics of Smoking in a Large Social Network." *New England Journal of Medicine.* 358: 2249–58.

27. Bell, R., Pliner, P. (2003) "Time to Eat: The Relationship Between the Number of People Eating and Meal Duration in Three Lunch Settings." *Appetite.* 41 (2): 215–18.

28. Wansink, B. (2004) "Environmental Factors That Increase the Food Intake and Consumption Volume of Unknowing Consumers." *Annual Review of Nutrition.* 24: 455–79.

29. Wu, H., Sturm, R. (2012) "What's on the Menu? A Review of the Energy and Nutritional Content of US Chain Restaurant Menus." *Public Health Nutrition.* 16 (1): 87–96.

30. "Fooled By Food." (2013) *Nutrition Action Healthletter.* April.

31. Wu, H., Sturm, R. (2012) "What's on the Menu? A Review of the Energy and Nutritional Content of US Chain Restaurant Menus." *Public Health Nutrition.* 16 (1): 87–96.

32. Thorp, A., Owen, N., Neuhaus, M., Dunstan, D. (2011) "Sedentary Behaviors and Subsequent Health Outcomes in Adults a Systematic Review of Longitudinal Studies, 1996–2011." *American Journal of Preventative Medicine.* 41: 207–15.

33. Thielman, Sam. (2013) "You Endure More Commercials When Watching Cable Networks Compared to Broadcast." *Adweek.* 23 June. http://www.adweek.com/news/television/you-endure-more-commercials-when-watching-cable-networks-150575. Retrieved 17 Dec. 2013.

34. Kilmer, G. et al. (2006) "Surveillance of Certain Health Behaviors and Conditions Among States and Selected Local Areas—Behavior Risk Factor Surveillance System (BRFSS), United States." *Morbidity and Mortality Weekly Report.* 57 (SS07): 1–188.

35. Eaton, D., et al. (2008) "Youth Risk Behavior Surveillance—United States." *Morbidity and Mortality Weekly Report*. 57 (SS04): 1–131.

36. Buettner, Dan. (2008) *The Blue Zones. Lessons for Living Longer from the People Who've Lived the Longest*. Washington, DC: National Geographic.

Chapter 6: Change

1. Kochanek, K., Xu, J., Murphy, S., Miniño, A., Kung, H. (2011) "Deaths: Final Data for 2009." *National Vital Statistics Reports*. 60 (3)

2. Jackevicius, C., Li, P., Tu, J. (2008) "Prevalence, Predictors, and Outcomes of Primary Nonadherence After Acute Myocardial Infarction." *Circulation*. 117: 1028–36.

3. Ho, P., et al. (2006) "Impact of Medication Therapy Discontinuation on Mortality After Myocardial Infarction." *Archives of Internal Medicine*. 166: 1842–47.

4. Deutschman, Alan. (2007) "Change or Die." *Fast Company*. December 19. Web. December 2007.

5. Wansink, B., Sobal, J. (2007) "Mindless Eating. Environment and Behavior." 39: 106–123.

6. Peterson, Christopher, Seligman, Martin. (2004) *Character Strengths and Virtues*. (1st ed.) American Psychological Association / Oxford University Press. April 8

7. Souza, G. G. L., et al. (2007) "Resilience and Vagal Tone Predict Cardiac Recovery From Acute Social Stress." *Stress*. 10 (4), 368–74.

8. Ingjaldsson, J., Laberg, J., Thayer, J. (2003) "Reduced Heart Rate Variability in Chronic Alcohol Abuse: Relationship with Negative Mood, Chronic Thought Suppression, and Compulsive Drinking." *Biological Psychiatry*. 54: 1427–36.

9. Buch, A., Coote, J., Townend, J. (2002) "Mortality, Cardiac Vagal Control and Physical Training: What's the Link?" *Experimental Psychology*. 87 (4): 423–35.

10. Hansen, A. L. et al. (2004) "Heart Rate Variability and Its Relation to Prefrontal Cognitive Function: The Effect of Training and Detraining." *European Journal of Applied Physiology*. 93, 263–72.

11. Barton, J., Pretty, J. (2010) "What Is the Best Dose of Nature and Green Exercise for Improving Mental Health? A Multi-Study Analysis." *Environmental Science & Technology*. 44: 3947–55.

12. McGonigal, Kelly. (2012) *The Willpower Instinct: How Self-Control Works,*

Why it Matters, and What You Can Do to Get More of It. London: Penguin Group.

13. Cozolino, L. (2010) *The Neuroscience of Psychotherapy: Building and Rebuilding the Human Brain.* (2nd ed.) New York: Norton.

14. Dweck, C. (2006) *Mindset: The New Psychology of Success.* New York: Random House.

15. Sapolsky, R. (2004) *Why Zebras Don't Get Ulcers.* New York: Holt.

16. Oaten, M., Cheng, K. (2005) "Academic Examination Stress Impairs Self-Control." *Journal of Social and Clinical Psychology.* 24: 254–79.

17. Vohs, K., Heatherton, T. (2000) "Self-Regulatory Failure: A Resource Depletion Approach." *Psychological Science.* 11 (3): 249–54.

18. Vohs, K., et al. (2008) "Making Choices Impairs Subsequent Self-Control: A Limited Resource Account of Decision Making, Self-Regulation, and Active Initiative." *Journal of Personality and Social Psychology.* 94: 883–98.

19. Hoffman, W., Baumeister, R., Förster, G., Vohs, K., (2012) "Everyday Temptations: An Experience Sampling Study of Desire, Conflict, and Self-Control." *Journal of Personality and Social Psychology.* 102. (6): 1318–35.

20. Crescioni, A., et al. (2011) "High Trait Self-Control Predicts Positive Health Behaviors and Success in Weight Loss." *Journal of Health Psychology.* 16 (5): 750–59.

21. Gailliot, M. et al. (2007) "Self-control Relies on Glucose as a Limited Energy Source: Willpower Is More Than a Metaphor." *Journal of Personality and Social Psychology.* 92 (2): 325–36.

22. Ibid.

23. Hoffman, W., Baumeister, R., Förster, G., Vohs, K., (2012) "Everyday Temptations: An Experience Sampling Study of Desire, Conflict, and Self-Control." *Journal of Personality and Social Psychology.* 102 (6): 1318–35.

24. Gailliot, M., et al. (2007) "Self-Control Relies on Glucose as a Limited Energy Source: Willpower Is More Than a Metaphor." *Journal of Personality and Social Psychology.* 92: 325–36.

25. Bray, S., Martin Ginis, A., Hicks, A., Woodgate, J. (2007) "Effects of Self-Regulatory Strength Depletion on Muscular Performance and EMG Activation." *Psychophysiology.* 45 (2): 337–43.

26. Danziger, S., Levav, J., Avnaim-Pesso, L. (2011) "Extraneous Factors in Judicial Decisions." *Proceedings of the National Academy of Sciences of the United States of America.* 108 (17): 6889–92.

27. McGonigal, Kelly. (2012) *The Willpower Instinct.* New York: Penguin Group.

28. Gailliot, M., Baumeister, F. (2007) "The Physiology of Willpower: Linking Blood Glucose to Self-Control." *Personality and Social Psychology Review.* 11 (4): 303–27.

29. Gailliot, M. et al. (2007) "Self-Control Relies on Glucose as a Limited Energy Source: Willpower Is More Than a Metaphor." *Journal of Personality and Social Psychology.* 92 (2): 325–26.

30. Muraven, M., Baumeister, R., Tice, D., (1999) "Longitudinal Improvement of Self-Regulation Through Practice: Building Self-Control Strength Through Repeated Exercise." *Journal of Social Psychology.* 139 (4): 446–57.

31. Oaten, M., Cheng, K. (2006) "Improved Self-Control: The Benefits of a Regular Program of Academic Study." *Basic and Applied Social Psychology.* 28 (1): 1–16.

32. Ibid.

33. Oaten, M., and K. Cheng. (2006) "Longitudinal Gains in Self-Regulation from Regular Physical Exercise." *British Journal of Healthy Psychology.* 11, 717–33.

34. Ibid.

35. Snowling, N., Hopkins, W. (2006) "Effects of Different Modes of Exercise Training on Glucose Control and Risk Factors for Complications in Type 2 Diabetic Patients: A Meta-Analysis." *Diabetes Care.* 29 (11): 2528–27.

36. Mead, N., & Patrick, V. (2012) "In Praise of Putting Things Off: Postponing Consumption Pleasures Facilitates Self-Control." Available at SSRN 2089152.

37. McGonigal, Kelly. (2012) *The Willpower Instinct.* New York: Penguin Group.

38. "Stress in America." (2007) *American Psychological Association.* Washington, DC.

39. Finlay, K., Trafimow, D., Villarreal, A. (2006) "Predicting Exercise and Health Behavioral Intentions: Attitudes, Subjective Norms, and Other Behavioral Determinants." *Journal of Applied Social Psychology.* 32 (2): 342–56.

40. Ibid.

41. Norcross, J., Ratzin, A., Payne, D. (1989) "Ringing in the New Year: The Change Process and Reported Outcomes of Resolutions." *Addictive Behaviors.* 14 (2): 205–12.

42. Grant Halvorson, Heidi. "Nine Things Successful People Do Differently." (2011) *Harvard Business Review.* February 25. http://blogs.hbr.org/2011/02/nine-things-successful-people/

43. Sniehotta, F., et al. (2005) "Long-term Effects of Two Psychological Inter-
    ventions on Physical Exercise and Self-Regulation Following Coronary
    Rehabilitation." *International Journal of Behavioral Medicine.* 12 (4): 244–55.

44. Fowler, J., Christakis, N. (2008) "Estimating Peer Effects on Health in Social
    Networks: A Response to Cohen-Cole and Fletcher; Trogdon, Nonnemake,
    Pais." *Journal of Health Economics.* 27 (5): 1400–05.

45. Trumpeter, N., Watson, P., O'Leary, B. (2006) "Factors within Multidimen-
    sional Perfectionism Scales: Complexity of Relationships with Self-Esteem,
    Narcissism, Self-Control, and Self-Criticism." *Personality and Individual
    Differences.* 41 (5): 849–60.

Index

About the Author

Jenny C. Evans is a speaker, author, and on-air expert on resiliency, stress, exercise physiology, nutrition, and health. Jenny is the founder and CEO of PowerHouse Performance. Working with thousands of C-suite executives, leaders, and employees worldwide, her dynamic presentations inspire and educate audiences to increase their capacity for stress and to recover from it more quickly and effectively. Clients improve their performance and productivity, all while enhancing their health. Her corporate client list includes Yale School of Management, AT&T, Estée Lauder Companies, Comcast, Nationwide, and Ameriprise Financial. She is also the creator of PowerHouse Hit the Deck—the ultimate tool for combating stress and increasing fitness.

Jenny serves on many advisory boards, writes as a blogger for *The Huffington Post*, and was NBC KARE 11's Health & Fitness expert for over four years. She has been featured on National Public Radio and Lifehacker. com as well as in *Shape*, *Elle*, *Women's Health*, *Redbook*, and *Woman's World*.

Jenny has a bachelor of science degree in kinesiology with an emphasis in psychology from the University of Minnesota and has been an American Council on Exercise Certified Personal Trainer and Group Fitness Instructor for close to twenty years.

She lives with her wife and daughter in Minneapolis, Minnesota. In her spare time, she's a competitive athlete and a yoga addict. She races duathlons and performs aerial arts on her backyard trapeze rig. She also loves to travel off the beaten path around the world.

Join the rEvolution

If you are ready to join the rEvolution or want more information on building resiliency, please visit the book's website:

www.ph-performance.com

Once there you can:
- Sign up for special resiliency training content and new blog post alerts (we never share or sell your information).
- Purchase PowerHouse Hit the Deck.
- Read the blog to learn more information relating to each chapter of the book.

You can also join the rEvolution by following @PowerHousePC on Twitter and liking **Jenny Evans - PowerHouse Performance** Facebook page.

Book Jenny Evans to Speak At Your Next Event

Jenny Evans transforms cultures from stressed to resilient. She speaks to corporations, associations, and universities around the world on how to improve resiliency, performance and health.

Anything but run of the mill, these events are active, high-energy, engaging and life-changing. Whether you have one hour, a half, or a full day, Jenny will leave you and your audience inspired, informed and on your way to leading a more resilient life.

Jenny will help you:

- Increase your threshold for stress

- Learn how to recover from stress more quickly and efficiently

- Elevate your levels of productivity, performance and energy

- Improve your fitness, health, sleep and body fat

- Successfully implement resiliency training tools

- Empower yourself to thrive in an increasingly demanding business environment

Made in the USA
Monee, IL
17 July 2021